THE BUSINESS OF GOD

The Business of Modern Life Series

Series Editors: Justin Bronson Barringer and James McCarty

The Business of Modern Life Series explores the ways that neoliberal global capitalism has infiltrated and come to dominate virtually all spheres of modern life including incarceration, healthcare, agriculture, technology, education, non-profit organizations, immigration, and church along with, of course, war. Various industrial complexes have popped up all around us, and this series will grapple with the effects that they have on our daily lives. It will be the first series of its kind—that is, one addressing a variety of theological and ethical issues of the modern world through the lens of capitalism's pervasive domination. Many books have been published on the areas we hope this series will explore, but for the most part they have neglected how finance capitalism, global markets, and economic philosophy and policy drive, or often eschew, theological and ethical concerns. Each book in this series will take on one of the industrial complexes (e.g., the military-industrial complex, the prison-industrial complex, the agricultural-industrial complex, etc.), all following the same basic format, which first addresses the biblical and theological foundations relevant to the topic, then reflects on the theological and moral state of affairs in history and in the world today, before finally closing with some uniquely Christian proposals for responding to the issues raised.

The Business of God

Theological and Ethical Reflections on the Church Industrial Complex

Edited by
Sheryl Johnson
and
Dannis Matteson

CASCADE *Books* • Eugene, Oregon

THE BUSINESS OF GOD
Theological and Ethical Reflections on the Church Industrial Complex

The Business of Modern Life Series

Copyright © 2025 Wipf and Stock Publishers. All rights reserved. Except for brief quotations in critical publications or reviews, no part of this book may be reproduced in any manner without prior written permission from the publisher. Write: Permissions, Wipf and Stock Publishers, 199 W. 8th Ave., Suite 3, Eugene, OR 97401.

Cascade Books
An Imprint of Wipf and Stock Publishers
199 W. 8th Ave., Suite 3
Eugene, OR 97401

www.wipfandstock.com

PAPERBACK ISBN: 978-1-6667-6784-1
HARDCOVER ISBN: 978-1-6667-6785-8
EBOOK ISBN: 978-1-6667-6786-5

Cataloguing-in-Publication data:

Names: Johnson, Sheryl, editor. | Matteson, Dannis, editor.
Title: The business of God : theological and ethical reflections on the church industrial complex / edited by Sheryl Johnson and Dannis Matteson.
Description: Eugene, OR : Cascade Books, 2025 | The Business of Modern Life Series | Includes bibliographical references.
Identifiers: ISBN 978-1-6667-6784-1 (paperback) | ISBN 978-1-6667-6785-8 (hardcover) | ISBN 978-1-6667-6786-5 (ebook)
Subjects: LCSH: Capitalism—Religious aspects—Christianity. | Business—Religious aspects—Christianity. | Church and the world. | Church finance. | Economics—Religious aspects—Christianity.
Classification: BR115.C3 B88 2025 (paperback) | BR115.C3 (ebook)

VERSION NUMBER 08/12/25

Scriptures taken from the Holy Bible, New International Version®, NIV®. Copyright © 1973, 1978, 1984, 2011 by Biblica, Inc.™ Used by permission of Zondervan. All rights reserved worldwide. www.zondervan.com The "NIV" and "New International Version" are trademarks registered in the United States Patent and Trademark Office by Biblica, Inc.™

Scripture quotations are taken from the New Revised Standard Version Updated Edition. Copyright © 2021 National Council of Churches of Christ in the United States of America. Used by permission. All rights reserved worldwide.

Scripture quotations taken from the (NASB®) New American Standard Bible®, Copyright © 1960, 1971, 1977, 1995, 2020 by The Lockman Foundation. Used by permission. All rights reserved. lockman.org.

This book is dedicated to all of the dreamers and visionaries working and creating beyond and in spite of the Church Industrial Complex, past, present, and future.

How we are at the small scale is how we are at the large scale. The patterns of the universe repeat at scale . . . what we practice at a small scale can reverberate to the largest scale.

—ADRIENNE MAREE BROWN

Contents

Series Foreword | ix

Contributors | xi

The Business of God: An Introduction | 1
  Sheryl Johnson and Dannis Matteson

Section 1: Historical and Biblical Insights

Chapter 1
Challenging the Church Industrial Complex:
Historical Lessons from Francisco de Vitoria | 17
  Molly Greening

Chapter 2
A Tower That Reaches to the Heavens:
Deconstructing Industrial Complexes Using Biblical Text | 31
  Erika Katske

Chapter 3
The Widow "Mite" Not Give Online:
Gifts, Accounting, and Community Formation | 45
  Daniel F. Sebastian

Section 2: Ethical Resources and Critiques

Chapter 4
Materialism, Economism, and the Modern Catholic Social Teaching:
What Would Be the Roles of the Church in an Era of Neoliberalism? | 67
  David Kwon

Chapter 5
The Specter of Capitalism: Dorothy Day and the Catholic Worker Movement as Response to Magisterial Financial Trends | 87
  Martin Tomszak

Section 3: Theological Reflections on Church Practices

Chapter 6
Challenging the Metrics of Ministry | 109
    Darryl W. Stephens

Chapter 7
Curiosity Killed the Cat(echism):
The Managerial Church and the Intellectual Appetites | 127
    Matthew J. Dodrill

Chapter 8
Neoliberal Homesteading in the Life of Churches | 148
    Christy M. Newton

Chapter 9
COVID-19 Pandemic, Technology,
and the Church Industrial Complex | 161
    Kelly Colwell

Chapter 10
Mentoring for Village Leadership:
Refounding Seminary in the Ways of Kinship | 175
    John Nelson with Jin S. Kim and Laura Newby

Conclusion | 198
    Sheryl Johnson and Dannis Matteson

Series Foreword

OVER THE CENTURIES THE CHURCH has been a source of guidance to many about the provision of goods and services that contribute to the common good. St. Basil started what may be considered one of the first hotels and hospitals in his Basiliad in the fourth century. Monastic communities served as a model for modern educational institutions, and sometimes served as places of sanctuary for those whose lives were in danger. And countless Christians through the centuries have sought guidance from the church about their participation in warfare or how they were going to run their businesses. To many in the modern world such a role for the church seems absurd, because we have come to believe that state actors and business leaders should dictate the what and why and how of our lives, often even letting business trends or patriotic commitments order the life of the church. However, there has also been resistance to the rise of nation-state and business logics ordering our moral lives.

In 1961 Dwight Eisenhower warned us that the ever-deepening relationship of private companies' profits to the United States' participation in war was creating a "military-industrial complex" that threatened the very practice of democracy.[1] In 1983 political philosopher Michael Walzer warned us that the moral logic of the market is imperialistic and threatens to become the dominant way we relate to each other by turning nearly every human interaction into a market transaction.[2] And Christian theologian-activists—from Martin Luther King Jr. to Dorothy Day to Desmond Tutu—have shown us ways to resist these trends through social movements and lives of radical hospitality. These phenomena—the rise of various industrial complexes, the colonialist expansion of market logics into every aspect of our lives, and the seeming completion of market expansion around the world—have become so commonplace that we rarely question them anymore.

1. Eisenhower, "Farewell Address."
2. Walzer, *Spheres of Justice*.

We now speak not only of the military-industrial complex, but of the prison-industrial complex, the medical-industrial complex, and even the nonprofit-industrial complex (to name only a few). These industrial complexes are economic subsystems within the larger global market that are dependent on private actors influencing, and even shaping, public policies and practices to promote their continual expansion. Increasingly and with growing speed, sectors of our common life once considered public and shared are becoming privatized and dominated by market forces: our schools, our medical institutions, and even our churches. The books in The Business of Modern Life take these developments seriously as theological and ethical problems to be examined, critiqued, and resisted. The Christian tradition has long taught us that humans are more than consumers or commodities but bearers of God's image. The church has long reminded us that we belong not only to ourselves or our appetites but to each other and to God. And the words of Jesus have long challenged us to believe that it is the poor rather than the rich, the oppressed rather than the powerful, who are blessed by God.

In The Business of Modern Life you will find a series of books examining the social ethics of our contemporary economic life in ways that seek to resist turning everything we do into "business" and reclaiming a vision of shared life that orients us toward the business of loving God and our neighbors. The books in this series will address these topics through four primary lenses: theological foundations for understanding and addressing the industrial complex in question; the history of that particular industrial complex; the global impact of that industrial complex today; and finally, possible Christian responses to the industrial complex being addressed. Collectively, then, these volumes should be a compendium of neoliberal, global capitalism's effects on nearly the entirety of human lives. They will also suggest ways that followers of Jesus may think about and act faithfully in response to these realities, seeking out the good, the true, and the beautiful as a declaration that it is not the market and Mammon that ultimately reign, but Jesus Christ.

Contributors

Kelly Colwell, Co-Senior Minister, First Congregational Church of Berkeley United Church of Christ and Adjunct Faculty, Pacific School of Religion, Berkeley

Matthew Dodrill, Upper School Humanities Teacher at Trinity School of Durham and Chapel Hill, Durham, North Carolina

Molly Greening, Instructor, Loyola University Chicago, Chicago

Sheryl Johnson, Faculty Lecturer in Ethics at Pacific Lutheran Theological Seminary, Berkeley

Erika Katske, Training Coordinator, Institute for Social Transformation, University of California at Santa Cruz and Doctoral Candidate, Graduate Theological Union, Berkeley

Jin S. Kim, Founder and Teacher at Underground Seminary, Minneapolis

David Kwon, Assistant Professor at Seattle University, Seattle

Dannis Matteson, Visiting Assistant Professor at Saint Mary's College, Notre Dame

John Nelson, Assistant Instructor at Underground Seminary, Minneapolis

Laura Newby, Pedagogue & Catalyst at Underground Seminary, Minneapolis

Christy Newton, Executive Director, Disciples Seminary Foundation, Oakland, California

Daniel F. Sebastian, Provisional Assistant Professor at Evangel University, Springfield, Missouri

Darryl W. Stephens, Director of United Methodist Studies and Director of the Pennsylvania Academy of Ministry, Lancaster Theological Seminary, Lancaster, Pennsylvania

Martin Tomszak, Visiting Assistant Professor at Valparaiso University, Valparaiso, Indiana

The Business of God

An Introduction

SHERYL JOHNSON AND DANNIS MATTESON

The term "Church Industrial Complex" can bring many images to mind. For some, it is the stadium-like sanctuaries of megachurches with large screens and bright lights, or the lavish bookstores and coffee shops in the atrium on the way in. For others, it may be the proliferation of "Christian" goods and services that are sold worldwide, ranging from music to books to courses to Bibles (in a proliferation of forms) to educational curricula. It may bring to mind thoughts of celebrity preachers and televangelists or the opulence of the Vatican. One might think about the industry of present-day missionaries and short-term mission trips, or the endeavor of the early twentieth century to "evangelize the world in this generation," or the entwining of church, economy, trade, and colonialism going back centuries.

The theoretical framework behind the term "Industrial Complex" explores how institutions established with a purpose external to themselves can become focused on their own self-perpetuation—pursuing power, growth, and profits—in ways that may well contradict and undermine that original purpose. The first use of the term is credited to sociologist C. Wright Mills and was popularized by former US President Dwight D. Eisenhower in his 1961 Farewell Address to the nation. In this speech, he warned of the growing power of a "military-industrial complex" where the economic benefits of war (to the nation, weapons manufacturers, defense contractors, and other related industries) were undermining democratic processes and encouraging ongoing war for the sake of financial return, all under the guise of national security.[1] The military was also increasingly organized under

---

1. Best, "Introduction," xvi.

business models with profit serving as the central motive.[2] We can see that it is not only the military but many other industries and sectors that are shaped by these same market interests. Over the past decades, features of post-industrial capitalism such as hierarchical power systems, commodification, privatization, repression, mass production/standardization, a focus on growth and efficiency, and extreme profit motivations have become prevalent in nearly every corner of our lives and our world such that it can be difficult to even imagine an alternative.[3] The sectors and institutions that are impacted include healthcare, education, entertainment, agriculture, non-profits, prisons, and religion—including Christian churches, which we will focus on in this book.

Due to the very phenomenon of Industrial Complexes and embedded within the context of racial and market capitalism, these sectors are increasingly interrelated in ways that serve power and increase profits for each. Take academia, for example. Henry Giroux reveals the way that, in many cases, higher education no longer serves to promote and advance knowledge for its own sake but now does research to benefit and cut costs for certain industries (i.e., pharmaceuticals, agriculture, the military), create direct revenue for businesses through exclusive contracts and privatization (i.e., outsourcing dining hall services), and increase its own revenue by cutting costs wherever possible (i.e., decreasing tenured faculty and increasing part-time and adjunct roles).[4] In a volume focused on the broad phenomena of Industrial Complexes, Steven Best argues that "the powerful logics of industrialization and capitalism, symbiotically interlocked at least since the nineteenth century, have expanded, diversified, and colonized ever more institutions and organizing systems, and expanded into a world system."[5]

These trends, of course, have not gone unnoticed. Much theorizing and activism have critically engaged with a whole variety of other "Industrial Complexes," ranging from the military, healthcare, prison, wedding, athletic, celebrity, global, and non-profit sectors. The insights gained in these spheres and others are highly pertinent to the situation of Christian churches and Christian institutions. Although the purpose, mission, identity, and role of these institutions vary, all have been swayed in similar ways by the phenomenon of Industrial Complexes. Naturally, we do not wish to suggest that these institutions should be "returned" to a prior state or need not be critiqued beyond their entwinement with other Industrial

2. Best, "Introduction," xvi.
3. Best, "Introduction," xvi, xx.
4. Giroux, *University in Chains*, 102–8.
5. Best, "Introduction," xx.

Complexes. The same is true for churches and Christian institutions: There is need for a more focused critique that is more narrow than the phenomenon of the church's entwinement in other societal Industrial Complexes. The primary focus of our work, therefore, is the influence of profit and power in the Church Industrial Complex.

This book draws attention to and explores this framework of the Industrial Complex in relation to churches. How do churches, intended to worship God, preach the gospel, nurture discipleship, and serve those in need, become focused on factors such as profit accumulation, limitless growth, and the expansion and consolidation of power? It is critical to explore the ways that systems like colonialism, capitalism, white supremacy, and patriarchy also intersect as oppressive forces within this sphere. As Industrial Complexes function to accumulate profits and consolidate power, there is often an element of extracting and appropriating resources from more marginalized groups (be they classed, gendered, racialized, etc.) for the benefit of more privileged groups and to further their interests. These examples of injustice in the Church Industrial Complex are of critical import.

We also need to address critical questions that detail what is at stake. What are the impacts of the Church Industrial Complex on various facets of church life and parties involved? Where do we find the Church Industrial Complex particularly manifest, and how can those instances help us to see where it may be operating in more subtle and less visible ways, particularly among those in positions of privilege and power? Finally, we must consider what can be done to resist these "temptations" of power and profit. We must locate the corners of church that have and continue to be witness to alternative, liberative approaches. Often these corners can be found in more marginalized communities and spaces. Yet we must not romanticize oppression nor suggest that in some way these communities are "pure" or "uncorrupted" in a manner that is infantilizing, essentializing, or otherwise oppressive. It is critical to be nuanced as we amplify voices and spaces of resistance, while attempting to resist our own Industrial Complex-style of extraction of theology, ethics, and praxis in oppressed spaces to serve the desires of those of us with greater privilege and power in the church.

Exploring the Church Industrial Complex

As the editors of this book, we acknowledge that we are certainly not the first to coin the term "Church Industrial Complex." This is a term that has been popping up in various places in recent years, particularly in blogs, podcasts, and other newer media. It seems the concept is defined and understood in somewhat differing ways, but generally speaking, most use this term to explain the structures of the church in the modern day, including all of the financial and power relationships that exist in denominations, parachurch organizations, congregations, Christian media, and so forth. Some also explore the relationship between church-specific institutions and other systems such as those connected to politics and the media. Most sources take a critical perspective on the Church Industrial Complex, but this is not universally true. Some, writing from a more evangelical perspective, speak positively about the ways that the Church Industrial Complex functions to spread the gospel effectively and efficiently, perhaps even gaining valuable insight from emulating or intersecting with other Industrial Complexes. However, for the most part, many using this term seem concerned and dismayed by the ways that churches have become disconnected from key elements of Christian faith as they have pursued power and profit—the antithesis of standing with the marginalized and decrying unjust systems.

While it is not possible or necessary to cite every instance of theorizing related to the Church Industrial Complex, we will introduce a few of these as a way to give a flavor of the arguments and scope of discussions. A 2009 blog post by Peter Laarman in *Religion Dispatches*, an independent online magazine, names the Religion Industrial Complex as a system that has entwined politics and religion to domesticate Protestantism and dissuade churches from taking strong stands that diverge from mainstream political opinions.[6] Laarman suggests that Protestant churches have become "chaplains" to the US Democratic Party in the ways that they offer uncritical, unquestioning support rather than prophetically calling the entire political realm to conscience.[7] On a related topic but with a distinct approach, Jacques Berlinerblau articulates a Religion-Industrial Complex that came together in preparation for the 2008 US election to analyze the role religion played in that election as well as the more practical elements of religious lobbyists and consultants serving to enhance the image and reception of political candidates.[8] Here, we see writers arguing that religion (and, more specifically, Christianity) operates in service to broader Industrial Complexes.

Others reflect more specifically on the systems and situations that are internal to the church's own workings. Lutheran pastor Jay Winters blogs that we can understand the various levels of church governance and intersecting institutions, such as seminaries, as a sort of Church Industrial Complex that has developed alongside other Industrial Complexes and is now

---

6. Laarman, "Putting the 'Protest' Back in Protestant."
7. Laarman, "Putting the 'Protest' Back in Protestant."
8. Berlinerblau, "Religion-Industrial Complex."

being re-evaluated alongside these others at the present moment.[9] There are also numerous articles that cite specific aspects of the Church Industrial Complex. Introducing another critical perspective, David W. Congdon argues that there is currently a "global-church Industrial Complex" operating to "mine the resource of 'non-Western Christianity' for the sake of fixing 'Western Christianity.'"[10] He argues that this view romanticizes and essentializes the church of the Global South precisely because it is seen to be less co-opted by "secular" forces. Here we see the complexities and diversity of the Global Church erased and elements extracted by churches in the Global North to serve a particular agenda, with little benefit to those in the Global South.

Modern Christian missionary engagement has also been described as operating through the framework of an Industrial Complex. Scott A. Bessenecker argues that a "capitalist mindset" has infiltrated the church's engagement in mission and that these ventures have become shaped by corporate models.[11] According to Bessenecker, features of this capitalist influence include mission organizational structures, employee relationships, financial focus, marketing, and definitions of success.[12] While he does not question the project of conversion and the need to engage in mission, he suggests that it can be done in ways that are more just, such as emphasizing simplicity, long-term accountability in relationships, discipleship over numerical growth, and collaborative engagement with Christians in various parts of the world.

In studying the Church Industrial Complex, many scholars focus specifically on evangelicalism, some even suggesting that the Church Industrial Complex is a uniquely evangelical phenomenon. A piece by blogger Anthony G. Siegrist proposes a Church-Industrial-Celebrity-Complex that operates similarly to secular celebrity industries to do whatever it takes to expand their reach and monetize their message.[13] Skye Jethani also focuses on the connection between Christian media organizations and evangelical celebrities which mutually seek to enhance one another's wealth and influence.[14] It seems that the focus on conversion and growth in evangelical spaces—understood as a core aspect of the church—may make it especially

9. Winters, "Church Industrial Complex."
10. Congdon, "Global-Church Industrial Complex."
11. Bessenecker, *Overturning the Tables*, 23.
12. Bessenecker, *Overturning the Tables*, 23.
13. Siegrist, "Understanding the Church-Industrial-Celebrity-Complex."
14. Jethani, "Evangelical Industrial Complex and the Rise of Celebrity Pastors (Pt. 1)."

susceptible to other elements of Church Industrial Complex and particularly complex to discern what counts as truly living out mission versus what is a corruption of the gospel.

On the other hand, others argue that the Church Industrial Complex impacts all Christian churches. Dan White Jr., consultant with an alternative church planting movement called V3, analyzes the Church Industrial Complex. He argues that it has borrowed from mainstream culture to define church success as requiring features such as continuous growth, accumulation of resources, increased power, and hierarchical structures.[15] White focuses on the values and worldview of the Church Industrial Complex and the ways that it has defined the goals of many churches, goals which are not aligned with the way of Jesus and the model of the Early Church. Many writers use theological and scriptural foundations to ground the values and metrics we should hold for evaluating the church and use those as a point of comparison for current practices and models.

While the specific features of the Church Industrial Complex that are analyzed are all somewhat distinct, it appears that most are using this concept to explore the ways that the church is not holding true to its own stated values and is instead becoming complicit in systems of power, politics, money, and prestige. Most do not see this shift as inevitable, but instead offer an immanent critique rooted in the long tradition of theological skepticism and the rejection of elements of these systems, if not the systems in their entirety. There is the sense that Christianity can and should take new forms and ones that are deeply rooted in Christian values, rather than replicating or reinforcing systems and institutions of power in our world.

In *The Business of God*, we highlight some historical, biblical, theological and ethical considerations of the Church Industrial Complex (CIC) and give examples of ways that Christian institutions perpetuate structures and practices that cement the CIC. The various writers collected in this book, as scholars within seminaries and Christian institutions, as well as ministers of churches, are therefore examining the Church Industrial Complex from within. This means that our work interrogates our own contexts within the CIC as we struggle against it ourselves.

Many of us are intimately intertwined with the tension of keeping churches and institutions afloat financially in a market-based economy. We feel the pressure bearing down upon us to attract new community members or students so that we can increase the revenue for our workplaces. Some of us witness those hardline decisions that compromise community values but seem to be the only option for keeping the building maintained. Many

---

15. White, "Discover the Grassroots Work of Movement."

of us experience the precarity of being exploited while at the same time feeling like we have put one foot inside the door of exploitation by our very institutional participation. All of this is to say that, as we critique the CIC, we are not critiquing from an ivory tower outside of the CIC's reality. In fact, that would be impossible, for we acknowledge that "ivory towers" are pinnacles of the CIC structure itself. Instead, we are critiquing, reflecting and envisioning with full acknowledgment that we, too, are participants in the CIC in one way or another. And we believe that this critique, reflection, and envisioning work can help to articulate pathways of liberation away from both the Church Industrial Complexes as well as the many other entwined Industrial Complexes of our time. We hope that this work will provide insight into repairing the historical and present-day harm that these Complexes have left in their wake.[16]

Readers will notice that we have woven common themes throughout our chapters in both unique and similar ways. We critique neoliberalism heavily as an ideology that distorts gospel values as well as the dominant blueprint for structuring Christian institutions. We stand upon the work of Rebecca Todd Peters, for example, in defining neoliberal globalization for the *Ecumenical Review* of the World Council of Churches. With Todd Peters, we take neoliberalism to point to the *kind* of market capitalism around which Christian institutional economic practices revolve. Neoliberalism, in the context of globalization, describes the ways that political leaders gain power by yielding to corporate pressure to deregulate governmental intervention of the market.[17] Neoliberalism also shapes culture through an ideology that says the race for profit transcends any kind of ethical critique of the economic practices that profit requires.[18] Neoliberalism as an ideology is fueled by a culture that promotes individualism, self-interest, and competition.[19] Authors of this book draw on diverse resources to further define neoliberalism and to illuminate how churches and Christian institutions have been built upon neoliberal values and reify these structures.

Given the North American context of this book, it is critical to acknowledge that neoliberalism is an iteration of the structure of colonization

---

16. At the same time, we also acknowledge that this book does not by any means illuminate all perspectives relating to the CIC. We want to contribute to the conversation while listening to voices not captured in this work. As we emphasize in the conclusion, there are critical voices and elements that we were not able to include in this book, and we look forward to continuing to expand the conversation beyond the limits of our immediate considerations.

17. Todd Peters, "Feminist Critical Discourse," 283.

18. Todd Peters, "Feminist Critical Discourse," 298.

19. Todd Peters, "Feminist Critical Discourse," 294.

and a reflection of coloniality. This awareness is woven through each and every chapter of this book because we cannot speak about the CIC without speaking about its ties to the historical and present-day violence of colonization. For instance, in chapter 1, Greening highlights important definitions of colonization and summarizes these definitions emphasizing that colonization is not just an event but a "structure of power relations that continues today in settler societies like the United States, Canada, New Zealand, and Australia." Coloniality is a term that has been expressed by colonized and Indigenous people to critically resist European domination. Coloniality describes both a system and a way of thinking and being that either submits to or enforces this kind of domination. Catherine Walsh and Walter Mignolo describe this system operating as a "complex structure of management and control."[20] Our chapters give examples of Christian institutions complying with this very structure of management and control as well as forming Christians to think and act in colonial terms and habits.

Many chapters also rely on the theoretical frameworks of both Catholic Social Teaching (CST) and Marxist thought to critique the capitalist structures of the Church Industrial Complex. On the one hand, CST can be viewed as a doctrinal stand against capitalist exploitation and extraction set down by the Magisterium of the Roman Catholic Church. In chapter 4, David Kwon points to CST documents that warn against the "culture of death" grounded in market capitalism. By naming this "culture of death," *Evangelium Vitae* (no. 12) shows how economy influences culture and in the end, our church communities as well.[21] Another example of Catholic Social Teaching's strong critique of capitalism can be found in Pope Francis's criticism of the "technocratic paradigm" in *Laudato Si'*.[22] On the other hand, a number of authors lean on Marxist critique of capitalism. Multiple authors examine the adoption of *commodity fetishism* within churches and Christian institutions. This fetishism becomes problematic, and even dangerous, when the church becomes obsessed with turning ministry into the production of commodities to attract members or consumers. Ultimately, this fetishistic obsession manipulates social relationships and eats away at the fabric of a community.

20. Mignolo and Walsh, *On Decoloniality*, 125.
21. John Paul II, *Evangelium Vitae*, sec. 97.
22. Francis, *Laudato Si'*, sec. 106–14.

Overview of Chapters

This book comprises three main sections: Historical and Biblical Insights, Ethical Resources and Critiques, and Theological Reflections on Church Practices. We end the book with a case study that provides a constructive example of forming church leaders to resist the CIC. The Church Industrial Complex carries with it long-standing historical contexts, and it is a present-day iteration of histories of colonial empire building and the theologies that justified and empowered it. Conversely, there is also a long history of critique about the CIC. In chapter 1, "Challenging the Church Industrial Complex," Molly Greening provides historical context for understanding the CIC by examining the influence of Francisco de Vitoria and his simultaneous proliferation and critique of political and ecclesial forces of colonization in what is today's North America. Greening shows how the polemical example of Vitoria can stand as a warning for church leaders. Greening flags how North American Christians should be wary of Christian institutions purporting to uphold social justice while remaining beholden to the financial bottom line because this often thwarts concrete forms of solidarity.

The project of empire building and the justification of its violent conquest has long influenced the interpretation of biblical passages. In chapters 2 and 3, Erika Katske and Daniel Sebastian provide examples of how the interpretation of scripture has been commonly used as an ideological foundation for the Church Industrial Complex. Paradoxically, both authors argue that the passages they examine can, in fact, disrupt ideologies that build the Church Industrial Complex.

In chapter 2, "A Tower That Reaches to the Heavens," Katske analyzes mythologies of tower-building and highlights the symbol of the tower woven into the fictions that undergird the Church Industrial Complex. This very phenomenon leads North American Christians to interpret the pericope of Gen 11:1–9 through an industrial lens. Katske shows how a close read of the Tower of Babel leads to the re-examination of God's character and God's role in this story. And, when read side by side with Marx, the story instead provides a pointed critique of commodity fetishism, specifically when structures (i.e., towers) take on meaning and value of their own. God's disruption of the Tower of Babel is here interpreted to interrogate the role of commodity fetishism within the Church Industrial Complex.

Daniel Sebastian considers in chapter 3, "The Widow 'Mite' Not Give Online," how online donation practices of congregational giving have the potential to cement an "accounting" mindset for Christian communities. When counting the amount of funds donated is given priority and the largest donations are given the highest value, Sebastian argues that this signals the loss of meaning behind those very rituals. Sebastian shows how the widow in the Gospel of Mark imposes her physical presence in a dominating space and thereby confronts religious leaders who are concerned with recording dollar amounts. Not only that, Sebastian suggests that this figure's physical presence carves out a space for community members who are often ostracized because of their incapacity to give large sums of money.

Section 2 identifies some important ethical resources and critiques for examining the function of the CIC in Christian institutions, starting with "Materialism, Economism, and the Modern Catholic Social Teaching: What Would Be the Roles of the Church in an Era of Neoliberalism?" by David Kwon. Through a Marxian critique of commodity fetishism and Catholic Social Teaching's theological critique of materialism, this fourth chapter explains how neoliberal structures are not just an individual problem but the very culture in which church life is embedded. Kwon argues that Christians, and Catholics specifically, have ethical resources to draw on for critiquing the way capitalism is imbued in Christian culture. Kwon points out the dangers of neoliberal globalization shaping church culture because it can distort our concepts of morality. Catholic Social Teaching (CST) can address this by redefining freedom beyond simply a license to do anything one wants and ensuring basic needs and rights are met and protected.

Martin Tomszak responds with chapter 5, "The Specter of Capitalism," which mines the Catholic tradition to critique the church's own participation in capitalism. Tomszak's critique draws on Matthew's parable of the vineyard, CST, the example of radical lay communities, and the thought of Dorothy Day. This chapter sheds light on how, in their construction of CST, the Catholic hierarchy proposes a "third way" beyond capitalism and Marxism, but fails to flesh out the practical and material examples of what that would look like. To fill in this gap left by CST, Dorothy Day, Peter Maurin, and the Catholic Worker Movement exemplify ways of living out the principles of CST. In doing so, they create a map forward to live in contrast to capitalist values and transform communities through direct service and the fostering of relationships.

The third section of this book provides theological reflections on how church practices translate community belief and how some of these practices prop up the Church Industrial Complex. In chapter 6, "Challenging the Metrics of Ministry," Darryl Stephens argues that the empire of Christendom haunts us today when Christian institutions are modeled after the "market-driven economic system." Stephens claims that this tendency can be seen when market logic interprets divine favor through wealth accumulation and prosperity. In fact, he argues that the very life of a Christian community often rests upon metrics that reflect this market logic. Stephens laments that these metrics sideline core components that make Christian communities unique and vital. This is partially because, as Stephens states, evaluating the life of a Christian community through market metrics tells the story that "quantification yields value; what cannot be measured cannot be valued." Stephens questions these facets of the CIC and proposes methods for disrupting the scarcity mindset.

In chapter 7, "Curiosity Killed the (Cat)echism," Matthew Dodrill provides the theoretical background for understanding the "technocratic paradigm" and its impacts on church practices. Dodrill critiques how the "Fresh Expressions" model represents trendy appeals to consumerist desires essentially invoking innovation as the primary "virtue" by which to live and upon which to build a church community. These trends toward innovation become problematic because pastors essentially become managers and entrepreneurs. Meanwhile, as Dodrill notes, "questions about the good life and the kingdom of God are replaced by questions about growth and maximizing outputs."

Christy M. Newton invokes the metaphor of homesteading in chapter 8, "Neoliberal Homesteading in the Life of Churches," to critique how the CIC charts a blueprint for church life that serves economic interests rather than community needs. Through what Newton calls "spiritual homesteading," neoliberal values dominate community processes of making meaning about the purpose of church, which ultimately, in her words, "takes up residence in the life of churches." Newton suggests concrete forms of resistance against these new metaphorical homesteading patterns that so often lay claim to church life in the era of the CIC.

A research study by Kelly Colwell provides practical examples of ways that the pandemic revealed the intensification of the use of technology among churches. In chapter 9, "COVID-19 Pandemic, Technology, and the Church Industrial Complex," Colwell documents the diverse ways churches felt forced to lean on technology to keep communities in connection. At the same time, Colwell evaluates how this phenomenon reveals the common pitfalls of technology, which have served to reinforce the Church Industrial Complex.

The Business of God ends with a case study in chapter 10 entitled "Mentoring for Village Leadership," by John Nelson, Laura Newby, and Pastor Jin S. Kim. The authors of this chapter describe an alternative seminary disrupting the CIC trend that turns pastors into managers of corporations. The Underground Seminary, founded in 2014, is a mentorship and formation program for church leaders as well as a community of people committed to reviving kinship culture. Underground Seminary is a community characterized by values that include upholding the sacredness of the earth, sustainable mutuality, relationality, communal ethos that serves a gift economy, and cooperation and advocacy. This chapter shows that there are already Christian communities dedicated to resisting both the CIC and the neoliberal capitalist pressures that reinforce it.

Our hope is that after reading *The Business of God* readers will have tools and language for critiquing the Church Industrial Complex in their own contexts. As we have demonstrated, these contexts may include churches, universities, not-for-profit agencies, or other Christian institutions. It is impossible to escape the influence of the CIC because of how Christian institutions support political platforms by providing funding to lobbyists, for example. As an Industrial Complex, the CIC's structure has a forceful grasp on policy and economics, and for this reason, it is pertinent that Christians not only look at their own community contexts for evidence of the CIC but more broadly interrogate how the CIC is interwoven with other Industrial Complexes that dominate our society.

This book focuses explicitly on the Church Industrial Complex with a particular emphasis on the North American context. It is not to say that other religions do not in their own ways function as Industrial Complexes, but because of the position of power held by Christianity in a historical sense and on the global level, there are certainly nuances and perhaps particular challenges that are distinct to this tradition. We write from this position as we both strive to unmask the ways that Christianity so often supports unjust structures and systems and also desire to show that this system is not inevitable or unavoidable. We write to both show what *is* as well as to begin to envision what *could be* and to lift up what already exists in some corners of the church.

Bibliography

Berlinerblau, Jacques. "The Religion-Industrial Complex." Berkley Center for Religion, Peace, and World Affairs, July 9, 2007. https://berkleycenter.georgetown.edu/posts/the-religion-industrial-complex.

Bessenecker, Scott A. *Overturning the Tables: Freeing Missions from the Christian-Industrial Complex*. Downers Grove, IL: InterVarsity, 2014.

Best, Steven. "Introduction." In *The Global Industrial Complex: Systems of Domination*, edited by Steven Best et al., ix–xxv. Lanham, MD: Lexington, 2011.

Congdon, David W. "The Global-Church Industrial Complex." *Patheos*, May 17, 2018, https://www.patheos.com/blogs/anxiousbench/2018/05/the-global-church-industrial-complex/.

Francis. *Laudato Si'*. Encyclical Letter of the Holy Father on the Care for Our Common Home. The Holy See, May 24, 2015. https://www.vatican.va/content/francesco/en/encyclicals/documents/papa-francesco_20150524_enciclica-laudato-si.html.

Giroux, Henry A. *The University in Chains: Confronting the Military-Industrial-Academic Complex*. Boulder, CO: Paradigm, 2007.

Jethani, Skye. "The Evangelical Industrial Complex and the Rise of Celebrity Pastors (Pt. 1)." *Christianity Today*, February 20, 2012, https://www.christianitytoday.com/pastors/2012/february-online-only/evangelical-industrial-complex-rise-of-celebrity-pastors.html.

John Paul II. *Evangelium Vitae*. Encyclical Letter on the Value and Inviolability of Human Life. The Holy See, March 25, 1995. https://www.vatican.va/content/john-paul-ii/en/encyclicals/documents/hf_jp-ii_enc_25031995_evangelium-vitae.html.

Laarman, Peter. "Putting the 'Protest' Back in Protestant: Reclaiming the Spirit of Resistance." *Religion Dispatches*, June 1, 2009. https://religiondispatches.org/putting-the-protest-back-in-protestant-reclaiming-the-spirit-of-resistance/.

Mignolo, Walter, and Catherine E. Walsh. *On Decoloniality: Concepts, Analytics, Praxis*. Durham, NC: Duke University Press, 2018.

Siegrist, Anthony G. "Understanding the Church-Industrial-Celebrity-Complex." Anthony G. Siegrist, February 11, 2021. https://anthonysiegrist.com/2021/02/11/understanding-the-church-industrial-celebrity-complex/.

Todd Peters, Rebecca. "Feminist Critical Discourse on Globalization, Economy, Ecology and Empire." *The Ecumenical Review* 64 (2012) 281–98.

White, Dan, Jr. "Discover the Grassroots Work of Movement." V3, August 8, 2016. https://thev3movement.org/2016/08/08/church-as-movement-not-industrial-complex/.

Winters, Jay. "The Church Industrial Complex." JWinters, May 7, 2021. https://jwinters.com/post/650530506120790016/the-church-industrial-complex.

SECTION 1

Historical and Biblical Insights

Chapter 1

Challenging the Church Industrial Complex
Historical Lessons from Francisco de Vitoria

MOLLY GREENING

Introduction

In the United Nations gardens located in New York City, there is a bust of sixteenth-century theologian Francisco de Vitoria (1485–1546). Under this statue, a plaque reads "Fundador del Derecho de Gentes," or Founder of the Law of Peoples. Vitoria was a Dominican friar at the University of Salamanca in Spain a few decades after the beginnings of colonization. Vitoria is known for his theological and political contributions to sixteenth-century Catholic Spanish thought. Many contemporary Catholics view Francisco de Vitoria as a courageous voice of conscience during a time when truly Christian values of human dignity were corrupted by greed. About fifty years after the colonization began of what is now called the Americas, Vitoria synthesized natural law theory and revived the Roman legal framework of the *ius gentium* or law of nations. With these legal theories, he argued against theological adversaries for the full humanity of Indigenous people and their inherent human dignity due to their God-given capacity for rationality. He also defended Indigenous land rights by challenging the Doctrine of Discovery, or the right given through a papal bull from Pope Alexander VI for Spanish colonizers to claim the land they "discovered" during conquest. His legacy has led some to celebrate him as the "grandfather of international law" since humanists like Grotius who came after him would build on his writings to construct more formalized universal rights frameworks that were not dependent on religious justification.

Other scholars, however, depict Vitoria's legacy in less charitable ways. They say that his law of nations framework further entrenched an emergent economic system that relied on private property, profit accumulation, and endless war that made the values of settler colonialism seem natural and beneficial for all. Martti Koskenniemi argues that Vitoria provided justifications for states to wage endless wars to continue an exploitative global economic system based on profits yielded from private property ownership.[1] By including Indigenous people into a law of nations framework that claimed universality but benefited European conquest, Vitoria put Indigenous people in a double bind, Ashley Bohrer argues, of accepting the terms of their own exploitation while affirming their dignity at the same time. Bohrer claims that Vitoria normalized an incredibly unequal set of terms by claiming Indigenous inclusion under the guise of equality.[2]

So, was Vitoria paving the way toward international justice or was he an architect of colonial power and oppression? Depending on your conversation partners, the story told of Vitoria's legacy usually falls on either side of this dichotomy. But I want to hold on to this tension within Vitoria's reception history to glean insights for challenging the Catholic Church Industrial Complex today. I hold that Vitoria did attempt to challenge Church expansion and the unjust accumulation of resources. He also challenged state power linked to upholding these structures. But his legacy is a helpful reminder for any church leaders in positions of power who may claim to be solely focused on justice when economic factors are also at play: If colonialism is a structure, not an event, then important insights can be gleaned from Vitoria's theological negotiations at the beginning that may hold import for realizing global justice today.

A Structure, Not an Event: Colonial Genealogies

Maile Arvin, Eve Tuck, and Angie Morrill argue that colonialism is not just a historical event but a structure of power relations that continues today in settler societies like the United States, Canada, New Zealand, and Australia.[3] Decolonial thinkers like Nelson Maldonado-Torres point to the racialization of religion as an important pivot point for continuing these

---

1. See Koskenniemi, "Empire and International Law," 1–36.
2. Bohrer, "Just Wars of Accumulation," 28–29.
3. Arvin et al., "Decolonizing Feminism," 12.

structures,[4] which Anibal Quijano coined as the "coloniality of power."[5] A historical overview of this specific theological negotiation of colonial Church expansion emphasizes structures of power that are still operative today. Foucault's theory of genealogy is instructive here, since we can use it to investigate what has influenced the multiple lines of power within the Catholic Church.[6] Vitoria shows that even the Doctrine of Discovery was contested by differing papal authorities in contradictory papal documents, proving that the Catholic Church is not monolithic, even where it claims itself to be.

These voices of contestation are particularly important for assessing the ideological histories of terms like *human rights*, *land rights*, and *human dignity*. Arvin, Tuck, and Morrill also argue that a critique of structures set in place by settler colonialism is incomplete without a critique of the ways that the nation state is gendered and sexed through heteropatriarchal norms.[7] Native feminists importantly show how many of these concepts still uphold structures of power that perpetuate white supremacy, patriarchy, and cis-heterosexuality. I draw attention to the ways that Vitoria claims neutrality and universality in ways that reinforce colonial domination connected to race, religion, and gender.

Defining Church Industrial Complex

I understand the term Church Industrial Complex in multiple ways. In one way, it names how churches engage in practices of self-perpetuation at the expense of their own morals. Dan White Jr. characterizes the Church Industrial Complex as focused on (1) rapid expansion, (2) the accumulation of larger and larger amounts of wealth/resources, and (3) increasing church power through (4) establishing hierarchical governance structures that consolidate power for a select few in positions of leadership. One of the benefits of naming church power as an Industrial Complex is that it points to how churches and settler states are interlocking structures. Thus, I also understand the Church Industrial Complex as inseparably linked to the other forms of Industrial Complexes.

The Church Industrial Complex not only functions with the same logic of expansion and accumulation as the Military Industrial Complex, the Immigration Industrial Complex, the Prison Industrial Complex, to

---

4. See Maldonado-Torres, "AAR Centennial Roundtable," 636–65.
5. See Quijano, "Coloniality of Power, Eurocentrism, and Latin America," 533–80.
6. See Foucault, "Nietzsche Genealogy, History."
7. Arvin et al., "Decolonizing Feminism," 8.

name a few, but churches and Christian denominations sometimes (1) work in tandem with these structures; (2) profit from them and (3) are always embedded within them in the dailiness of ministry. For example, in the case of prisons and immigration detention centers, churches often work for governments as intermediary actors, occupying a blurry space where they are neither representatives of the state nor completely outside of its jurisdiction. Religiously affiliated chaplains and workers for state-sponsored immigration shelters, for example, can use this blurry space to be advocates, even if their paycheck is coming from the same structure they may critique. Churches can also profit from other Industrial Complexes through direct business or contracts or through financial investments that benefit from militarization, warfare, and the exploitation of land and bodies for the accumulation of natural resources.

Even the minutiae of church life is entangled in these webs of exploitation. For example, in the winter of 2023, the *New York Times* exposed how unaccompanied migrant children as young as thirteen coming to the United States from Central America were being exploited for cheap labor in factories owned by Fruit of the Loom, Frito-Lay, Whole Foods, Walmart, and J. Crew.[8] From the fresh socks and underwear in the donation basket at a church clothing drive to the donuts, coffee, wine, and cheese used for church socials, these seemingly inconspicuous items are intimately connected to this structure of exploitation.

A historical overview speaks to the ways that we need models of church leaders in positions of power challenging the church around issues of expansion, accumulation, and power hoarding. However, we do not need heroes—where Vitoria gets it wrong is as important for this analysis today as where he gets it right.

Justifying or Challenging Colonialism?

One of Vitoria's most famous works was *Relectio De Indis* (1539), where he defended the land rights of Indigenous people in the Americas using a combination of natural law reasoning and a revival of *ius gentium*, or the law of nations that originated in Roman law texts. He was also credited with establishing the "School of Salamanca," which left a serious political legacy while ushering in a new era of scholasticism during a time of significant political and religious upheaval.

A closer look at Vitoria's argumentation shows complexity in the role Catholic theologians in positions of power played in the negotiation of this

---

8. Dreier and Luce, "Alone and Exploited."

new colonial world order. At this period of the sixteenth century, church and state were both distinguishable from each other in Spain, though impossible to *completely* separate. Theologians were negotiating a space in between shifting power constellations while looking for universal frameworks that could speak to the new realities of conquest. Oftentimes, Catholic missionaries and clerics were key actors in establishing *or* challenging the newly emergent material constellations of power, even if they saw their role as primarily spiritual. Theologians were confessors for the conquistadors, holding a level of moral power over those who may have been looking for absolution or guidance regarding their guilty consciences over their methods of conquest. Missionaries trying to evangelize Indigenous communities were both prophetic witnesses against *and* accomplices to the death-dealing devastation caused by the emergent global order that led to murder, sexual violence, and forced labor of Indigenous people and people from West Africa sold into slavery. Whether Catholic theologians or missionaries were challenging or justifying particular colonial practices, conversion to Christianity was usually seen as the utmost priority.

Colonial practices that solidified during the first forty years of colonization were being heavily debated in Europe, especially since economic, political, and spiritual motivations were often intertwined. Some theologians, such as Vitoria and Juan Ginés de Sepúlveda, speculated on the humanity and rationality of human beings they had never met before while sitting in their universities across the ocean. Both sides consulted the *same* ancient philosophers and medieval theologians, using the work of Aristotle and Aquinas to either justify or challenge aspects of the new circumstances of colonization.

Sepúlveda would be known as one of the biggest advocates of colonialism, debating against Bartolome de las Casas in the Valladolid debates of 1550. He also argued that Indigenous people were slaves by nature, using natural law to say that it was natural for certain people to rule over others, just as it is natural for men to have power over their wives and their children. In Sepúlveda's words:

> The man rules over the woman, the adult over the child, the father over his children. That is to say, the most powerful and most perfect rule over the weakest and most imperfect. This same relationship exists among men, there being some who by nature are masters and others who by nature are slaves.[9]

---

9. McNeil and Mintz, "Juan Ginés de Sepúlveda (1547)."

Similarly, Sepúlveda used natural law and divine law to try and justify the subordination of Indigenous peoples:

> Those who surpass the rest in prudence and intelligence, although not in physical strength, are by nature the masters. On the other hand, those who are dim-witted and mentally lazy, although they may be physically strong enough to fulfill all the necessary tasks, are by nature slaves . . . . It will always be just and in conformity with natural law that such people submit to the rule of more cultured and humane princes and nations . . . . Thanks to their virtues and the practical wisdom of their laws, the latter can destroy barbarism and educate these [inferior] people to a more humane and virtuous life.[10]

Vitoria also used natural law theory, but he asserted the full personhood of Indigenous people and challenged the scope of the power of both the Castilian Crown and the authority of the papacy. It is important to note that during this time, there was hardly consensus about the church's authority, even within the papacy. These insights can be important for church leaders today.

Amplifying Contestation within the Church

It was the papal bull *Inter Caetera*, issued by Pope Alexander VI, that granted "all non-Christian lands" to the Spanish Crown in 1493. Citing *Inter Caetera*, many claimed that the right of the Spanish Crown to rule in the Americas had *already* been given by the Pope in 1493. Vitoria challenged the authority of the Crown and the Pope by asking three questions: (1) "by what right (*ius*) were the barbarians subjected to Spanish rule?"; (2) "What powers has the Spanish monarchy over the Indians in temporal and civil matters?"; (3) "What powers has either the monarchy or the Church with regard to the Indians in spiritual and religious matters?"[11] But did the Pope, or the Spanish Crown, *really* have any right to such authority?

Though Pope Alexander VI granted the Spanish Crown dominion over all non-Christian lands with a papal bull, in 1537 Pope Paul III nullified this bull through another papal bull, *Sublimus Deus*, which asserted that Indigenous people had property rights, were not slaves by nature, and could not be forcibly converted. There was even a document called *Pastorale Officium*, which enforced sanctions on people who disobeyed this new decree, claiming to excommunicate people who did not comply. However, Vitoria's

---

10. McNeil and Mintz, "Juan Ginés de Sepúlveda (1547)."
11. Vitoria, *Vitoria*, 233.

treatise was delivered shortly after this document was quietly revoked. Knowing this background of contestation, Vitoria argued against both the right of the church and the crown to "dominion" over non-Christian lands by negotiating the differences between human law, natural law, and divine law.

Just How Universal Is the Law of Nations?

Vitoria revived the law of nations, or *ius gentium*, after disproving that the Spanish Crown or the Pope could claim power over the Americas. According to Vitoria, neither the "most serene Emperor" or the "supreme pontiff" is the "master of the whole world";[12] the "right of discovery" is illegitimate since: Indigenous people had public and private dominion;[13] refusing to convert to Christianity or committing mortal sins is not grounds for just war;[14] and claims that Indigenous people voluntarily accepted papal or Spanish authority are invalid. Vitoria also argued that the *Requerimiento*, where Spanish troops would read a statement, ask for immediate conversion and, if there was not agreement, wage war, were coercive and not clearly communicated in a rational way,[15] and he claimed, finally, that the Americas are not a providential gift from God in response to "barbarian" abominations,[16] such as transgressing binary gender norms or practicing non-Christian religions.

In the final section of his treatise, Vitoria presented "seven just titles" that constituted his law of nations framework. This includes the right to travel (*ius peregrinandi*), the right to preach (*ius praedicandi*), and the right to trade. Since Vitoria already proved that neither the Pope nor the Crown had the authority to make laws in the Americas, his appeal to the law of nations importantly established a framework that, he argued, was built on consent and already observable custom. However, we can ask whether these understandings of universal law were actually consensual and commonly held.

He also argued for a global concept of the commons, where he claimed that *all* people should be entitled access to waterways, along with unrestrained travel. Vitoria said:

12. Vitoria, *Vitoria*, 252–58.
13. Vitoria, *Vitoria*, 264.
14. Vitoria, *Vitoria*, 265–72.
15. Vitoria, *Vitoria*, 275.
16. Vitoria, *Vitoria*, 276.

> In the beginning of the world, when all things were held in common, everyone was allowed to visit and travel through any land he wished. This right was clearly not taken away by the division of property (diusio rerum); it was never the intention of nations to prevent men's free mutual intercourse with one another by this division.[17]

Vitoria defended land rights of Indigenous people and denied the right of discovery for Spaniards since Indigenous people had dominion over their land. However, access to the commons was more universal for some than others. Extraction from Indigenous lands was a crucial economic interest of the Crown and Pope. Vitoria claimed that "if there are any things among the barbarians which are held in common both by their own people and by strangers, it is not lawful for the barbarians to prohibit the Spaniards from sharing and enjoying them."[18] Vitoria claimed that digging for gold or fishing for pearls is permitted, as long as Spaniards do it "without causing offense to the native inhabitants and citizens."[19]

Vitoria used a notion of the commons to claim that the right of discovery, or the way that anything "unoccupied or deserted" becomes the property of the discoverer, is maintained by both natural law and the law of nations: "All things which are unoccupied or deserted become the property of the occupier by natural law and the law of nations ... the law of nations ... expressly states that goods which belong to no owner pass to the occupier."[20] Though Vitoria argued that Indigenous people had dominion over their land, access to the resources of land became predicated on the lack of a particular form of private ownership coupled with an accelerated pace of extraction geared toward accumulating profits.

An Intolerable Loss to the Royal Exchequer: Justifying War for Continued Profits

Even Vitoria himself acknowledges that economic loss and the end of the current practices could not be accepted: for, "if all these titles were inapplicable, that is to say if the barbarians gave no just cause for war and did not wish to have Spaniards as princes and so on," Vitoria reasons, "the whole Indian expedition and trade would cease, to the great loss of the Spaniards.

---

17. Vitoria, *Vitoria*, 278.
18. Vitoria, *Vitoria*, 280.
19. Vitoria, *Vitoria*, 280.
20. Vitoria, *Vitoria*, 264.

And this in turn would mean a huge loss to the royal exchequer, which would be intolerable."[21] There was an economic bottom line that was beyond question, and Vitoria used the law of nations to declare the practices of buying and selling as natural, even if colonial methods accelerated extraction (and profit) on a global scale. Critics like Ashley Bohrer write:

> The inclusion of indigenous peoples in the universal brotherhood of humanity had the effect of binding them to a putatively equal and universal system, even if it had vastly unequal effects ... precisely because Amerindians are rational humans, they are bound by the laws of nature to accept the Spanish colonial presence.[22]

Indeed, it is difficult to believe that if Indigenous people came to Spain and began to mine, deforest, or fish at the pace of colonizers that their actions would also be protected under the law of nations. By arguing for the full humanity of Indigenous people, Vitoria also locked them into a supposedly universal system that greatly privileged colonial economic interests.

According to Vitoria, if any of these laws are violated, then the Spaniards, if they have *caused no harm*, have grounds for a just war. Important to this discussion is the way that he assumes colonial innocence while using Christian values like neighbor love and hospitality to assert grounds for just war through the supposed neutrality of the law of nations. For example, Vitoria references "natural partnership and communication" to establish the right to travel and the principle of hospitality: "It is a law of nature to welcome strangers ... the Spaniards are the barbarians' neighbours ... and the barbarians are obliged to love their neighbors as themselves (Matt 22:39) and may not lawfully bar them from their homeland without due cause."[23]

Due to the epistemology of natural law theory and rationality, Vitoria's framework reinforced assimilation to Christian norms as the only rational outcome.[24] Vitoria's arguments about the right to preach came with a caveat, especially because, if Indigenous people *do* have the same capacity for reason, within the natural law framework they would be irrational to not accept the gospel preached in a reasonable way. Thus, "if reasoning fails to win the acquiescence of the barbarians, and they insist on replying with violence, the Spaniards may defend themselves, and do everything needful

---

21. Vitoria, *Vitoria*, 291.
22. Bohrer, "Just Wars of Accumulation," 28–29.
23. Vitoria, *Vitoria*, 279.
24. For more on the connection between faith and reason during colonial debates, see Greening, *Belonging in the Borderlands*.

for their own safety. It is lawful to meet force with force."[25] Statements that seemed to protect religious freedom under the revamped Roman category of *ius gentium* asserted the right to war and justified forced conversion all through this same line of thinking about the connection between faith and reason.

But it is not just self-defense that Vitoria argues for, since within a just war framework, "if it is lawful to declare war on them, then it is lawful to exercise to the full the rights of war."[26] A just war could include not only self-defense, but also the "rights of war" that come with a situation where force is justified. According to this logic, the taking of land and resources, forcing people to work for no wages, and upending already existing political structures would be justified. Thus, the Spaniards "may then treat them no longer as innocent enemies, but as treacherous foes against whom all rights of war can be exercised, including plunder, enslavement, deposition of their former masters, and the institution of new ones."[27] Vitoria reminded his listeners that the sovereign has the authority to judge what the outcome should be for the combatants, reinforcing Spanish authority. Rationality, conversion, and national power end up being intertwined through a paternalistic developmental model undergirded by education into Christian rationality.

The connection between religious identity and land rights was central to the justification of colonization in the Americas. Paradoxically, both resisting conversion and converting to Christianity reinstated the power to the Pope and the Crown that Vitoria disproved in the first half of his treatise. If enough people in the Americas converted, Vitoria claims the Pope may be able to claim Indigenous people as under his jurisdiction.[28] If enough Indigenous people converted, then Spain would also be "responsible" for continued protection since "it would be neither expedient nor lawful for our prince to abandon altogether the administration of those territories."[29]

Thus, though he argued for Indigenous land rights in the first half of the treatise, Vitoria leaves many justified avenues for continued Spanish rule. Although we have already seen the economic and political benefits of continued colonial domination, Vitoria claimed that this rule was valid as long as it was of "benefit" for Indigenous people. Using curious language, Vitoria states, "I myself do not dare either to affirm or condemn" the eighth

---

25. Vitoria, *Vitoria*, 282.
26. Vitoria, *Vitoria*, 283.
27. Vitoria, *Vitoria*, 283.
28. Vitoria, *Vitoria*, 261.
29. Vitoria, *Vitoria*, 292.

possible title in his treatise, a title that left room for a patriarchal, colonial habituation:

> These barbarians, though not totally mad, as explained before, are nevertheless so close to being mad, that they are unsuited to setting up or administering a commonwealth both legitimate and ordered in human or civil terms.... They are unsuited even to governing their own households (res familiaris); hence, their lack of letters, of arts and crafts (not merely liberal, but even mechanical), of systematic agriculture, of manufacture, and of many other things useful, or rather indispensable, for human use. It might therefore be argued that for their own benefit the princes of Spain might take over their administration, and set up urban officers and governors on their behalf, or even give them new masters, so long as this could be proved to be in their interest.[30]

The phrase "unsuited to govern their own households" references Indigenous family structures that did not mimic the *res familiaris*, or the extremely patriarchal Roman household codes that placed a man as head of household with full control over his wives, his children, and his enslaved people. This structure was akin to the rational soul that controlled the "lower" inclinations, which became associated with wives, children, and slaves. While Vitoria claimed to neither agree or disagree with the statement above, benevolent paternalism was interwoven with the claim that these actions must only serve the benefit of Indigenous peoples, whose lack of heteropatriarchal models of governance and family structure shows their need for intervention.

Conclusion

Was Vitoria a forerunner for international rights, or did his framework offer theological and legal justification for exploitative economic expansion? Vitoria leaves ample space for justifying much of what he speaks against in the first half of the text. The law of nations established rights to travel, trade, and preach outside of the jurisdiction of human law and divine law; however, this also legitimated war against any resistance to Christian preaching, the unrestrained extraction of land and bodies, and the false argument that colonization was benefiting the colonized, and not the colonizer. This uneven applicability may signal discrepancies in Vitoria's thinking; the

---

30. Vitoria, *Vitoria*, 290.

political nature of arguing against both Pope and Crown meant Vitoria was up against the major power structures of his time. Did his final reflections assuage the fears of the powers that be, assuring them that economic gain and the winning of souls would continue? Are there times when speaking against power might reinforce other power dynamics that go unnamed?

It is important to remember that speaking against the Church Industrial Complex may upset financial sponsors and people in positions of power. A prophetic witness must not acquiesce to the status quo, even if doing so will come with financial loss. Church leaders may similarly be faced with decisions that, like Vitoria, weigh human dignity against the Royal Exchequer. In this case, trying to value both obscures power differentials within policies that claim to be advocating universal equality. It requires a lack of accountability for harm and an arrogant self-perception to pretend that exploitation is in the best interest of all.

Laurel Schneider and Nikki Young write about colonial patterns that claim protection while furthering exploitation in important ways for Church leaders to consider:

> Religiously legitimated heteropatriarchal ideologies anchor the notion that colonization—of resources, bodies, ideas, desires—is both a huge responsibility of the colonizer and an act of great generosity that rescues the colonized from the error of their ways. The gaslight? Responsibility and generosity rather than robbery and usury; civilization and progress rather than enslavement and subordination.[31]

When decision-making happens among a small group of elite individuals in positions of power who claim generosity and responsibility without including the people most impacted by such decisions, harm is the more likely outcome.

Mission work similarly needs to be reconsidered through the lens of Vitoria. Returning to Dan White's definition of Church Industrial Complex is important when considering the role of mission work, even for churches that are trying to move outside of models of endless growth, profit accumulation, and hierarchical leadership. According to White, "boundary-crossing" church missions that value close-knit community and transformative discipleship rooted in a local context contrast with Church Industrial Complex.[32] However, Vitoria's arguments show how boundary-crossing and Christian values can still be used to cover ulterior motives.

---

31. Schneider and Young, *Queer Soul and Queer Theology*, 94.
32. White, "Discover the Grassroots Work of Movement."

We cannot dismantle the Church Industrial Complex without looking at the broader networks that churches participate in, economically or through governments, and Vitoria provides an important example of negotiating the interconnections of church and state. This inseparability of church and state may have been more obvious during the time of Vitoria, but Janet Jakobsen and Ann Pellegrini show how supposedly secular states like the United States still fall back on thinly veiled religious values, particularly when sexuality or gender are being debated.[33] Even today, church and state cannot be so easily untangled, and if colonialism is a structure, not an event, then this insight becomes all the more relevant. This becomes especially clear while seeing the ways church denominations can work in tandem with prisons and detention centers, occupying a blurry space of being both within said systems and distant enough to be a voice of critique. These blurry spaces are complex, and church leaders can lean into the internal contestation that proves such structures are not as monolithic as they may claim to be. Lines of power are multiple, and resistance can always be found. The same terms, even the same authors, can be used to claim liberation *and* oppression. The logic of othering can be built into a framework *intended* to establish universal rights that still ranks human beings based on narrowly conceived concepts of civilization and rationality. Conversion, rationality, consent, and the justified use of force all must be carefully examined under this line of thinking. Church leaders challenging expansion and accumulation should take Vitoria's example as a warning: economic, political, and spiritual motivations are frequently intertwined, but the sting is that much greater when people who claim to be striving for justice reinforce the powers they claim to be dismantling.

Bibliography

Arvin, Maile, et al. "Decolonizing Feminism: Challenging Connections Between Settler Colonialism and Heteropatriarchy." *Feminist Formations* 25 (2013) 8–34.

Bohrer, Ashley J. "Just Wars of Accumulation: The Salamanca School, Race and Colonial Capitalism." *Race and Class* 59 (2018) 20–37.

Dreier, Hannah, and Kirsten Luce. "Alone and Exploited, Migrant Children Work Brutal Jobs Across the U.S." *New York Times*, February 25, 2023. https://www.nytimes.com/2023/02/25/us/unaccompanied-migrant-child-workers-exploitation.html.

Foucault, Michel. "Nietzsche Genealogy, History." In *Language, Counter-Memory, Practice: Selected Essays and Interviews*, edited by D. F. Bouchar, 139–64. Ithaca, NY: Cornell University Press, 1977.

Greening, Molly. *Belonging in the Borderlands: Questioning Catholic Ethics*. Forthcoming.

---

33. See Jakobsen and Pellegrini, *Love the Sin*.

Jakobsen, Janet, and Ann Pellegrini. *Love the Sin: Sexual Regulation and the Limits of Religious Tolerance*. Boston: Beacon Press, 2004.

Koskenniemi, Martti. "Empire and International Law: The Real Spanish Contribution." *University of Toronto Law Journal* 61 (2011) 1–36.

Maldonado-Torres, Nelson. "AAR Centennial Roundtable: Religion, Conquest, and Race in the Foundations of the Modern/Colonial World." *Journal of the American Academy of Religion* 82 (2014) 636–65.

McNeil, Sara, and Steve Mintz. "Juan Ginés de Sepúlveda (1547)." Digital History, 2018. https://www.digitalhistory.uh.edu/active_learning/explorations/spain/spain_sepulveda.cfm.

Quijano, Anibal. "Coloniality of Power, Eurocentrism, and Latin America." Translated by Michael Ennis. *Nepantla: Views from South* 1 (2000) 533–80.

Schneider, Laurel C., and Thelathia Nikki Young. *Queer Soul and Queer Theology: Ethics and Redemption in Real Life*. New York: Routledge, 2021.

Vitoria, Francisco de. *Vitoria: Political Writings*. Edited by Anthony Pagden and Jeremy Lawrance. Cambridge: Cambridge University Press, 1991.

White, Dan, Jr. "Discover the Grassroots Work of Movement." *V3*, August 8, 2016. https://thev3movement.org/2016/08/08/church-as-movement-not-industrial-complex/.

Chapter 2

A Tower That Reaches to the Heavens
Deconstructing Industrial Complexes Using Biblical Text

ERIKA KATSKE

Is it a human thing to be fascinated by towers? Even early in the Bible, in the book of Genesis following the story of the Flood, the illusive, mystical story of the Tower of Babel describes an ancient pull toward tower building. Popular culture's version of the narrative goes something like this: humans arrogantly aspire to be like God, building an edifice to reach the heavens; God is angered by their hubris; God ragefully destroys the tower and scatters the people to the ends of the earth, separating them physically and forcing them to speak different languages.

The text, however, gives very few details about what happened in the Valley of Shinar. The story, after all, is only nine verses. The people's motivation is abstract, and the narrative gives few clues about the connection between their acts and God's response. In fact, the text does not state that the community's actions were sinful—nor that God's response was punishment. Compared to other biblical stories (the enslavement of the Israelites by the Egyptians, for example), the text of Gen 11:1–9 is vague and emotionally neutral.

I revisited this odd story several years ago while living and working in San Francisco under the growing shadow created by construction of the Salesforce Tower, downtown's newest and tallest building. At the time, the world was also witnessing the rise to power of Donald Trump, whose fame stemmed from hotel towers with his name in New York City and beyond. I was immediately struck by—and perhaps hopeful about—the story's potential to offer theological insight into the seemingly ubiquitous obsession with infinite growth and profit that defines our tower-building era.

I was also working as a community organizer in faith communities on a variety of justice campaigns. Having spent my career helping to create collective action toward systemic change, I found it hard to accept common readings of the story. Why would God be threatened by, or displeased with, this human effort toward a common goal? More importantly, living in a moment defined by virulent racism and xenophobia, I could not accept that God created different languages (or made humans otherwise distinct from each other) as a form of punishment.

Rereading the story in the Hebrew text, I also could not find any basis for understanding God as angry. God does redirect human activity away from the tower—indicating some divine insight that called for change—but contrary to popular retelling, God does not destroy the tower, and God's language throughout seems calm and observational. Anger is certainly a possible reading of the verses, but it is far from explicit and not the only explanation for God's actions. And yet, interpretations of the story that persist in American culture almost all agree that God is upset by the people's project and acts, in turn, to punish their wrongdoing.[1] This telling of mischievous humans rebelling against their creator echoes a long Christian tradition of understanding human beings as inherently flawed and characteristically defiant.[2] Noted contemporary ethicist and philosopher Jeffrey Stout goes so far as to cite the Tower of Babel in the introduction to his award-winning book, *Ethics After Babel*, as a symbol that "continues to exert its power over the imagination. Whenever we desire to penetrate the strangeness of alien speech or dispel the confusion of tongues," he explains, "the image of the ruined tower recurs. It is, among other things, a symbol of our moral condition."[3]

---

1. A simple internet search for "meaning of Babel in the Bible," for example, points readers to a Wikipedia page with the tagline "Biblical pericope about hubris and the origin of languages" as well as an array of Jewish and Christian Bible study websites that tout the Babel story as a warning against competing with God. The popular online magazine *Grunge* features an article that examines the biblical tale, presenting it as a "goldmine for artists and poets" as well as "a metaphor for any project that aggrandizes its builders while also suggesting an inevitable fall. Big Tech has been compared to the biblical tower, and critics of the planned corporate headquarters for Amazon, designed as a whirling spire, also used the analogy." See Perry, "Tower of Babel Explained."

2. While biblical humans are often characterized as defiant in Jewish tradition, generally speaking, rabbinic Judaism understands human beings as first and foremost created in the image of the Divine and therefore essentially good.

3. Stout, *Ethics After Babel*, 1.

Feminist theologian Elisabeth Schüssler Fiorenza remarks on the ways in which "biblical texts affect the perceptions, values, and imagination not only of Christians, but of Western cultures and societies."[4] She cites the *Postmodern Bible* noting that "the Bible has exerted more cultural influence in the West than any other single document."[5] Reflected in norms, policies, and rules of conduct, the influence of the Bible—specifically as interpreted by Christian tradition—is unmistakable in American culture and in other cultures where biblical teachings, used as tools of colonization, have intertwined with local traditions. The lessons that are accepted as derived from biblical scripture have concrete impact on the lives of individuals and communities globally—whether those people ascribe to the Bible's teachings or not. As a result, common interpretations of this culturally significant narrative continue to play a role in framing cultural values, morality, and ethics (understanding multiplicity as "chaotic," destructive, and undermining to human community or seeing human beings as arrogant and harmfully ambitious, to name two examples).

But what if the accepted interpretation of the Babel narrative is questioned? What if this story is interpreted with an eye toward offering insight into the ethics around relationships with the contemporary towers we build—real and imagined? How might the dominant narrative shift if it is read as a theological response to the "shared fictions" of Industrial Complexes? I will argue that even in its pre-capitalist context, the Babel narrative contains keys to unpacking the human tendency to fall in love with the things we create, leaving behind the people, partnerships, and goals of even the most sacred projects.

Examining the Text: Genesis 11:1–9

Readers of Gen 11 are greeted with a rather curious repetition in the first verse. The text echoes itself, in common biblical style, stating that "the whole world had one language and a common speech."[6] The word translated as speech, דְּבָרִים (*devarim*), has several meanings. Since, according to Jewish teaching, Torah does not repeat without significance, a religious reading would question why the text specifies both language and speech in the same verse. If readers instead understand דְּבָרִים as "manner" or "purpose,"

---

4. Dube, *Postcolonial Feminist Interpretation of the Bible*, 23.
5. Dube, *Postcolonial Feminist Interpretation of the Bible*, 23.
6. The New International Version translation is quoted here, but both the NIV and the King James translations use the words "language" followed by the word "speech" in Gen 11:1.

however—an equally valid translation—a slightly different meaning of the verse emerges.[7] The text would seem to emphasize something else about how humans were acting—that they were somehow homogeneous beyond communication.

The people begin to act in the third and fourth verses. They say to each other, "Let's mold bricks and burn them in the fire."[8] Common interpretations would have readers believe that, once settled in Shinar, humanity sets out with a vision of a city and tower. However, verses 3 and 4 describe a different process. In the third verse, humanity makes a technical discovery; they can produce durable bricks by baking them. The same verse continues, explaining that "the bricks became like stone to them, and bitumen served them as mortar."[9] The second half of the verse suggests that the bricks they made became for them like natural, God-created stone. In addition, bitumen, a sticky, black substance mined from the ground, became their mortar. It is likely that wet clay had sufficed for building up to this point, but in this story, the people seem to (literally) unearth a new, stronger substance, one that is only available through extraction.

Contrary to popular recounts, it is not until the fourth verse—after producing new bricks and extracting bitumen—that the idea of the city and tower emerges. The order of these two verses is significant; it is important to note that the idea of building a city and tower develops *after* the means become available—not before. The production of bricks and mining of bitumen seem to unleash a new sense of possibility and a new desire.

The second half of the fourth verse reveals another aspect to humanity's motivation for building the city and tower beyond ambition or creativity. The full verse tells us that the people said to each other, "Let us establish a city and a great tower, its head in the heavens, and make for ourselves a name [or place, reputation] to avoid being scattered over the face of the whole earth."[10] Many interpretations point to this statement as the crux of humanity's sinfulness. According to these readings, humans act arrogantly, competing with God. But, given the story's placement directly after the destruction caused by the flood, this verse could reflect something different—that humanity's idea for building the city and tower was fueled on one side by the discovery of the means and on the other by a fear of being displaced, a communal response to recent trauma.

---

7. The Stone Edition of the Torah (Orthodox Jewish) does use the word "purpose" instead of "speech" in Gen 11:1.

8. Gen 11:3, my translation.

9. Gen 11:3, my translation.

10. Gen 11:4, my translation.

God enters the narrative in verses 5 and 6: "God came down to take a look at the city and the tower that humanity's children had established. God said, 'Behold, they are one people, and [there is] one language for all of them, and this is what they have started to do. Surely then, there is no holding them back from anything they might consider doing.'"[11] What does God observe that prompts the peculiar statement in the sixth verse? Popular interpretations imagine God as displeased with the sight of the city and tower. Continuing the theme of humans as arrogant, these readings infuse God's statement with a sense of anger, jealousy, or perhaps threat in response to humanity's attempt to become more powerful.

The text, however, is far from clear about God's response to what humans have begun to do. Reading anger or even disappointment into God's statement, while possible, seems a stretch. God's remarks could just as easily contain a sense of surprise, interest, or even pride in the work that God's creations have managed to undertake. This moment—and the interpretation of God's reaction—is critical to how we understand the story's meaning. Clearly God feels the need for a shift, but what exactly God sees in humanity's actions is unclear from the sixth verse.

God states the solution to the situation as the creation of different languages in the seventh verse. Grammatically, the text presents readers with several options for understanding God's motivation. Most interpretations of the seventh verse imagine that God acts to correct (or, more popularly, punish) humanity: "Come, let us go down and confuse their language so they will not understand each other."[12] However, the word אֲשֶׁר (asher), which is most often translated as "so," could also be read as "since." With that change, the new verse reads quite differently: "Come, let us go down there and stir up [or mingle, mix, confuse] their language, *since* they will not pay attention, each to the language of the other."[13] Instead of understanding the result of humanity speaking the same language as unity and cooperation (and perhaps over-ambition), readers are now pushed to consider how having the same language leads humanity to hear and understand each other *less*. In this light, God's actions shift from punishment and separation to a means of *reconnecting* people to each other.

The remaining two verses conclude the narrative with many unanswered questions. Genesis 11:8–9 offers this ending: "And God dispersed them from there over the whole face of the earth, and they ceased to build the city. Because of this, its name is called Babel, because there God stirred

---

11. Gen 11:5–6, my translation.
12. Gen 11:7, NIV translation.
13. Gen 11:7, my translation; emphasis added.

up [or mingled, mixed, confused] the whole earth's language, and from there God caused them to be dispersed over the face of all the earth."[14] Neither the city nor the tower is destroyed; humans are distracted from their building project by the change in their language and their dispersal—a redirected purpose.

Using the alternative interpretation of the seventh verse suggested above, it is not clear if the confusion of human language led human beings to stop *understanding* one another. What is explicit in the text is that God's actions succeed in shifting humanity's attention away from the tower and back to fulfilling the instruction to fill the earth; that is, horizontal growth instead of vertical. With this shift in the narrative, readers may be able to extract theological wisdom helpful for navigating contemporary towers—the Industrial Complexes of our time—the construction of which demand our constant attention.

Reinterpreting Babel

When God descends to view the city and the tower at Babel, what does God observe that prompts action? What issue does God try to resolve by creating different languages and dispersing the people? The text is surprisingly mute on these points. I propose reading this text in a way that sheds light on the relationship that humanity had developed with the tower and, by extension, the relationships that human beings form with many of our creations and the fictitious power those creations exert. In this reading of the story, God is troubled by the way in which the human-produced bricks are not only transformed into a tower but also imbued with social and political significance, becoming humanity's singular purpose. Babel was certainly not the last time that humanity created an entity that took on a life of its own. The Tower of Babel is just one example of the many hungry, growing, and consuming Industrial Complexes that human communities become compelled to maintain. In God's reaction to the events at Babel, however, lies a message about resistance and a reminder to turn toward each other as opposed to remaining focused on our creations.

As many social scientists (and, recently, economists and theologians) have pointed out, the individualistic narrative of the market would have us believe that personal preferences and desires drive what is produced, marketed, and made available to consumers. The power of the market is ultimately constrained by the needs and wants of the people and, in that

---

14. Gen 11:8–9, my translation.

way, can only be democratic in nature and lead to common good.[15] Given that cultural frame, it is easy to read humanity's desire as the primary driver of the events at Babel. The people felt they *needed* an eternal tower, so they started to build one. Read this way, the text teaches that acts driven by wanting too much or imagining and creating something larger than life are not God's idea of the best use of human energy and creativity.

However, such a reading stems more from capitalist cultural and ethical norms than from the text itself. The verses place the bricks before the tower, production before desire. This order is a more accurate description of human interactions with goods of the market generally. Realizing the "power" of the bricks and bitumen spurs human imagination and desire. That desire, in turn (and fueled by a combination of fear and hope following the flood), becomes the tower that humanity imagines can prevent a painful scattering. But the fantasy about the abilities of the tower is just that—a fantasy. I imagine God descending (Gen 11:5) and wondering why humanity is behaving so oddly toward what appears to God to be a pile of baked clay. What do humans see in this strange construction project that has somehow taken on meaning and life beyond its materials? What may have not been clear to humanity was likely obvious to God: the relationship between the creators and creation had changed significantly.

The shift in significance of the tower could be interpreted as the first biblical case of an Industrial Complex. Further, for readers familiar with the writings of Karl Marx, the dynamic between the people and their tower might look surprisingly similar to commodity fetishism—Marx's term for the ways in which products are endowed by their producers and consumers with independent, life-altering powers. The term *commodity fetishism* signifies, as theologian Franz Hinkelammert describes, "a break between producer and product of such nature that the product gets beyond the control of the producer. This may not be seen, but it is felt, experienced, and lived."[16]

Karl Marx first described the process by which the things we produce become more to us than the materials of which they are composed:

> In reality, [a commodity is] a very queer thing, abounding in metaphysical subtleties and theological niceties . . . . It is as clear as noon-day, that man, by his industry, changes the forms of the materials furnished by Nature, in such a way as to make them useful to him. The form of wood, for instance, is altered,

---

15. Several theologians describe and critique the assumption that the market is democratic because it is directed by individual desires. See Cavanaugh, *Being Consumed*; Bell, *Economy and Desire*; and Cox, *Market as God*, for example.

16. Hinkelammert, *Ideological Weapons of Death*, xvi.

by making a table out of it. Yet, for all that, the table continues to be that common, every-day thing, wood. But, so soon as it steps forth as a commodity, it is changed into something transcendent. It not only stands with its feet on the ground, but, in relation to all other commodities, it stands on its head, and evolves out of its wooden brain grotesque ideas, far more wonderful than "table-turning" ever was.[17]

Note that Marx discusses the process of fetishization using theological language. The relationships that Marx observes between people and things are metaphysical and, in that way, take on a life separate from and beyond their materials. That "life" comes with shared meaning-making.

Based on Marx, Franz Hinkelammert extends this fetishism to human institutions and systems. His observations echo what we might imagine happening among the people at Babel as well as the ways we describe the phenomenon of Industrial Complexes. As Hinkelammert explains:

Strange as it may seem, no one has ever seen a business, a school, a state, or an ownership system. What one sees are the *elements* of such institutions—that is, the building where the school or business operates, or the persons who carry out the particular activities of such institutions. The concept of these institutions nevertheless points to the whole of their activities and therefore points toward an invisible object.[18]

Like the tower, institutions and systems become endowed with collective meaning and power even though both are fabricated and arbitrary. The tower does not do anything to demonstrate its significance or inspire loyalty. Humanity not only creates the physical edifice but also ascribes to it shared significance, influence, and imagined salvific ability. The people develop a collective relationship with the tower, giving it life.

Why would a fantastical relationship with the tower be troubling? After all, human beings were created with creative imaginations and capacity for fantasy. Why would this shift in their relationship to the tower concern God? Why did commodity fetishism concern Marx? I will argue three reasons that are relevant to our exegesis of the Babel story. First, for Marx, commodity fetishism indicates alienation between the producer/consumer and the product, the earth, other people, and oneself. Second, the economic enterprise—the unending work of building the tower and striving for its mystical powers—comes to define human life. This kind of sole focus on

---

17. McLellan, *Karl Marx*, 435.
18. Hinkelammert, *Ideological Weapons of Death*, 1.

the enterprise—driven by a fantasy relationship and the imagined power of the entity—begins to reorder a community's sense of purpose, worth, and value. In the story of Babel, the center of humanity's energy and culture becomes the tower. In our era, Industrial Complexes—though products of our creativity, hope, and values—play a similar role in reconfiguring our relationships and perceptions of what is right and good. This shift in purpose occurs regardless of the intentions for creating and serving communities (as with a congregation or school). Over time, these goals, and the community itself, must take a backseat to the created structure's perpetuation. Third, alienation combined with the unending work of building the tower combine to make life painful and lonely for individuals. For those who believe in a loving and caring God, it is not hard to imagine God intervening at Babel to quell humanity's suffering.

Using Marx's theory of alienation as a tool for interpreting the events at Babel reveals timely insights into what God may have seen upon descending. Had the people become so focused on the production of bricks that they had lost connection to themselves, to the earth, and to each other? A *midrash* (or, Jewish narrative commentary) on the Tower of Babel seems to posit just that: "the builders brought the bricks up on one side and came down on the other. If a man fell down and died, no heed was given to him. But when a brick fell down, they stopped work and wept."[19] The rabbis suggest that human beings had become more attached to the imagined abilities of the tower and to the significance embedded in the project than they were to each other. In other words, they had lost all sense of humanity's sacredness; the tower had become more important to them than life.

Once the idea for building the tower and city emerges, we can imagine, its construction becomes all-encompassing, the focus of the entire human community. The centrality of the tower, it follows, redefines what the community, culture, and each individual hold as valuable. The tower becomes humanity's first Industrial Complex. If society exists with the sole purpose of erecting a tower—one that is believed to hold the keys to safety and salvation—then life becomes defined by the project. As Joerg Rieger describes in his book *No Rising Tide*, "what is at stake here are not just values but what is of ultimate value or, to use Paul Tillich's descriptor of God, what is of ultimate concern."[20]

In the passage above, however, Rieger is not talking about Babel. He is making a case for the ways in which market-driven logic replaces other forms of meaning-making in our global capitalist reality. Like humanity's

---

19. Bialik and Ravnitzky, *Book of Legends* (*Sefer Ha-Aggadah*), 29.
20. Rieger, *No Rising Tide*, 9.

relationship with the ever-growing tower, a society and culture defined by the Industrial Complexes it creates maintains an almost exclusive focus on spurring growth—particularly economic growth. As a result, individual and collective purposes become reconfigured to serve the need for perpetuation of the project. Theologian Daniel Bell calls this the "totalizing" effect of capitalism, emphasizing the ways in which it sets the stage for "a market that is at the center of life and society."[21] This observation describes the way in which capitalist mental models—the same ones that transform human creations into complexes—squeeze out other values and belief systems that could serve to challenge their logic.

The tower thus becomes the only touchstone for construction of meaning at Babel. As in the creation of any Industrial Complex, even those intended to serve and foster community, human consciousness reconfigures around the growth and preservation of the enterprise. Hinkelammert stresses this point, and its implications for faith values and practices, throughout much of his writing. "From the moment when commodities begin to become 'personified,'" he explains, "the human being (the producer) has to become subordinated to them in order to live. This is where the corresponding religious spirit of the capitalist system takes root."[22] Theologian William Cavanaugh, quoting Pope John Paul II, echoes Hinkelammert, focusing on the impact on human beings as workers and pointing out that "in a reversal of Genesis, 'man is treated as an instrument of production, whereas he . . . ought to be treated as the effective subject of work and its true maker and creator.'"[23]

Daniel Bell goes further to cite the work of philosophers Michel Foucault and Gilles Deleuze. Challenging individualistic notions of human consciousness, Bell reminds us that "as Deleuze and Foucault argued, capitalism does not simply act on a pregiven human subject; rather, it forms a particular kind of human subject."[24] Like the power that market-driven Industrial Complexes exert in our era, the tower at Babel can be understood as an entity that reshaped human sense of self and meaning, producing people "who are 'oddly alone' in the midst of society."[25] This process of consciousness and identity formation, however, could mean the acceptance of harmful, self-defeating, or simply false understandings. We can see this clearly within our global market reality, and several thinkers have written in

21. Bell, *Economy of Desire*, 26.
22. Hinkelammert, *Ideological Weapons of Death*, xvi.
23. Cavanaugh, *Being Consumed*, 39.
24. Bell, *Economy of Desire*, 94.
25. Bell, *Economy of Desire*, 97.

detail about the ways in which these insidious core beliefs become believable. Bell, for example, argues that identity formation based on market rules causes individuals and communities "*to desire the very thing that dominates and exploits us.*"[26] Bell finds this striking because individualist notions of identity formation would have us "think of domination and exploitation as both obvious and abhorrent by those who experience them."[27] We choose not to see this reality, he explains, because desire and self-understanding have already been formed by the enterprise—be it a market-driven Industrial Complex or the tower.

The tower, however, does not—and could never—provide the protection and immortality that humanity sought. Instead, its shared mythology traps human beings in a false reality based in what Joerg Rieger terms "a transcendent fix."[28] Rieger emphasizes that the promise of future growth and production holds our attention "no matter how badly it may perform this function at present."[29] But the false reality continually stokes our desire—perhaps even desperation—for a deeper experience of belonging, safety, or hope for the future.[30] It becomes all-consuming and demands our commitment.

As Marx taught, the process of production that creates alienated human beings and commodity fetishism is one in which human capacity is separated and extracted, rendering human beings mere shells of their spiritual selves. Alienation leaves human beings empty and incomplete—detached from themselves and each other—and thus not only prone to continuing to project metaphysical powers onto created entities but also driven toward imagined ends that can never be achieved. We can read in the Babel story a concerned and loving God who witnesses how these dynamics change humanity. The divinely created beings are suffering, anxious and frustrated by the impossible task of building the tower. This is as valid a reading as one that casts God as patriarchal, angry, and eager to guard Divine power. A reading in which God sees humanity suffering and acts to alleviate the pain of their treadmill-like existence redefines the lessons we take from the narrative.

This reading also leads to the final question in the reinterpretation of the Babel narrative: Why would God choose to intervene by diversifying the whole earth's speech? What can contemporary readers learn from

26. Bell, *Economy of Desire*, 60.
27. Bell, *Economy of Desire*, 60.
28. Rieger, *No Rising Tide*, 18.
29. Rieger, *No Rising Tide*, 18.
30. Rieger, *No Rising Tide*, 96.

God's strategy of interrupting the commodity fetishism of humans, and how might that learning be applied to our work as justice-seeking theologians, congregation builders, and faith leaders in our tower-building era?

The confusion of language at Babel is often understood as the moment when God creates diversity in general. God can be seen not only as creating different ways of communicating but also multiplying human lifeways—that is, not only in linguistic diversity but also in ways of experiencing the world, in thinking about and approaching challenges, and perhaps, in generating different personalities, strengths, and learning styles. In fact, linguists and other social scientists have long been intrigued by the way that variations in language reflect differences in cognition and understandings of the world.[31] Contrary to accepted interpretations, this diversification of the earth need not be seen as God's attempt to *divide* humanity. Readers can instead interpret God's strategy as ensuring the possibility for challenge and resistance to injustice and suffering. Absent the kind of difference that God creates, humanity did not seem able to question the power and centrality of the tower. We can imagine human beings behaving in passive, unthinking, machine-like ways while focused solely on their construction project. We can also begin to comprehend why God stepped in after observing these carefully fashioned creatures (in charge of creation, no less) behaving in such a manner. God, who created humanity to participate as co-creators, would likely be concerned by the anxious and mechanistic production surveyed at Babel. Seeing only uniformity in purpose and action among human beings ("Behold, they are one people, and [there is] one language for all of them, and this is what they have started to do"[32]), God creates room for disagreement, for contrasting perspectives—even messy arguments—that interrupt the power of the fetishized tower.

In addition, God's act of complicating earth's speech does not make unity impossible. On the contrary, it might make right-intentioned unity *more* possible. Theologian Jung Mo Sung differentiates between relational desire—craving for what he terms "encounter"—and the alienated desire for commodities. He explains that "many who have experienced 'a spiritual' experience (with or without calling it 'divine') which humanizes the person and leads to an encounter with the neighbor, the poor, the source of mutual humanization, discovers ... something which opens in him the

---

31. Probably the most familiar example in the United States of the interest in the way language differences determine worldviews comes from the work of anthropologist Franz Boaz, who noted that while English speakers had only one word for "snow," the Inuit people had multiple, giving them the ability to communicate different types and states.

32. Gen 11:6, my translation.

impossibility of living without it."[33] He refers to encounter as a "firm place" from which individuals connect authentically and become able to recognize the humanity in others and in themselves.[34] "This is the experience which permits people to meet one another as subjects meeting subjects," he states, "and not subjects meeting others who have been reduced to the condition of objects of observation, manipulation, or conquest."[35] Within an encounter, a self-aware human, reflecting the Divine image, connects with another, an act in which both affirm the other's essence—an unalienated connection that has the potential to reveal the alienated state in which many of us live much of the time. Sung quotes Eric Fromm, noting that "the difference between having and being is . . . between a society centered on persons and one centered on things."[36]

For Sung, the power of an encounter transcends language. He suggests that authentic understanding does not depend on using the same words. As the Babel story suggests, shared language may *prevent* the kind of spirit-to-spirit connection Sung discusses. When we forget, either as speakers or listeners, that human experience is more than words—and that words are only useful in as much as they point to that deeper reality—we forfeit the opportunity to find each other. Anyone who has tried to communicate across languages knows well that both speaking and listening require careful attention to the other person. Those attempts often facilitate deeper knowing and connectedness. This lesson could be one of the most important for congregations in particular to take from a new interpretation of Babel.

The Work Ahead

While there are many biblical texts whose accepted meanings are infused into our political and social realities, the story of the Tower of Babel remains one of the least examined. This narrative, however, serves as a starting point for forging new meaning of and resistance to our contemporary tower-building era. Reconstructing these nine verses helps surface the impact of economic systems on our congregations and communities. It can shed light both on the ways in which our holiest communities become fetishes that demand resources for endless growth and also the ways in which they can become sites of resistance. Because our market economy uses the powers of desire and hope to foster movement toward the twin goals of growth

33. Sung, *Desire, Market, and Religion*, 133.
34. Sung, *Desire, Market, and Religion*, 148.
35. Sung, *Desire, Market, and Religion*, 148.
36. Sung, *Desire, Market, and Religion*, 49.

and profit, faith and spiritual communities and their leaders are poised to examine, reclaim, and liberate that desire, redirecting it back toward the holy work of honoring human particularity and ensuring that people are connected in webs of relationships. But we must make sure that our congregations are places where that work is occurring—where we are actively bringing diversity to the fore inside our communities, engaging with neighboring communities who have different experiences and worldviews, and continuing to stretch ourselves and bridge and change in ways that bring us into broader connection and relationship.

The story of Babel could serve as a reminder that our Divine desire directs us toward authentic, spiritual connection with ourselves, with each other, and with the earth. That type of authentic communion can never be fulfilled by any capitalist endeavor—even when it looks like the holy work of building a congregation. That desire, as re-imagined by God at Babel, can only be realized through deep relationships—with each other, with the wider creation, and with the Divine.

Bibliography

Bell, Daniel M., Jr. *The Economy of Desire: Christianity and Capitalism in a Postmodern World*. Grand Rapids: Baker, 2012.

Bialik, Hayim Nahman, and Yehoshua Hana Ravnitzky, eds. *The Book of Legends (Sefer Ha-Aggadah): Legends from the Talmud and Midrash*. Translated by William Braude. New York: Schocken, 1992.

Cavanaugh, William T. *Being Consumed: Economics and Christian Desire*. Grand Rapids: Eerdmans, 2008.

Cox, Harvey. *The Market as God*. Cambridge, MA: Harvard University Press, 2016.

Dube, Musa. *Postcolonial Feminist Interpretation of the Bible*. St. Louis, MO: Chalice, 2000.

Hinkelammert, Franz J. *The Ideological Weapons of Death: A Theological Critique of Capitalism*. Maryknoll, NY: Orbis, 1986.

McLellan, David, ed. *Karl Marx: Selected Writings*. Oxford: Oxford University Press, 1977.

Perry, David. "Tower of Babel Explained." *Grunge*, August 16, 2021. https://www.grunge.com/488636/the-tower-of-babel-explained/.

Rieger, Joerg. *No Rising Tide: Theology, Economics, and the Future*. Minneapolis: Fortress, 2009.

Stout, Jeffrey. *Ethics After Babel: The Languages of Morals and Their Discontents*. Princeton, NJ: Princeton University Press, 2001.

Sung, Jung Mo. *Desire, Market, and Religion*. London: SCM, 2007.

Chapter 3

The Widow "Mite" Not Give Online

Gifts, Accounting, and Community Formation

DANIEL F. SEBASTIAN

This essay considers how online and digital forms of offerings might tempt practitioners into viewing church giving in the offering through an accounting lens, which is a view of the world that only counts "how much?" By illuminating this point, I demonstrate that how offerings are conducted is vital to what they accomplish. I begin by considering how a number-centric accounting lens loses sight of the importance of the shape and form of offering practices themselves. I suggest that online and digital forms of giving are a growing trend in churches that exemplify this accounting perspective. The essay moves to an evaluation of the story of the widow's offering in Mark's Gospel that highlights the importance of the widow's physical participation, something for which accounting cannot count. By identifying the limitations of an accounting perspective for understanding the significance of the widow's offering, I consider the communal implications of the widow's gift and the insight that it might provide for current offering practices. The chapter takes seriously the form of offerings in order to provide a constructive vision for the possibilities of community formation through offering practices.[1] In contrast to the Industrial Complex where the

---

1. By offering practices I refer to two things. The first is the moment within a church's liturgy devoted to the offering, whether this involves passing plates, processing to the front of the church, an announcement about giving from the front, or even flashing instructions for how to give on a screen. The second is the actual mechanism that facilitates financial transfers. This may be the plate being passed, but it might also be a

ends usurp the means, the constructive vision proposed in this essay identifies the means of offerings as essential to the offering's ultimate ends.

Accounting and Offerings

The Industrial Complex is a concept that names, in part, those moments when means become ends in themselves. Viewing church offerings through an accounting lens can lead to offering practices where the end is the collection of as much money as efficiently as possible rather than the flourishing of the church. Through such a lens, offering practices are reduced to mechanisms of monetary collection foreclosing possibilities for communal formation that can bolster the life of the church in ways beyond gathering financial resources. There are two ways in which an accounting framework can strip the actual performance of offering practices—the means of collection—of significance or connection to the church's flourishing and therefore become an end in itself.

First, accounting is a way of viewing the world that involves constant counting. In doing so, accounting not only "counts" but also determines "what counts." It decides what is extraneous and can be stripped away. In other words, accounting's "counting" defines the ends through its calculative and quantifying framework. Whereas the offering should be ordered toward facilitating the life of the church and the formation of a flourishing community, when the offering becomes confined by an accounting framework, its aim becomes narrowed to that of maximizing financial intake—asking only, "how much?" This emphasis constrains the imaginative potential for the practice of the offering to establish a thick community, one in which individuals participate together in the shared life of the church rather than simply sharing physical proximity as an audience.

Second, by foregrounding numbers, accounting presents its assessments as facts. As the cultural historian Mary Poovey describes, "numbers have come to epitomize the modern fact."[2] The information presented by accounting is thereby taken as neutral, objective, and detached from any personal values. The ostensible objectivity of accounting allows it to portray itself as value-free, functioning without regard for any particular end. It operates, so it seems, as the means by which decision-makers can accumulate the information they need to make decisions based upon their own personal values. In this description, accounting appears capable of being employed on behalf of any end. It is assumed to be an ends-neutral mean.

---

kiosk or offering box in the lobby or pre-authorized automatic transactions.

2. Poovey, *Modern Fact*, xii.

Thus, despite the fact that accounting determines what counts, it is taken as ends-neutral, which makes it easy for accounting to be exported and used for framing thoughts and attitudes about interactions in every realm of life.[3] I assert that online and digital practices of offerings too easily strip offerings of significance outside of the amount given and cause us to lose sight of the importance of offerings as a practice that contributes to the community's flourishing beyond just its function as a collection of financial resources. While offerings may function to collect finances, this function should not exhaust the entirety of their importance.

Church offering practices vary across communities based upon tradition, geography, and various other factors. The churches that I find most susceptible to the critique of this chapter are those that have adopted a megachurch aesthetic.[4] These churches, often following the model of leaders like Bill Hybels, an early pioneer and former pastor of a megachurch, try to develop "the feeling of worry-free comfort" that people experience in places such as malls.[5] The trend toward online and digital offerings, however, has also affected churches with a more traditional liturgy. Though the precise challenges presented to each church will vary, reflection on offering practices is warranted as new technologies are making digital and online forms of monetary transfer more common.

It is unsurprising that a spring 2022 survey conducted by the Barna Group found a drop from 34 percent to 25 percent over the course of the COVID-19 pandemic of Christians who reported having given "via the standard offering plate" at church using cash or checks.[6] This paralleled the report of fewer "practicing Christians" having given across every form of collection (online or web giving, automated clearing house [ACH], automatic withdrawal, mobile or app, text-to-give, terminal or kiosk, etc.), though the

---

3. Accounting undoubtedly frames financial and business transactions and interactions, but it also categorizes and frames non-financial interactions, which is visible when people begin to describe social engagements as ways of transferring social or political capital. The fact that economists can describe "marriage 'markets'" where potential partners are trying to maximize their own efficiency, outputs, and capital points to the broad reach that an accounting framework can have in counting interactions, whether that be a purchase at a store or the profitability of one's choice of a spouse; see Becker, "Economic Way," 394.

4. By highlighting an aesthetic, I am pointing out that even a small church might be shaped with an ethos (often displayed through architecture, lighting, and music) that mirrors that of a megachurch though it would not be classified as one based on attendance. While megachurches are often associated with Evangelical, Pentecostal, or non-denominational churches, mainline Protestant churches can also fall in this category.

5. Kilde, *When Church Became Theatre*, 219. For an account that highlights positive aspects of megachurches, see Wellman et al., *High on God*.

6. Barna Group, *Heart of the Giver*, 66–67.

decrease in giving to physical offering plates was the most significant.[7] It is unclear whether in the spring of 2022 fewer people were giving in person because those people were now giving digitally or if they had ceased their giving altogether. As a whole, however, online and digital forms of giving constitute a higher percentage of church giving than they had previously. Though, perhaps surprisingly, this survey reports that 49 percent of pastors think the majority of the givers in their churches donate in person by check or cash and only 16 percent of pastors think the majority of their givers donate digitally.[8] Thirty percent report an even mix of in-person and digital giving.[9] In other words, online giving is no longer novel and is certainly mainstream, but it has not surpassed in-person forms of giving in most churches based upon the pastors' responses to the Barna poll.

The critique I raise about online giving stems from the propensity for online giving to negate the significance of physical and embodied participation in offering practices. This embodied giving can contribute to community formation in ways that cannot be measured by the amount of money given. Online and digital offerings typify a kind of practice that is easily reduced to accounts and amounts, thereby contributing to the adoption of an accounting lens and its assumed ends. The next section considers the widow's offering in Mark 12 by foregrounding the physical dynamics that are often considered to be mere background. This reading emphasizes the significance of the physical and embodied realities of church offerings to understand how they contribute to the overall life and health of communities.

The Widow's Mi(gh)te

While lauding the widow as a model of sacrificial giving is perhaps the most widespread reading of Mark's story of the widow's gift of two mites (Mark 12:41–44), other provocative interpretations have been proposed.[10] I will briefly note alternate readings provided by biblical scholars that highlight

---

7. Barna Group, *Heart of the Giver*, 66.
8. Barna Group, *Heart of the Giver*, 65–67.
9. Barna Group, *Heart of the Giver*, 65–67.
10. Mites were the Roman coin of least value. Commentators have noted that the mites were also referred to as "coppers" due to the material used to make them; see Marcus, *Mark 8–16*, 858. Their use is noteworthy in contrast to Tyrian coinage that was the official "money of the sanctuary." The use of mites could symbolize either the widow's exclusion from even operating within the standard currency of the temple or that the money changers had not yet returned since Jesus's clearing of the temple (Mark 11:15–19), highlighting further the connection to Jesus's protest of the temple noted below; see Freyne, *Galilee*, 280.

the complexity and ambiguity of this narrative before presenting my own reading of the passage through the use of critical spatial theory. My interpretation resists focusing on the amounts given and instead concentrates on the importance of the physical aspects at play in the offerings and the relational work being carried out.

Addison G. Wright challenges the common assumption that the widow's actions are praiseworthy. Wright posits instead that the story's placement immediately following Jesus's rebuke of scribes that "devour widows' houses" suggests that the actions of the widow are to be lamented.[11] He argues that it is possible that the widow "acts out of despair, out of guilt, out of a desire to be seen contributing."[12] In a similar vein, André Resner notes that the author does not provide any outright approval of the widow's actions, nor is anyone in the text described as doing so. There are no instructions to go and imitate the widow's actions using classic phrases such as "blessed is she" or "go and do likewise."[13] Perhaps the reader should be stunned and upset. What compelled the widow to give her last pennies? Is this an example of the scribes' practice of devouring widows' houses that Jesus has just condemned? The ambiguity of the meaning of the phrase "devour widows' houses" makes it impossible to answer with certainty, but Wright and Resner help us imagine that there may be more to this passage than simply an exemplar of sacrificial giving.[14]

In fact, interpretations of the widow's action as exemplary and as an opportunity to lament her situation can both hold merit. The two interpretations are not necessarily mutually exclusive.[15] In both of these interpretations, however, Joseph V. Kozar notes the widow's diminished importance. He states that "the interpretation of the widow as a 'model of giving' imprisons her in a 'jail' of domestic and common place truths," and an interpretation that focuses on a condemnation of the scribes pushes the widow "aside by a preordained exegetical focus on male conflict."[16] Utilizing a comparison to Mark 14:3–9, which recounts the story of a woman anointing Jesus despite the rebuffs by all of the men present, Kozar sees these two women as their own distinct literary type. Rather than simply victims of

---

11. All biblical citations, unless otherwise noted, come from the New Revised Standard Version Updated Edition.

12. Wright, "Widow's Mite," 258.

13. Resner, "Widow's Mite or Widow's Plight," 547.

14. For discussions of possible interpretations of the phrase "devour widows' houses," see Smith, "Closer Look at the Widow's Offering"; Derrett, "'Eating Up the Houses of Widows.'"

15. Blomberg, *Jesus and the Gospels*, 374n69.

16. Kozar, "Owl and the Pussycat," 41–42.

the scribes or other men, these women stand as the "ideal opposite of the scribes." While the scribes embody an ethos of "self-aggrandizement," the widow is resolutely "doing the will of God."[17]

This reading also ties the widow directly to Jesus. The literal translation from Greek states that the widow "gives her whole life" (Mark 12:44c), the same sacrifice that Jesus will soon offer.[18] Casting her coins into the temple treasury thus adumbrates Jesus's sacrifice. Given that Christians view Jesus's death as the ultimate contestation of the temple, the widow's actions, which foreshadow that event, could also be considered a protest of temple authority.[19] I argue that the widow's actions contest the temple authority by re-imagining and re-configuring the temple community. Contemporary Christians can draw upon the widow's example of contesting power in her own tradition for thinking about how to challenge entrenched interests within their own Christian tradition.

Imagining the widow's offering as a protest to the temple community has relevance outside of the realm of accounting. Accounting reduces offerings to quantities. By utilizing critical spatial theory, I illuminate the aspects in the widow's story beyond what lands on the accountant's ledger to expand our understanding of the offering's significance. Paying close attention to the dynamics of space and the role that the physical environs play in understanding the force of the widow's actions will help uncover meaning in what is often called background. This background, of course, does not count in the accountant's journal.

Victor Matthews, in exploring the use of critical spatial theory for biblical studies, notes that critical spatial theory attends to three arenas.[20] Firstspace is considered the "'real' or physical world."[21] One could, for instance, use a measuring tape to determine the actual measurements of a room in order to assess firstspace. The importance of the temple in Mark's Gospel, both as it is challenged by Jesus and as it looms in the widow's story, is connected largely to its stature after its refurbishment by Herod. While the story takes place in what was technically the Second Temple Period, the temple in the Gospels is nothing like the original second temple that

---

17. Kozar, "Owl and the Pussycat," 43.

18. Kozar, "Owl and the Pussycat," 43.

19. For discussions of Jesus contesting the temple, consider Sleeman, "Mark, the Temple, and Space," 338–49; Wenell, "Contested Temple Space," 323–37; Wenell, *Jesus and Land*, 44–47.

20. Matthews, *More Than Meets the Ear*, 132. Matthews's use of this tripartite description is based upon theorists such as Edward W. Soja and Henri Lefebvre; see Soja, *Thirdspace*; Lefebvre, *Production of Space*.

21. Matthews, *More Than Meets the Ear*, 132.

was a sad shadow of Solomon's original temple depicted in Ezra 3:12.[22] In fact, Herod's temple was twice the size of Solomon's temple and evoked awe-inspired descriptions by commentators such as Josephus.[23] The Court of Women in the temple, where the offerings were collected, was ornamented with "thirteen trumpet-shaped offertory boxes."[24] The temple then was an imposing physical presence hovering over the widow as she gave. Failure to foreground the magnificence of the temple in contrast to the poverty of the widow loses sight of the reality that "space replicates power in societies. Like everything else, power exists within space."[25] The widow could not be present in the temple without tangible reminders of the power to which the temple was attached—power that she lacked.

The power manifested by the physical and measurable qualities of Herod's temple is best assessed in relation to secondspace, which is the imagined space of the temple. Imagined space is the meaning and significance overlaid on firstspace by various individuals. Considering a place as sacred or profane is an example of secondspace. For while two places may be identical in terms of firstspace (i.e., have the exact same dimensions), the meaning inhered in them—their "imagined representation"—can vary.[26] Determinations about how one should act and comport oneself in a specific space (a church, a courtroom, a national monument, etc.) are reflections of secondspace, or the imagined meaning and significance of space. Francis Schmidt argues that a particular process of thinking was inculcated through the physical construct of the temple building.[27] This manner of thinking is the temple's secondspace. An important component of secondspace is that it is not homogeneous across all individuals. Every person has the potential to imagine space and its meanings in a unique fashion. As Karen Wenell says, "even dominant and culturally pervasive meanings of place will always be open to challenge and change."[28] In Mark's narrative, Jesus's overturning of the money changers tables (Mark 11:15–19) and the description of the widow's offering might best be understood as challenges to the entrenched logic of the temple that dispute the temple's commonly ascribed secondspace.

While there can be almost endless secondspaces (as each person can project and imagine any meaning they want on a space), there can be only

---

22. Jacobson, "Herod's Roman Temple," 18–27.
23. Ritmeyer and Ritmeyer, "Reconstructing Herod's Temple Mount," 26.
24. Marshall et al., *New Bible Dictionary*, s.v. "Treasure, Treasury."
25. Stewart, "New Testament Space/Spaciality," 141.
26. Matthews, *More Than Meets the Ear*, 132.
27. Schmidt, *How the Temple Thinks*.
28. Wenell, "Contested Temple Space," 329.

one thirdspace. This refers to the lived reality unfolding in space.[29] Thirdspace is where the conflict over secondspace occurs as each person tries to live out the meaning they attach to a place. Clearly, Herod had left his mark of wealth and grandeur on the lived space of the temple. The way the temple was inhabited and used as a public place where offerings were given—its thirdspace—was crucial for maintaining the dominant secondspace. Scribes would likely spend time viewing and tracking gifts being given. Scribes were, after all, engaged in "counting, tallying, verifying ... not merely transcribing words."[30] For this reason, Marty Stevens suggests that understanding a scribe as a "recorder, a ledger-keeper," and "an enumerator" captures better the role of the scribes, as does the translation "storehouse accountant."[31] The scribes count the donations and as a result note who counts in the community.

The ritual of giving is a performance of the relationship that individuals have with the temple. This ritual plays out in the lived thirdspace of the temple and thus displays and enacts a particular secondspace (the significance attributed to the temple, its meaning and value, and who belongs there). The donations demonstrate the power that the economic sociologist Viviana Zelizer ascribes to money as "a means of creating, transforming, and differentiating" social relations.[32] As wealthy individuals publicly display their large gifts, they are asserting their prominence in the temple community. The performative power is expressed by Juronn Økland who notes the tautological nature of rituals that "construct what they declare."[33] One cannot help but imagine the possibility that the wealthy individuals were ostentatiously delivering their "large sums" to the trumpet-shaped receptacles in a way that recalls Jesus's warning in Matthew against sounding a trumpet while giving (Matt 6:2).[34] The orchestration of these public displays formed, maintained, and monitored the temple community.

It is into this thirdspace that the widow enters. Her destitution was visible, given that Jesus remarks on it. She steps into a space where she does not belong, an environment whose firstspace foregrounds the wealth and power of the temple and its community whose dominant secondspace is enacted through the performances of the wealthy. Yet, in participating in

---

29. Matthews, *More Than Meets the Ear*, 132.
30. Stevens, *Temples, Tithes, and Taxes*, 76.
31. Stevens, *Temples, Tithes, and Taxes*, 77.
32. Zelizer, *Economic Lives*, 89.
33. Økland, *Women in Their Place*, 34.
34. For further details on the physical environs where the offering was given, see Marcus, *Mark 8–16*, 857–58.

the offering, by forcing her presence in the lived space of the temple, she imposes her own imagined space of the temple—one where she is a vital member and contributor. In this sense, the widow's offering can be taken as a form of resistance to the exclusivity represented by the temple's assumed secondspace (a community circumscribed by wealth and power) through a challenge of its thirdspace (her physical presence asserts her place, and that of others who are frequently marginalized, within the temple community). Even though the widow could not afford to contribute to the temple offering, she does. She gives a free-will offering, however small, that nonetheless serves as an act of resistance against the imagined community of the temple—attached as it is to wealth and power—and includes herself in the lived reality of the community. She enters into the public realm in her visibly impoverished state and participates in the community. By participating in the offering, the widow resists the dominant imagination of who belongs in the temple community and enacts her own more inclusive community.

The scribes, or accountants, cannot account for the relational significance of the widow's coins on their ledgers. Their calculations constrain the possibility for imagining the entirety of the relationality enacted at the offering receptacles. What they see and record are transactions that can be captured in debits and credits, not gifts whose significance expands beyond a journal entry. It is the performative power enacted through the widow's gift, her physical presence, that challenges the imagined space of the temple and serves as a spark for reflection upon the offering practices within modern churches. Reflecting on Mark's story of the widow's offering through critical spatial theory demonstrates how an accounting lens limits this story's importance.

Ledgers and Limitations

The accounting ledger despoils interactions of everything except the information which it deems important. Poovey describes this process of denuding the details of interactions in sixteenth-century bookkeeping practices.[35] Bookkeeping required several sets of books at this time that represent steps along the way from the first recording of a comprehensive description of the initial interaction to a final entry in the ledger that presents little more than the relevant accounts and amounts. One particularly important part of this process was the conversion of all of the goods and monies that had been exchanged "into a single currency, the money of account."[36] Measuring and

---

35. Poovey, *Modern Fact*, 41–54.
36. Poovey, *Modern Fact*, 43.

representing all actions according to a single unit of account is fundamental for accounting. Reading Mark's story through an accounting lens provides little to reflect on other than the sheer discrepancy of amounts between the wealthy and the widow. But the significance of what is going on in this offering, in my reading, simply cannot be accounted for in a manner that reduces offerings to a single number—how much? There is a complex meaning of the financial interactions that goes beyond amounts.

The sociologist Viviana Zelizer has noted that when it comes to legal negotiations, people are not only concerned with price and amounts, "but it is impressive how often they argue over the form of payment and its appropriateness for the relation in question."[37] Attending to the complexity within interactions helps identify the meaning embedded in the transaction. In doing precisely this, Zelizer brings out that the amount of any exchange is only one of the relevant elements for considering how people define, negotiate, and maintain relationships through financial interactions.[38] The concern that I want to raise with the practice of online giving is that it primarily focuses on "how much," too easily lapsing into an accounting way of thinking. As such, it does not attend adequately to the significance for defining, negotiating, and maintaining relationships that is built into the form that a gift takes. The loss of physically engaging thick offering practices—those where practitioners can participate in and perform together the life of the church regardless of "how much" money they contribute—portends, from this perspective, the loss or distortion of crucial relational work within the offering. If the widow had given online, would her challenge to the temple's imagined community have been made invisible?

Gift theory starkly contrasts with accounting for its focus on elements beyond just monetary value.[39] Reducing gifts and counter-gifts to a single unit of account and formatting them for the accountant's ledger erases the information most crucial for evaluating their significance. For example, timing is critical with gifts. A counter-gift cannot be given immediately, and it certainly could not be identical to the original gift given, for that would amount to rejecting the original gift. The interval between the gift and counter-gift is central to gift exchanges functioning as intended.[40] The French

---

37. Zelizer, *Purchase of Intimacy*, 28.

38. Zelizer, *Purchase of Intimacy*, 37.

39. Gift theory refers to anthropological and sociological studies of societies that are built upon gift-giving and reciprocity rather than transactions considered to be discretely economic and governed by contracts. These studies often highlight the significance of the form of exchange and transactions on the social structure of the society in realms beyond just the economy.

40. Bourdieu, *Outline of a Theory*, 5–6.

philosopher and sociologist Pierre Bourdieu summarizes the consequence of all of these nebulous features stating, "Everyone knows that 'it's not what you give but the way you give it' that counts, that what distinguishes the gift from mere 'fair exchange' is the labour devoted to *form*: the *presentation*."[41]

Considering the spatial dynamics in Mark's story of the widow is a way of drawing out the form of her gift—her physical presence and participation in the offering, how she gives. Her presence, her participation was charged with meaning. One would, of course, need to know precisely the way in which she carried herself to truly capture the depth of social meaning at work. I have imagined that she carried herself with dignity and assertiveness that protested the possibility of her exclusion from the temple community because of her social position. The meaning of her offering, however, remains ambiguous and open to interpretation. This is, of course, because the more fundamental point I have made in my assessment of the widow's story is that gifts contain a host of meanings that cannot be encapsulated in the amount given. We know how much the widow gave, but the significance of the widow's offering cannot be captured simply in accounts and amounts.

Gifts and Community Formation

Identifying the significance of the offering as a gift rather than a financial exchange allows one to recognize that imagining the offering as merely a mechanism for fundraising fails to consider its full possibilities and implications. I am advocating for attending to the way in which offerings are structured for their performative significance in facilitating the flourishing of the church community. The way a church goes about its various tasks is imbued with importance. Returning to Bourdieu, he outlines the pedagogical significance of embodiment in defining some of life's most important realities.

> The principles em-bodied in this way are placed beyond the grasp of consciousness, and hence cannot be touched by voluntary, deliberate transformation, cannot even be made explicit; nothing seems more ineffable, more incommunicable, more inimitable, and, therefore, more precious, than the values given body, *made* body by the transubstantiation achieved by the hidden persuasion of an implicit pedagogy, capable of instilling a whole cosmology, an ethic, a metaphysic, a political philosophy,

---

41. Bourdieu, *Outline of a Theory*, 194.

through injunctions as insignificant as "stand up straight" or "don't hold your knife in your left hand."[42]

Bourdieu has a flare for toying with theological language, but his use of "transubstantiation" here—making real the presence and body of Christ—contains more theological import than he might have intended. The Eucharist is the central act of the Christian liturgy in which, by consuming the body of Christ, practitioners are themselves consumed and drawn into the body of Christ.[43] The offering historically was the precursor to the eucharistic table, and they were deeply connected. The offerings (in kind) presented would quite literally be used as the elements of the Eucharist. In other words, if the widow's offering of "her whole life" was a preamble to Jesus's own gift, the offering and Eucharist repeat this practice where congregants come and give their lives, which are in turn given back to them in the Eucharist. The body of Christ is constituted, in part, through the practices of the offering and Eucharist.[44] More powerful than being told one is part of the body is enacting that reality through physical practice.

Offering practices are thus deeply connected to community formation. Churches and communities that do not default to an accounting framework demonstrate the possibilities of community formation through the practice of the offering. The ethnographer and scholar of religion Devaka Premawardhana offers a fascinating account of one such neo-Pentecostal church in Boston where he outlines various practices that foreground the gift nature of tithes, including visible participation and gifts given in kind. Offerings are conceived of as "more important than the quantitative value of what passes between the sacrificer and divinity, between giver and receiver," encapsulating "the quality of the relationship to which the exchange binds the two parties."[45] What Premawardhana illuminates in exploring closely the offering practices in a context that some might quickly dismiss as exemplary of prosperity gospel abuses is that,

> the efficacy appears to be less about the quantifiable commodities prayed for—a physical healing, a financial windfall, an employment opening—than about the insertion of the self into relations of reciprocity. These relations are the mutually-obligating bonds

---

42. Bourdieu, *Outline of a Theory*, 94.

43. Cavanaugh, *Being Consumed*, 84.

44. Long and York, "Offering Our Gifts," 185–89. For an argument on how communal worship, through the lens of sacrifice and stewardship, is connected to the offering in some Evangelical and Charismatic churches, see Bialecki, "Between Stewardship and Sacrifice."

45. Premawardhana, "Transformational Tithing," 90.

of gift exchange that extend one's sense of self beyond atomistic individualism. They help satisfy the existential imperative for belonging to fields of being that include, in this case, a cosmology, a church community, and family, even family separated by an ocean and unseen for years.[46]

This kind of community formation is the possibility waiting to be stirred in many churches' practice of offerings, but it requires attention to the form and embodiment of the offering. Attending to the presentation of the offering could relate to two different elements—what is given and the way it is given. Online giving trends highlight the way in which the offering is too frequently treated as a painful portion of the liturgy or service that must be hurried along. But if the widow's offering was significant due to her ability to be visibly and physically a part of the community, then churches should consider how offerings can orchestrate the movements of congregants in order to enact the body of Christ.[47] Passing offering plates is a thin version of this; processionals—where participants bring their gifts forward to a receptacle or the altar at the front—are more fully embodied and offer a richer performance of communal formation where practitioners must adjust their own movements to correspond to and include those around them in service of jointly offering thanksgiving and glory to God.

Imagining offerings as rituals that orchestrate the bodies of practitioners in order to enact the body of Christ highlights the profound possibility of offerings. Online, and other ritually thin versions of offering collections, should not be imagined, however, as pedagogically empty. Those practices still shape and form practitioners but in different ways. Consider, for example, the way in which online giving platforms resemble online shopping. The user inhabits a digital world, but that world and the practices performed there have real significance. The church becomes one more consumer choice and preference, another means for individuals creating a particular image of themselves. Or, in the cases where a recurring gift is set up, it mirrors a subscription. The church is another form of entertainment consumption, with little contrasting it to television, movie, and music subscriptions. In other words, this form of offering does mold the participant, but not into

---

46. Premawardhana, "Transformational Tithing," 98.

47. The discussion here of offerings then could be extended even more broadly to buildings, space, and aesthetics that create boundaries for the community. Churches that aim to make attendees feel comfortable should always be cognizant of *who* will be made to feel comfortable and who might be made to feel uncomfortable. The offering is but one element of the church, all of which should be oriented toward creating a community where individuals can belong and flourish together as the body of Christ.

the body of Christ. It rehearses the practices of consumer capitalism, which is its own kind of temple marked by wealth, power, and individualism.[48]

Not only, however, do these kinds of practices enact performances that work against the potential of community formation, they also contain within them some of the same seeds of exclusion based upon wealth and power seen in Mark's story. The assumption that all attendees would be banked and/or have access to particular apps and giving mechanisms often required for online giving circumscribes the church's imagined community of those who belong and contribute to the church. The offering can be one more identity marker and community norm that is identified by the anthropologist and sociologist Susan Crawford Sullivan in her study of mothers in poverty who too often feel like they do "not belong at church" since the church often has a particular "functioning, self-sufficient, unified, respectful" parishioner in mind.[49] Online giving practices, their mechanisms, and their convenience can presume the sensibilities of a particular lifestyle, socioeconomic status, age, or ability.

Yet, if I am suggesting that we foreground the physical practices of the offering in order to make visible those who might be marginalized from an accounting perspective, I do not pretend that this is a panacea or without its own potential problems. Antonio Eduardo Alonso, a scholar of theology and culture and a composer of sacred music, offers a helpful critique against placing too much confidence in the efficacy of performing perfectly the church liturgy in order to "resist" larger cultural trends and establish justice.[50] Examples of how thickly embodied and highly visible offerings can become harmful demonstrate his concern about too quickly idealizing an imagined pristine performance. For example, Sullivan describes the stigma felt by women who were forced to go forward during an offering ritual but had no money to give.[51] The pressure felt to give, even if not so visible, can stray into detrimental arenas as well. Despite all of the positive descriptions of the offering given by Premawardhana, he says of the community

---

48. James K. A. Smith provides a provoking vignette of the way in which going to the mall can easily be described in terms that evoke the aura of going to a place of worship; see Smith, *Desiring the Kingdom*, 19–27. For examples of the many ways that Christian practices have been shaped by economic and cultural practices, see Kilde, *When Church Became Theatre*; Kruse, *One Nation Under God*; Vaca, *Evangelicals Incorporated*; Medina and Cornelia, "Prosperity Ethic."

49. Sullivan, *Living Faith*, 161.

50. Alonso, *Commodified Communion*. See also Winner, *Dangers of Christian Practice*.

51. Sullivan, *Living Faith*, 163.

he observed, "If tithing is a choice, it is hard to see the choice as genuine."[52] Mark's story might contain a seed for imagining the possibility of the offering on my reading, but churches should be wary of forgetting readings that recognize it as a reminder of Jesus's warning against devouring the houses of widows.

Unlike accounting logic, which has a universal quality to it, embodied practices must attend to bodies, which are necessarily particular. Thus, the particularity of specific communities should shape the performative and pedagogical elements of the offering practice. Each community should consider how their offering practice is shaping their community, thinking not least of how the widow in Mark might experience it. Churches must remain vigilant of physical forms of giving that become ostentatious shows of wealth and power or that stigmatize others. The suggestions below about the offerings' content can help mitigate the potential for these problems. Likewise, digital media, in some instances, might facilitate the participation of those who are sick and disabled in ways that are necessary for inclusion and the flourishing of the church.[53] Decisions for using different offering practices cannot simply be made based upon maximizing efficiency and "how much" but must ensure that the means of offerings are oriented toward—and therefore enact—the true ends of the offering.

Sullivan's account of women without money being stigmatized in offering practices brings questions to the fore about the content of the offering. If the focus on online giving raises the issue of how offerings are performed, it also clarifies an assumption about the content of contemporary offerings, namely, that they are solely, or at the very least primarily, about collecting

---

52. Premawardhana, "Transformational Tithing," 89.

53. I have not, due to space limitations, been able to address the broader topic of online church. My emphasis on the significance of physical practice highlights potential concerns that I have with online church. Though just as online forms of giving may open the possibility for more inclusive participation, the same is clearly true for online church. For an account of someone previously skeptical of digital media's ability to form church community whose perspective was changed through her own physical illness, see Thompson, *Virtual Body of Christ in a Suffering World*. The complexity of these questions was seen on a wide scale during the COVID-19 pandemic when churches transitioned *en masse* to online formats. The use of online church was, in this case, of course quite clearly not done out of a neglect of physical realities but in taking them seriously. This essay should highlight that the use of online church was not a neutral shift, but rather a tangible expression of neighbor love fitting to the particular challenges posed during the height of the COVID-19 pandemic. In the same way, then, that I note both the potential and pitfalls of physical offering practices, there are undoubtedly possibilities and potential for online church. We should, however, not assume that the use of online church is neutral. We must, instead, attend to the significance—good and bad—of how different media shape the ends of experiences and practices themselves.

money. Thus, an automatic withdrawal may mark a financial prioritization of contributing to the church, but that alone cannot exhaust the significance of participating in the offering. The theological implications of such a narrow construal of the offering are evident when claiming that some persons have nothing to contribute. If the offering is a liturgical sacrifice of prayer and thanksgiving to God, how could anyone not have something to offer? Poetry, testimonies, art, produce from a garden, written or spoken prayers, and pledges to pray or volunteer are all potential gifts. Likewise, tokens, be they dollar bills, pennies, small crafts, etc., could be handed out to everyone as they process toward the front to give in the offering, a tangible reminder that no person's gift is solely of their own doing—they are always already participating in God's gift of creation—while simultaneously ensuring everyone has a physical token to embody their gifts.

I do not think that churches must eradicate money entirely from the offering. Zelizer comments that while money is often perceived as venal, even our most intimate relationships are intertwined with financial transactions; money does not necessarily corrupt an interaction.[54] Churches err, however, when they assume offerings are only, or primarily, about money. That reflects an accounting logic, which online giving often lapses into, and signals a framework where the offering is shaped by money rather than the inverse. The offering should not be denominated and thereby defined by a monetary unit of account. The offering can incorporate money, but it is too capacious to be reduced by it.

The End . . . and Means

Many contemporary churches are structured and organized according to managerial principles. The roots of management theory are in accounting, detailed measuring, and counting that maximizes efficiency.[55] Online giving is efficient because it centers around the question, how much? The offering's end goal becomes to collect the maximum amount of funds with the minimum amount of disturbance to the "real work" of the church. If Industrial Complexes tempt one to unmoor the means from their ends and become ends in themselves, then shaping practices of offerings through an accounting framework unmoors the significance of the offering for community formation and focuses instead on income maximization. The means of monetary collection become the end of the offering.

---

54. Zelizer, *Purchase of Intimacy*, 20–26.
55. Rosenthal, *Accounting for Slavery*.

By highlighting the relational work accomplished through the physical and embodied elements of the widow's offering in Mark, I point to the significance of offerings for community formation beyond the element of "how much?" Accounting, however, considers those elements, which were so central to the efficacy of the widow's gift, to be extraneous and therefore not to count. I urge careful reflection on the deep importance imbued in the practice of offerings, not just that money gets collected. Limiting the significance of the offering to that which can be captured by an accounting ledger constrains its possibilities. Because of this, online giving cannot replace the whole of the offering. To assume that it can lapses too easily into reducing the offering to the accountant's ledger and missing the theological, communal, and even ethical import of the offering practice. It allows the means of money collection to become the end. The offering must be oriented toward its proper end, which is more than maximizing monetary collections. The offering cannot be less than an enactment, a performance, and thus, a creation of shared lives drawn together as the body of Christ both returning and, like the widow's own gift, prefiguring the greatest gift—Christ's body to the church.[56]

Bibliography

Alonso, Antonio Eduardo. *Commodified Communion: Eucharist, Consumer Culture, and the Practice of Everyday Life*. New York: Fordham University Press, 2021.

Barna Group. *The Heart of the Giver*. Barna Group, 2022.

Becker, Gary S. "Nobel Lecture: The Economic Way of Looking at Behavior." *The Journal of Political Economy* 101 (1993) 385–409.

Bialecki, Jon. "Between Stewardship and Sacrifice: Agency and Economy in a Southern California Charismatic Church." *Journal of the Royal Anthropological Institute* 14 (2008) 372–90.

Blomberg, Craig L. *Jesus and the Gospels: An Introduction and Survey*. 2nd ed. Nashville: B&H, 2009.

Bourdieu, Pierre. *Outline of a Theory of Practice*. Translated by Richard Nice. Cambridge: Cambridge University Press, 1977.

Cavanaugh, William T. *Being Consumed: Economics and Christian Desire*. Grand Rapids: Eerdmans, 2008.

Derrett, J. Duncan M. "'Eating Up the Houses of Widows': Jesus's Comment on Lawyers?" *Novum Testamentum* 14 (1972) 1–9.

Freyne, Seán. *Galilee from Alexander the Great to Hadrian 323 B.C.E. to 135 C.E.: A Study of Second Temple Judaism*. Notre Dame, IN: University of Notre Dame Press, 1980.

---

56. An earlier version of this essay was presented at the Society for Pentecostal Studies in 2021. Thanks to Marie Olson Purcell and D. Stephen Long who read and commented on drafts of this essay.

Jacobson, David M. "Herod's Roman Temple." *Biblical Archaeology Review* 28 (2002) 18–27.

Kilde, Jeanne Halgren. *When Church Became Theatre: The Transformation of Evangelical Architecture and Worship in Nineteenth-Century America*. New York: Oxford University Press, 2002.

Kozar, Joseph V. "The Owl and the Pussycat: An Off Kilter Reading of the Widow's Honorable Action at the Temple Treasury in Mark 12:41–44." *Proceedings of the Eastern Great Lakes Biblical Society* 28 (2008) 41–53.

Kruse, Kevin M. *One Nation Under God: How Corporate America Invented Christian America*. New York: Basic, 2015.

Lefebvre, Henri. *The Production of Space*. Translated by Donald Nicholson-Smith. Cambridge, MA: Blackwell, 1991.

Long, D. Stephen, and Tripp York. "Offering Our Gifts: The Politics of Remembrance." In *Calculated Futures: Theology, Ethics, and Economics*, 185–205. Waco, TX: Baylor University Press, 2007.

Marcus, Joel. *Mark 8–16*. The Anchor Bible Commentary 27A. New Haven, CT: Yale University Press, 2009.

Marshall, I. Howard, et al., eds. *New Bible Dictionary*. 3rd ed. Downers Grove, IL: IVP, 1996.

Matthews, Victor H. *More Than Meets the Ear: Discovering the Hidden Contexts of Old Testament Conversations*. Grand Rapids: Eerdmans, 2008.

Medina, Erron, and Jayeel Cornelio. "The Prosperity Ethic: Neoliberal Christianity and the Rise of the New Prosperity Gospel in the Philippines." *Pneuma* 43 (2021) 72–93.

Økland, Juronn. *Women in Their Place: Paul and the Corinthian Discourse of Gender and Sanctuary Space*. London: T. & T. Clark, 2004.

Poovey, Mary. *A History of the Modern Fact: Problems of Knowledge in the Sciences of Wealth and Society*. Chicago: The University of Chicago Press, 1998.

Premawardhana, Devaka. "Transformational Tithing: Sacrifice and Reciprocity in a Neo-Pentecostal Church." *Nova Religio: The Journal of Alternative and Emergent Religions* 15 (2012) 85–109.

Resner, Andre. "Widow's Mite or Widow's Plight: On Exegetical Abuse, Textual Harassment and Learning Prophetic Exegesis." *Review and Expositor* 107 (2010) 545–54.

Ritmeyer, Kathleen, and Leen Ritmeyer. "Reconstructing Herod's Temple Mount in Jerusalem." *Biblical Archaeology Review* 15 (1989) 25–53.

Rosenthal, Caitlin. *Accounting for Slavery: Masters and Management*. Cambridge, MA: Harvard University Press, 2018.

Schmidt, Francis. *How the Temple Thinks: Identity and Social Cohesion in Ancient Judaism*. Translated by J. E. Crowley. Sheffield: Sheffield Academic, 2001.

Sleeman, Matthew. "Mark, the Temple, and Space: A Geographer's Response." *Biblical Interpretation* 15 (2007) 338–49.

Smith, Geoffrey. "A Closer Look at the Widow's Offering: Mark 12:42–44." *Journal of the Evangelical Theological Society* 40 (1997) 27–36.

Smith, James K. A. *Desiring the Kingdom: Worship, Worldview, and Cultural Formation*. Cultural Liturgies 1. Grand Rapids: Baker Academic, 2009.

Soja, Edward J. *Thirdspace: Journeys to Los Angeles and Other Real and Imagined Places*. Cambridge, MA: Blackwell, 1996.

Stevens, Marty E. *Temples, Tithes, and Taxes: The Temple and the Economic Life of Ancient Israel*. Peabody, MA: Hendrickson, 2006.

Stewart, Eric C. "New Testament Space/Spaciality." *Biblical Theology Bulletin* 42 (2012) 139–50.

Sullivan, Susan Crawford. *Living Faith: Everyday Religion and Mothers in Poverty*. Chicago: The University of Chicago Press, 2011.

Thompson, Deanna A. *The Virtual Body of Christ in a Suffering World*. Nashville: Abingdon, 2016.

Vaca, Daniel. *Evangelicals Incorporated: Books and the Business of Religion in America*. Cambridge, MA: Harvard University Press, 2019.

Wellman, James K., Jr., et al. *High on God: How Megachurches Won the Heart of America*. New York: Oxford University Press, 2020.

Wenell, Karen J. "Contested Temple Space and Visionary Kingdom Space in Mark 11–12." *Biblical Interpretation* 15 (2007) 323–37.

———. *Jesus and Land: Sacred and Social Space in Second Temple Judaism*. London: T.&T. Clark, 2007.

Winner, Lauren F. *The Dangers of Christian Practice: On Wayward Gifts, Characteristic Damage, and Sin*. New Haven, CT: Yale University Press, 2018.

Wright, Addison G. "The Widow's Mite: Praise or Lament—A Matter of Context." *Catholic Biblical Quarterly* 44 (1982) 256–65.

Zelizer, Viviana A. *Economic Lives: How Culture Shapes the Economy*. Princeton, NJ: Princeton University Press, 2011.

———. *The Purchase of Intimacy*. Princeton, NJ: Princeton University Press, 2005.

SECTION 2

Ethical Resources
and Critiques

Chapter 4

Materialism, Economism, and the Modern Catholic Social Teaching
What Would Be the Roles of the Church in an Era of Neoliberalism?

DAVID KWON

It is well recognized that materialistic and economic determinist views have caused many of the moral and social issues facing both church and society in the modern world. Such thoughts and behaviors, however, should not be viewed as solely the problems of the individual but also as problems that are deeply rooted in our social structure, a structure that is primarily based on the capitalist system. It is precisely that materialism (e.g., mammonism) and economism (e.g., the primacy of economic thinking) become predominant when the market turns amoral and/or asocial, when the market overruns its boundaries and invades other areas of social life, and when other social values originally guided by the church are directed by the economy. As a result, this excess of capitalism, operating in tandem with the advance of neoliberalism, can cause people, including many Christians, to worship commodities or false gods and values.

In this chapter, I will explore how this commodity fetishism can become dehumanizing, causing humans to sacrifice themselves and others to those idols and eventually exclude humans from the society where they deserve to be free subjects in social life. The dehumanizing effects of commodity fetishism will be examined through the discourse of political economy and its ethical implications on the one hand and modern Catholic

Social Teaching (CST) and its associated theological discourse on the other hand. At the same time, the relationship between these two discourses will be explored, but mainly directed from the CST perspectives to the other voices for the purposes of clarity in this chapter.

Capitalism and Commodity Fetishism: Karl Marx's Lesson for Today

As members of a capitalist, consumerist society, we encounter daily the fetishization of commodities in which goods take on more value than we would expect them to. For example, this fetishization of commodities is manifested in the way people dote upon their cars. At the extreme, some people will invest in a cherished car more of their time, money, and even affection than they will in another person. Likewise, this fetishization is observed in religious and moral spheres where contemporary churches operate in the business world; in some corporatized churches, appreciating commodities serve a self-preoccupied desire for greater power and riches, even at the expense of the churches' missions and religious charisms. Such subordination to the system of commodity production and exchange has inspired in Christian individuals and communities "a desire for mastery and control."[1]

In critical theory, commodity fetishism is often grounded in Karl Marx's theory that a commodity should be considered as a fetish since humans and human relations are often taken over by commodity relations.[2] In anthropology, *fetishism* refers to the primitive belief that godly powers can inhere in inanimate things.[3] Marx borrows this concept and argues that the fetish character of a commodity is enforced by the fact that commodities are produced by people who work in isolation from each other and consumers.[4]

---

1. Joel Suman and Keith Meador discuss the unconscious dynamic which causes commodity fetishism, as well as how the same dynamic can be found in religion and other ideologies. See their book *Heal Thyself*, chapter 3: "Religious Belief as Commodity Fetishism."

2. Marx, *Capital*, 1. Though, Marx's theory on commodity fetishism is incomplete; his theory cannot explain why a commodity would attract a consumer in the first place and why a consumer would find it irreplaceable. For details, see Brown, *Sense of Things*, 31.

3. For Marx, the notion of fetishism conjures up an image of African societies who created their own gods and then became controlled by them; however, his theory does not directly deal with the religious objects of these societies, rather it refers to the abstract process of reification itself that modern Westerns individuals create their own fetishes and are directed by them. Marx, *Capital*, 165.

4. Marx, *Capital*, 126–27, 139.

As a result of this masked production, the commodity reveals itself as separate from the labor process and is therefore viewed less as a product of labor than as a thing existing in the world in its own right.[5] Divorced from its production, the commodity appears to have a life of its own. According to Marx, a commodity becomes more than a mere object of use, allowing it to become fetishized as a social relation between individual workers, which turns to a material or transactional relation between things through the value exchange process.[6] In capitalist society, therefore, things like gold, money, and commodities become parts of "the direct incarnation of all human labor," while "[humans or workers] become alienated because their own relations of production assume a material shape which is independent of their control and their conscious individual action."[7]

What Marx has done with the idea of commodity fetishism is to articulate the problem of materiality endowed in the idea of the fetish. In particular, what we can learn from Marx's theory of commodity fetishism is not only that the true social meaning of individual persons or workers is hidden behind the relations between material objects but also that commodity fetishization or reification alienates humans from material objects as well as from humans themselves. When human labor is treated as a commodity or material object, the human is sold to an employer or taken as part of their material possessions. These possessions are material objects that have been acquired through a means considered to be personal property or a consequence of the process of production in capitalist society. This labor is not understood as an independent work, which is first and foremost meant to be the true dignity of the person's work. This mechanism projects the person's being into objectivity, making material objects as a subject of the projected image of the person themself. Ironically, the person is further dictated by those material objects, commodities, fetishes, or whatever was created by the person themself.

Plainly, with putting this reverse emphasis on the material over the person, commodity fetishism is understood as our tendency to worship commodities. In particular, the tendency is implicitly associated with our preoccupation with material wealth. Further, this tendency is maximized in an era of neoliberalism rooted in social atomism and economic individualism that pit all in a war-like competition of wills, which we will examine more carefully in the rest of this chapter.

---

5. Marx, *Capital*, 142.
6. Marx, *Capital*, 153, 164–65.
7. Marx, *Capital*, 187.

Neoliberalism and Commodity Fetishism

One prevailing narrative is that neoliberalism is a political ideology that originated in classical liberal antecedents in a neoclassical paradigm.[8] In other words, within the hegemony of neoclassical economics, departments of economics have more radically become political propaganda centers because of the ideological nature of their subject matter. In particular, drawing upon principles of neoclassical economics, neoliberalism's policies seek to create a laissez-faire atmosphere for maximum economic development.[9] These policies are deeply rooted in materialism and economism, resulting in the commodity fetishism theorized by Marx. In fact, the present-day situation is even worse than Marx's nineteenth-century context because the effects of commodity fetishism are highly correlated to the main ideological elements of neoliberalism such as social atomism and economic individualism: Both tenets require ideological separation of economics from the political process (e.g., privatization), define private life under the regime of capital (e.g., consumerism promoted as ways which should actually make life easier), and emphasize international competitiveness as positive (e.g., competing trade viewed as the engine of growth).[10]

In particular, in assessing and discovering these challenging impacts of neoliberalism on society, we can see that neoliberalism is thoroughly grounded in an absolute faith in the market economy and its new mechanism. This means putting too much faith in the market economy's power to create the perfect society. Even today, there is an increasing tendency of commodity fetishism to be embedded in church and society where it gradually channels into a form of *religious* faith or fallacy, and this channeling mechanism becomes more socially acceptable to the neoliberal world

---

8. I recognize that there is a great deal of controversy in how to define neoliberalism, and I do not wish to make this the focus of this chapter. However, for the purposes of creating a reference point, I define neoliberalism as an ideational and political movement centered around the reemergence of classical liberal principles, namely, the tenet that the market itself works toward market economy, and someday it will lead to renewed economic growth; in this sense, government exists only to stimulate a free market economy.

9. Harvey, *Brief History of Neoliberalism*, introduction.

10. Social atomism is an ideology that assigns the individual as the basic unit of analysis for all social implications, justifying social struggles of *only* self-interested individuals to run a society (e.g., John Locke and Thomas Hobbes extend social atomism to the political realm as in the case of the social contract). Economic individualism holds that each individual person should be allowed autonomy in making their own economic decisions as opposed to those decisions being made by such social domains as states, corporations, and churches for the individual person. This vision has been expanded to economic liberalism. See Olsaretti, *Liberty, Desert and the Market*, 14, 88–100.

order. Hugo Assmann highlights this social phenomenon, calling this fallacy "economic religion."[11] He regards it as an idolatrous process: "economic rationality 'kidnaps' and functionalizes essential aspects of Christianity . . . it constitutes an economic religion that unchains an idolatric process."[12]

Where then does this kind of religious fallacy come from? This way of thinking about economic religion or religious fallacy is in line with what Franz Hinkelammert has called the "transcendental imagination." To be clear, Hinkelammert makes a distinction between the transcendental imagination and transcendental concepts. For him, transcendental concepts:

> begin with the objective social relations between subjects and take them to the limits of concepts of institutional perfection. Transcendental imagination, in contrast, begins with the effectively experienced mutual recognition between subjects, [and] transcendentalizes them in a situation of perfection. In the face of the rigidity of the perfect institutions there appears the fluidity of great joy.[13]

Clearly, transcendental concepts are conservative by nature, always working from within the limits of the present political, economic, social, and cultural apparatus for the transformation of society; however, transcendental imagination "places human subjectivity at the core of what is possible, which, in turn, relativizes institutions."[14] In the same manner, neoliberalism has fallen into a category of transcendental imagination by putting too much faith in the market economy as the perfect society since it does not take human subjects to the limits of concepts of institutional perfection.

To be clear, I am thus far not suggesting that we, as Christians, should become Luddites who refuse to consume anything and insist on living within our own homogeneous communities. Nonetheless, the church would be

---

11. Hugo Assmann lists the elements that characterize the religious fallacies of economic religion: "the insistence on the messianic role of the market in neoliberal discourse; the inculcation of a mystique of the market; capitalist culture as a whole; the one-directional interpretation of the failure of 'real socialism'; talk of the 'end of history'; the naturalization of history; the peculiar view of the self-regulating nature of the market (superior to the potential for self-regulation found in living organisms or ecosystems); and, above all, the implication that the market is good news (gospel)." Assmann, "Liberation Theology," 41.

12. Assmann, *Idolatría del Mercado*, 27. This quotation has been translated by Tognato, "In the Name of Money," 4.

13. Hinkelammert and Senent de Frutos, *Critica de la razon utopica*, 343. This quotation was translated by Míguez et al., *Beyond the Spirit of Empire*, 122.

14. Míguez et al., *Beyond the Spirit of Empire*, 122.

wise to be alert and consider the path into the future carefully. What way of life might be worth following in our increasingly neoliberal society?

Catholic Social Teaching (CST) has criticized the materialistic thoughts and behaviors proliferative in neoliberal capitalism. This materialism evolves into idolatry, and this fetishization blocks out the Christian mission in churches where commodities serve as the obsessive focus of characters whose subordination to market logic has inspired in them a desire for mastery and control. This focus is a seed of the Church Industrial Complex as the church is reduced to an economic system captive to a sort of logical machine that presents itself as a new phase in the evolution of capitalism that claims human freedom and equity can be located in and achieved via the free market. What is at stake in my criticism of neoliberalism is a claim on global social justice that must be upheld if there is to be any clarity in socioeconomic thought from a moral perspective. From this proposition, there are three ethical elements to be explored, especially through modern CST: (i) the juridically circumscribed market economy, (ii) the priority of the whole person over solely material well-being, and (iii) the primacy of the common good over individual interest. In what follows, we will explore these puzzles as we learn how CST has responded.

Catholic Social Teaching and Neoliberalism: Materialism Evolving into Idolatry

CST recognizes that humans cannot do anything without material goods, corresponding to their primary needs and constituting the basic conditions for their existence.[15] Nonetheless, CST clarifies that this correlation between human beings and material goods does not mean that humans should succumb to the temptation of making an idol of materials, for the ultimate meaning of life is not to be found in material goods.[16] Further, this idolatry of materials, or the market, can be understood in the contest of atheism, which results "from the absolute character with which certain human values are unduly invested, and which thereby already accords them the stature of God."[17] John Paul II claims that this idolatry of materials is deeply related to the capitalist production process:

---

15. Pontifical Council of Justice and Peace, *Compendium of the Social Doctrine of the Church*, no. 129.

16. Pontifical Council of Justice and Peace, *Compendium of the Social Doctrine of the Church*, no. 181. Also see John Paul II, *Redemptor Hominis*, no. 16.

17. Paul VI, *Gaudium et Spes*, no. 19.

> All that we can say of everything in the production process which constitutes a whole collection of "things," the instruments, the capital, is that it *conditions* man's work; we cannot assert that it constitutes as if were an impersonal "subject" *putting* man and man's work *into a position of dependence.*[18]

This critical aspect of John Paul II's observation is consistent with Marx's criticism of commodity fetishism—capital puts a human's labor into a position of dependence while the human succumbs to the temptation of making an idol of capital and material goods.[19]

In particular, CST argues that these temptations of idolatry of market and commodity fetishism are not helpful in accomplishing the church's mission. *Populorum Progressio* argues that temptations fallen into the false values of excessive temporal prosperity do not merely preclude the activity of human spirit but more fundamentally complicate the approach to God.[20] This viewpoint is clarified in the *Puebla* Final Document: "Earthly goods become an idol and a serious obstacle to the Kingdom of God when human beings devote all their attention to possessing them or even coveting them."[21] On that account, it is clear that one of CST's priorities is to attend to the deepest crisis of humanity, the moral and spiritual depravity of the human heart, which results in such obstacles as the idolatry of market, materialism, and the relentless pursuit of consumption. Hence, this idolatry of market or commodity fetishism must be continuously criticized by the church as part of her mission.[22]

Furthermore, it is important to note Jon Sobrino's comments on the *Puebla* Final Document. He recognizes that the document warns against the dangerous temptations of materialism, economism, and atheism as the "idols of our time." He also agrees that the worship of such idols dehumanizes human beings, "causing them to sacrifice themselves and others to those idols." However, he cautiously suggests that these temptations are grounded in *active* atheism of idolatry: "But there is no little merit in pointing out that the great problem of our continent is not, strictly speaking, agnosticism or abstract, passive atheism but rather the active atheism of idolatry and

---

18. John Paul II, *Laborem Exercens*, no. 13.

19. John Paul II, *Centesimus Annus*, no. 40.

20. Paul VI, *Populorum Progressio*, no. 41.

21. III Conferencia General del Episcopado Latinoamericano, *Documento de Puebla*, no. 493.

22. III Conferencia General del Episcopado Latinoamericano, *Documento de Puebla*, no. 405. As I revisit this later in the chapter, modern CST authors certainly do not seem to want to align themselves with Marxian critique even as they critique capitalism.

its sacrifice of human lives and human values."²³ In my estimation, what he calls active atheism of idolatry can be interpreted as a new version of commodity fetishism in today's era of neoliberalism.²⁴ In fact, the *Puebla Final Document* concerns the forms of idolatry of the 1970s: liberal capitalism and its reactionary opposite—Marxist collectivism. However, since the fall of the Soviet Union, Marxist collectivism has not been as prominent as before. This is now an era in which liberal capitalism dominates across the world, even enslaving post-communist nations to the idols of new market mechanisms. Indeed, within the context of neoliberalism, earthly goods and material objects are more easily, aggressively, and largely turned into the absolute idols of our time.

Catholic Social Teaching, Neoliberalism, and Globalization: Culture of Death

Modern CST attends to the relationship between neoliberalism and globalization, mainly due to the increasingly inclusive nature of globalization, which embraces all sorts of evolving processes of building the world as more integrated and interconnected—with neoliberal-driven interdependent economies.²⁵ Further, John Paul II brings particular attention to the process of cultural globalization as he distinguishes it from the process of economic globalization: "Cultural and ethical features of globalization are of special interest and greater interest to the Christian community, compared to the purely economic and financial effects of the phenomenon"; therefore, the church, as the expert in humanity, "is called to discern and evaluate the cultural *novum* produced by globalization."²⁶ This also means that the global market interests in their playing field are certainly aware that there are no legal, social, ecological, national, or cultural boundaries. Thus, economic competition *de facto* plays out in a market beyond all cultural and spiritual domains as the global market's interests—their maximal profits—take on complete priority. The concern is that this profit-seeking globalized

---

23. Sobrino, "Significance of Puebla for the Catholic Church in Latin America," 303.

24. One may wonder if atheism is an appropriate label in an era of neoliberalism since a majority of people, including Christians and their institutions, participate in commodity fetishism in various ways. For this viewpoint, see McRorie, "Markets as Moral Contexts."

25. Globalization, which has often been tied up with neoliberal ideology or its economic and cultural forms in social encyclicals, was addressed for the first time in *Centesimus annus*. Also see Himes, "Globalization with a Human Face," 270.

26. John Paul II, "Address to the Sixth Public Session of the Pontifical Academies of Theology and of St. Thomas Aquinas," no. 2.

mechanism is *culturally* rationalized by alleging that the global market's interests mean everyone's interests; more precisely, each of our thoughts and behaviors can be habitually ritualized and spiritually hypnotized with this rationalization that the big players' well-being means our well-being, the conglomerates' well-being means small- and midsize enterprises' well-being, and the mega churches' well-being means each believer's well-being.[27]

Plainly, CST is highly critical of neoliberal-driven globalization. That form of globalization can cause numerous social problems, including materialistic economism and unfair competition, both of which put the poor in a situation of ever-increasing inferiority and exploitation, thus increasing social inequality. As a result, this form of neoliberal-driven globalization produces a "culture of death," or the devaluation of human dignity and life that in many ways is associated with the market mechanism: "[This] culture is actively fostered by powerful cultural, economic and political currents which encourage an idea of society excessively concerned with efficiency."[28]

In particular, two issues should be considered in relation to the culture of death. First, the neoliberal-driven global market tends to cause commodity fetishism by emphasizing the material over the person, including the person's right to live. As a result, humans are obsessed with an idol that absolutizes a highly competitive and merciless economic system that drives socially vulnerable populations out to death. Second, the neoliberal market mechanism emphasizes individual freedom in the pursuit of self-interest, which is placed before others' right to life. However, CST does not agree that individual freedom means free choice situated in free competition; rather, it emphasizes that freedom to choose is appropriate only as long as humans are first able to live. Here, CST understands the concept of freedom as relational, as opposed to the individualistic (i.e., socioatomic) perspective of neoliberalism: "[The] aim [of CST] is to recover a perspective on the human person that views relationality as a vital component for authentic

---

27. To be clear, rationalization itself has multiple facets—it can be used for both good and self-deception. Lisa Cahill's understanding of rationalization is helpful: "Rationalization is not just a willful, self-generated series of intellectual contortions. It is a biased yet plausible interpretation of events and possibilities, pulled together from among options, within an environment, by an interested agent, to constitute a viewpoint that legitimates action. Rationalization is a strategy of self-deception. Rationalization depends on preexisting contexts and relationships, and on already being invested in certain outcomes. It is a warped exercise of practical reason about real goods to be achieved, an exercise in which the self averts attention from the real worth of various goods, the relation among the goods, and the effects that seeking a good, at a certain time, in a certain way, will have on other beings." Cahill, *Global Justice, Christology, and Christian Ethics*, 57.

28. John Paul II, *Evangelium Vitae*, no. 12.

personhood. Such a viewpoint will necessarily be attentive to the prospect of a common good or set of shared goods."[29]

Therefore, for CST, a culture of death not only focuses on traditionally specified life event issues such as the death penalty, but it also includes protection of the rights of the socially vulnerable: "[It] cannot be denied that such a culture of death, taken as whole, betrays a completely individualistic concept of freedom, which ends up by becoming the freedom of 'the strong' against the weak who have no choice but to submit."[30] This standpoint from CST proposed by John Paul II in *Evangelium vitae* is also found in *Ecclesia in America*:

> Nowadays, in America as elsewhere in the world, a model of [neoliberal] society appears to be emerging in which the powerful predominate, setting aside and even eliminating the powerless: I am thinking here of . . . many other people relegated to the margins of society by consumerism and materialism . . . . This model of society bears the stamp of the culture of death, and is therefore in opposition to the Gospel message. Faced with this distressing reality, the Church community intends to commit itself all the more to the defense of the culture of life.[31]

This critical defense initiated by John Paul II developed into Benedict XVI's CST presented in *Caritas in veritate*. According to Archbishop Giampaolo Crepaldi, despite the fact that *Caritas in veritate* restated most of the points made in previous social encyclicals, one original aspect of the encyclical is its concerns about the culture of death as "a package deal."[32] In other words, the messages of *Caritas in veritate* "invite a new way of thinking, and a new praxis, that takes account of the systematic interconnections between the anthropological themes linked to life and human dignity, and the economic, social and cultural themes linked to development."[33]

In another sense, Benedict XVI is critical of the processes of globalization as he focuses on diverse socioeconomic issues that have emerged since the 1990s. However, *Caritas in veritate* uses a slightly different perspective than previous social encyclicals to approach the problem of (cultural) globalization. Previous social encyclicals mostly referred to John Paul II's teaching with the intent to demonstrate the power of the media and profit-seeking mechanism, both of which are *culturally* rationalized in our

29. Himes, "Globalization with a Human Face," 274.
30. John Paul II, *Evangelium Vitae*, no. 19.
31. John Paul II, *Ecclesia in America*, no. 63.
32. Allen, "Gut Check for American Catholicism."
33. Allen, "Gut Check for American Catholicism."

social and economic life. In contrast, Benedict XVI discusses the processes of globalization with respect to the increasing technology-led culture. This culture tends to make people believe that technology can even re-create humans themselves through its advances and that humans regard themselves as their own almighty beings thanks to technological progress; technology allows itself to become "an ideological power that threatens to confine us within an *a priori* that holds us back from encountering being and truth" and, above all, efficiency and utility become the sole criteria of the truth.[34]

Just as in capitalist society, materialistic economism tends to create or at least facilitate commodity fetishism so as to sustain a global market mechanism and consumerist growth. In a technocratic society, truth as efficiency and utility turn into other idols that help us achieve and enforce our desire to be almighty, as this definition of truth "draws us out of our physical limitations and broadens our horizon."[35] This is another form of commodity fetishism, but it is also another form of the culture of death. This is not only because of technology's inability to recognize intrinsic value (e.g., human dignity) and its bent toward narcissism (e.g., placing things before humans) but also because technological practices in the pursuit of efficiency and utility "in turn foster a materialistic and mechanistic understanding of human life."[36]

The Role of the Church beyond Neoliberalism

John Paul II urges the church to continue promoting solidarity and the common good despite the challenges of neoliberal-driven globalization processes.[37] It is clear that the moral and social aspects of neoliberal capitalism must be more directly addressed by not only the leaders of nations but also by church leaders. However, the church does not always support restriction on individual freedom or an open possibility of *strong* state intervention. Instead, the church has a different agenda than the state or market. The church does not claim to be an expert in economics, but an "expert in humanity" that serves as a "voice for the voiceless (voz dos sem voz)," recognizing fundamental values such as charity, social justice, and solidarity at the center of human life, and thus fighting for the human advancement

---

34. Benedict XVI, *Caritas in Veritate*, no. 68–70.
35. Benedict XVI, *Caritas in Veritate*, no. 70.
36. Benedict XVI, *Caritas in Veritate*, no. 75.
37. John Paul II, "Address to the Plenary Session on the Subject 'Globalization,'" no. 2.

of all.[38] In other words, for these fundamental values to be realized inside and outside the church, the church must give the world a *diaconia* of truth about human beings and proclaim this truth, presenting it as the path to *true* progress in the world today.[39] Therefore, apart from presenting these fundamental values or their shared principle that the economy exists for all the human beings of the world, even a new and revolutionary economic system can scarcely be imagined as leading humans to *true* happiness and well-being. It can only lead to failure—at least from the church's standpoint. The church is thus obliged to consider this fundamental principle, seeking ways to overcome the challenges arising from the neoliberal-driven global market capitalism.

Unfortunately, however, the practical concern is that the role of the market has replaced the role of the church since it has led us into a blind faith that the neoliberal market and its associated economic rationality mechanism can alleviate our suffering and promise human flourishing. Noticeably, the church has participated in both the neoliberal capitalist practices today as well as in its theological justification of colonization, genocide, and slavery, which were done in the name of God and economic power. One of the prevalent examples is that many Christian communities have embraced the social tendency of being only or predominantly composed of middle- and upper-economic classes of rich and influential people. Unfortunately, this phenomenon occurs in Western society where neoliberal market logic plays a key role in everyday life. Ulrich Duchrow points out that most Western churches have been ambiguous in their economic teachings, especially with regard to finding a target population for their ministry, which "represents a fundamental problem for theology and the Church in a western middle-class society—although scripture also clarifies who are the

---

38. Paul VI, *Populorum Progressio*, no. 13. Both *Compendium of the Social Doctrine of the Church* (2004), and "Presentation, no. 61. Message of Pope Benedict XVI for the World Day of Migrants and Refugees" (2013) refer to *Populorum Progressio* (1967), no. 13—although the phrase of "expert in humanity" is not found in the church document. Terence A. McGoldrick sees that the phrase appeared for the first time in Paul VI, "Speech to the United Nations, October 4, 1965." See McGoldrick, "Episcopal Conferences Worldwide and Catholic Social Thought, in Theory and Praxis," 397, 402.

39. "Diaconia is traditionally seen as care for the human person in his or her concrete bodily dimension . . . . The corporeal works of mercy reveal a classical interpretation of diaconia, namely as charitable work . . . . Various commentaries on *Deus caritas est* criticize the Pope's interpretation of *diaconia* in terms of charity and his position that justice is less the task of the Church than of Christians and others in the world . . . . The encyclical *Caritas in veritate* interprets charity (love) as 'the heart of the Church's social doctrine,' which means in fact a reinterpretation of CST that has been characterized by a focus on justice." Dillen, "Complex Relationship Between Body and Mind," 265.

people that the Church needs to pay attention."[40] He says: "Here the Bible is quite clear [that Jesus defines very precisely the place where he, the 'human one' of the Kingdom of God, must be met with those whose basic needs are unsatisfied (Matt 25:31ff)]. This is the pattern running through it, and seen from here all its statements about economics become unambiguous."[41]

Notable free market–friendly thinkers like Michael Novak and Robert Nelson have also admitted that the whole world favors this role of the market since no one can evade the global influence on human development led by the market. In particular, Nelson argues that "the market, with its global dimensions and rational efficiency, provides the possibility for a new kind of salvation in which every tear will be wiped away."[42] What this also means for him is that "the market can provide what the church tried but failed to offer: (i) the maximization of individual liberty; (ii) the annihilation of all coercive uses of power; (iii) the realization of all relationships based on voluntary consent; (iv) the achievement of perfect harmony; and (v) the equality of all humanity through the world." He even attempts to incorporate this neoliberal market-driven vision into a constructive theology in sync with the natural law tradition: "(i) [The] pursuit of self-interest is inherently good; (ii) to be rational is to be 'efficient'; (iii) the goal of communal life is increased productivity; and (iv) a select group of persons—economists and social scientists—now forms a new priesthood because they are the interpreters of the market."[43]

However, these approaches are dangerous. It is important to pose the question, how do we integrate rational morality into a perspective informed by faith? The sources of faith, which are integrated into moral thinking and moral life, are Scripture, Christ, the church, and the magisterium as well as reason and experience,[44] but not the market itself. The market is not the source of faith, but part of human experience. Even though human experience also "seeks to grasp the whole of moral reality and to probe the natures of moral knowledge, objectivity, and truth,"[45] it is also important to remind us that we should examine our common ground in a more cautious and nuanced way.[46] Human goods are not only our own constructions. All human beings, not exclusively those who are well-adapted to the market, require

---

40. Duchrow, *Alternatives to Global Capitalism*, 205.
41. Duchrow, *Alternatives to Global Capitalism*, 205.
42. Long, "Global Market/A Catholic Church," 360.
43. Long, "Global Market/A Catholic Church," 360.
44. Gula, *Reason Informed by Faith*, 2.
45. Gula, *Reason Informed by Faith*, 17.
46. Cahill, "Community Versus Universals," 6.

that their basic human needs be fulfilled so as to flourish.[47] In addition, human goods can be more fully achieved through practices of love and concern for one another. In doing so, self-interest-seeking mechanisms, the culture of death, commodity fetishism, and all other materialistic economism-led thoughts and behaviors can be defeated.[48]

Furthermore, according to Duane Stephen Long, the problem of Nelson's theological claims is that "God is not found dying on a cross but is merely a power that secures certain laws so that the market mechanism works smoothly if we cooperate with it," which presents "a false form of salvation." This is because "the global market is not based on the revelation of God in Jesus," as "it cannot be grounded in the Word."[49] This critique of Nelson's theological claim leads to a prophetic mission of the church, I suggest. The church does not suggest a certain treatment like a panacea or a supernatural solution like magic as the neoliberal market does, but proclaims messages of God's grace which free human beings and thus reach the conscience of love, justice, and peace.[50] On one hand, to actualize this conscience in a proper way, vigilance is required; hence, the church's prophetic mission should be based on *thinking* action: "A correct concept of conscience determines the positions which are assigned to the virtues of freedom and obedience (. . . .) The conscience wishes to listen to, to obey God's call in the situation with all vigilance. The conscious and free presentation of the objective claims of beings, of the law of God, is a moral good."[51] On the other hand, however, the message of the gospel should not be too abstract in the face of the complex and contradictory neoliberal-driven capitalist society of wealth and poverty intermingled. It should reflect the concrete symbols of the age as they are examined thoroughly in the current historic context. The eyes which look into the symbols of this generation can be wide open when the church is completely open to the Holy Spirit. Also, this prophetic declaration of the gospel becomes possible when we are willing to undergo the distress that consistent penitence and renovation bring about. In reality, numerous Christians and Christian churches that have been moved by the Holy Spirit and prophetic words have participated

---

47. Cahill, "Community Versus Universals," 7.

48. Cahill, "Community Versus Universals," 11.

49. Long, "Global Market/A Catholic Church," 361.

50. Pope Francis notes that "the Church is . . . conscious of the responsibility which all of us have for our world, for the whole of creation, which we must love and protect. There is much that we can do to benefit the poor, the needy, and those who suffer, and to favor justice, promote reconciliation, and build peace." Francis, "Audience with Representatives of the Churches and Ecclesial Communities and of the Different Religions."

51. Haring, *Christian Maturity*, 63.

in the fight to protect the lives of all, especially their poor and alienated neighbors. The church should follow the footsteps of our predecessors in faith, standing with life and exhausting our prophetic mission.

Above all, the market is not God, and it is not our savior. The church should remind us of what Hugo Assmann called "economic religion." As discussed earlier, for him, "economic religion" can be characterized as "an idolatric process" in which the market economy becomes an ultimate, sacred passageway to solutions for all human problems. In other words, within the context of neoliberalism, "the messianic role of the market" has emerged.[52] However, the church itself should not be tolerant of this messianic role of the market due to its idolatric process. When humans put anything before God and deny confessing God as the one and only almighty God, instead worshiping an idol, it eventually results in death (e.g., Num 21:4–9). To repeat, CST documents also express the concern that such idolatry of the market leads humans to the way of death instead of the way of life. It is clear that the messages of neoliberalism tend to brainwash us into serving the market as our new god. They challenge the fundamental messages of Christianity, which confesses God to be the living and true God. It is critical for the church to take action as shared in its prophetic mission. Most importantly, the church is responsible for exploring the hidden ideology of the economic system and market economy that have gained such iconic status, thereby disclosing the limited conditions of the economy and market-centered soteriology, and thus revealing how they can be related to victims of the advance of neoliberalism in our society.

In another sense, the market itself is not only becoming a messianic idol that disturbs our relationship with God, but it also destroys our relationship with other humans. In particular, the concern is that this messianic market mechanism limits our human relations only to economic relations in which the market mechanism motivates and, in turn, regulates all social relations. Therefore, this form of the idolatric process of the market is opposite to the broader concept of God's economy and, more precisely, it ruins the relational *imago Dei*. It is important to remember what Pope Francis said recently regarding the more serious ethical and social problems that have emerged where those who are more closely involved in the economic system exert their domination over those perceived to be less involved the system, namely, the socially vulnerable population:

> One cause of this situation is found in our relationship with money, since we calmly accept its dominion over ourselves and our societies. The current financial crisis can make us overlook

---

52. Assmann, "Liberation Theology," 41.

the fact that it originated in a profound human crisis: the denial of the primacy of the human person! We have created new idols .... The thirst for power and possessions knows no limits. In this system, which tends to devour everything which stands in the way of increased profits, whatever is fragile, like the environment, is defenseless before the interests of a deified market, which become the only rule.[53]

This papal statement offers a good summary of the argument of this chapter: The church should be the salt and the light of the world, not the market. As Paul instructs the Romans, "Do not conform to the pattern of this world, but be transformed by the renewing of your mind. Then you will be able to test and approve what God's will is—his good, pleasing and perfect will" (Rom 12:2).

Conclusion and Further Thoughts

Modern CST has attempted to combat the materialistic economism reflected in the modern capitalist society. In particular, more recent CST documents have responded to the question of how material goods are evaluated as certain values in an era of neoliberalism, which advocates a full-scale or perfect market economy. Since the 1990s, modern CST has particularly characterized this form of materialistic economism as an idolatry. This idolatry or idolatric process, like commodity fetishism, eventually places a reverse emphasis on the material over the person. Above all, in the context of a neoliberal-driven market mechanism, the maximized tendency to worship commodities turns to a form of economic religion or religious fallacy, thus pitting all in a war-like competition of wills. Both Catholic social ethicists and contemporary secular thinkers have explored how this form of commodity fetishism can dehumanize human beings, cause humans to sacrifice themselves and others to those idols, and eventually exclude humans from the society they deserve as a *free* part of human life. Also, they have concerns about the "culture of death" in which one's individual freedom is placed before the rights of others, especially when those who are more closely involved in this economic system exert their domination with the tacit consent of the less involved in the system.

The church of today, like early Christian communities, is required to be an exemplary model. That is, as the church aims to provide communion and fellowship in economic life, it gives the world the *diaconia* of truth about human beings. As emphasized, the church as an "expert in humanity"

---

53. Francis, *Evangelii Gaudium*, no. 55–56.

should place vital economic values at the center of human life.[54] However, this alternative, more than anything else, presupposes an internal renovation of the church in economic respects. In other words, to fully realize the church's mission for economic justice, it must first be refreshed, reformed, and renovated from the inside out.

It is without question that the church should overcome the materialistic and economic determinist views if it wants to criticize social problems grounded in the culture of materialism and economism in a neoliberal-driven market society. For example, materialistic economism can be defined as an attitude that places importance on external appearance, like the number of people in the congregation, the size of buildings, the scale of offerings, and what can be measured in numbers. Materialistic and growth-supremacist ways of thinking consider quantitative expansion of systems and increases in the number of people in the congregation as the most important standards of development for the church. This is evidence that the church is directly affected by the neoliberal-driven capitalistic culture. As long as the church justifies and even encourages materialistic success and quantitative expansion in the wider culture that so treasures efficiency, competition, and visible performance, the ability to live a holy, humble, and honest life (individually and communally) and to communally share (what you have of yourself spiritually and materially) is nothing more than empty echoes. The church thus cannot suggest an alternative life and a form of community to society.

In particular, our society increasingly is becoming almost incapable of thinking, speaking, and acting outside of market logic and relationships of utility. As our society tends to fall into commodity fetishism, many Christians tend to idolize a certain kind of effectiveness. We live in a *purpose-driven* age—an age that measures value in terms of achieving (usually self-benefiting) goals that we can contain rather than in terms of intrinsic goods that exceed us. In this sense, we almost always think of *accomplishment* as one's ability to grasp and wield something (e.g., the accomplishment of getting a stable job). This accomplishment is what follows mastery within a mode of cause-effect, cost-benefit analysis.

This way of thinking is not only secular: Such rationalization is characteristic of the economically colonized mind that challenges the moral vision of many Christian churches today. This challenge does not simply mean that materialism and economism run against the church's moral teachings or modern CST. Rather, this challenge affirms that, in reality, such

---

54. Paul VI, *Populorum Progressio*, no. 13; and Paul VI, "Speech to the United Nations, October 4, 1965."

an economically colonized mind is also often found as a greater threat of corrupting, distorting, and even shaking the root of the church's moral vision since it is (tacitly) immersed in church life and culture in the name of accomplishment and utility.

In this reality of our social life, we need to revive the tradition of idolatry criticism, which has stood against the idols that led to "death" throughout the history of the Christian tradition. Furthermore, the materialistic and economic determinist views that dominate our social life today should be monitored, filtered, and de-sacralized. At the same time, these views should be eradicated, especially when they oppress our socially vulnerable neighbors in the name of economic rationality. In doing so, it becomes possible for us to appreciate the true spirituality of Christianity living by the church and society in this era.

Bibliography

III Conferencia General del Episcopado Latinoamericano. *Documento de Puebla*. 1979. https://www.celam.org/documentos/Documento_Conclusivo_Puebla.pdf.

Allen, John L., Jr. "A Gut Check for American Catholicism." *National Catholic Reporter*, July 17, 2009. http://ncronline.org/blogs/all-things-catholic/gut-check-american-catholicism.

Assmann, Hugo. *La idolatría del Mercado*. San José, Costa Rica: DEI, 1997.

———. "Liberation Theology: Looking Forward." Translated by Francis McDonagh. *Religion, State and Society* 21 (1993) 39–52.

Benedict XVI. *Caritas in Veritate*. 2009. https://www.vatican.va/content/benedict-xvi/en/encyclicals/documents/hf_ben-xvi_enc_20090629_caritas-in-veritate.html.

Brown, Bill. *A Sense of Things*. Chicago: University of Chicago Press, 2003.

Cahill, Lisa Sowle. "Community Versus Universals: A Misplaced Debate in Christian Ethics." In *The Annual of the Society of Christian Ethics*, 18. Washington, DC: Georgetown University Press, 1998.

———. *Global Justice, Christology, and Christian Ethics*. Cambridge: Cambridge University Press, 2013.

Dillen, Annemie. "The Complex Relationship Between Body and Mind as a Key for a Renewed Catholic Reflection on Diaconal Work." In *Exploring the Boundaries of Bodiliness: Theological and Interdisciplinary Approaches to the Human Condition*, edited by Sigrid Müller et al., 261–70. Göttingen: Vandenhoeck and Ruprecht, 2013.

Duchrow, Ulrich. *Alternatives to Global Capitalism: Drawn from Biblical History, Designed for Political Action*. Utrecht: International, 1997.

Eagleson, John, and Philip Scharper, eds. *Puebla and Beyond*. Translated by John Drury. New York: Orbis, 1979.

Francis. "Audience with Representatives of the Churches and Ecclesial Communities and of the Different Religions." Message of Pontifical Council for Interreligious Dialogue for Feast of Vesakh. March 20, 2013. https://www.vatican.va/content/

francesco/en/speeches/2013/march/documents/papa-francesco_20130320_delegati-fraterni.html.
———. *Evangelii Gaudium*. 2013. https://www.vatican.va/content/francesco/en/apost_exhortations/documents/papa-francesco_esortazione-ap_20131124_evangelii-gaudium.html.
Gula, Richard. *Reason Informed by Faith: Foundations of Catholic Morality*. New York: Paulist, 1989.
Haring, Bernard. *Christian Maturity*. Translated by Arlene Swindler. Montreal: Palm, 1967.
Harvey, David. *A Brief History of Neoliberalism*. Oxford: Oxford University Press, 2005.
Himes, Kenneth. "Globalization with a Human Face: Catholic Social Teaching and Globalization." *Theological Studies* 69 (2008) 269–89.
Hinkelammert, Franz J., and Juan Antonio Senent de Frutos. *Critica de la razon utopica*. Bilbao, Spain: Desclee de Brouwer, 2002.
John Paul II. "Address to the Plenary Session on the Subject 'Globalisation: Ethical and Institutional Concerns.'" *Papal Addresses* no. 2, Vatican City, April 27, 2001. https://www.pass.va/content/pass/en/magisterium/saint-john-paul-ii/2001-27-april.pdf.
———. "Address to the Sixth Public Session of the Pontifical Academies of the Theology and of St. Thomas Aquinas." *Speeches* no. 2, Vatican City, November 8, 2001. https://www.vatican.va/content/john-paul-ii/en/speeches/2001/november/documents/hf_jp-ii_spe_20011108_pontificie-accademie.html.
———. *Centesimus Annus*. 1991. https://www.vatican.va/content/john-paul-ii/en/encyclicals/documents/hf_jp-ii_enc_01051991_centesimus-annus.html.
———. *Ecclesia in America*. 1999. https://www.vatican.va/content/john-paul-ii/en/apost_exhortations/documents/hf_jp-ii_exh_22011999_ecclesia-in-america.html.
———. *Evangelium Vitae*. 1995. https://www.vatican.va/content/john-paul-ii/en/encyclicals/documents/hf_jp-ii_enc_25031995_evangelium-vitae.html.
———. *Laborem Exercens*. 1981. https://www.vatican.va/content/john-paul-ii/en/encyclicals/documents/hf_jp-ii_enc_14091981_laborem-exercens.html.
———. *Redemptor Hominis*. 1979. https://www.vatican.va/content/john-paul-ii/en/encyclicals/documents/hf_jp-ii_enc_04031979_redemptor-hominis.html.
Long, Duane Stephen. "A Global Market/A Catholic Church: The New Political (Ir)Realism." *Theology Today* 52 (1995) 356–65.
Marx, Karl. *Capital: A Critique of Political Economy*. Vol. 1. Edited by Frederick Engels and translated by Samuel Moore et al. New York: Modern Library, 1906.
McGoldrick, Terence A. "Episcopal Conferences Worldwide and Catholic Social Thought, in Theory and Praxis: An Update." *Theological Studies* 75 (2014) 376–403.
McRorie, Christina. "Markets as Moral Contexts: An Account Based in Catholic Theological Anthropology." In *Democracy, Religion, and Commerce: Private Markets and the Public Regulation of Religion*, edited by Nathan Oman and Kathleen Flake, 162–76. Routledge, 2023.
Míguez, Néstor Oscar, et al. *Beyond the Spirit of Empire: Theology and Politics in a New Key*. London: SCM, 2009.
Olsaretti, Serena. *Liberty, Desert and the Market: A Philosophical Study*. Cambridge: Cambridge University Press, 2004.

Paul VI. *Gaudium et Spes*. 1965. https://www.vatican.va/archive/hist_councils/ii_vatican_council/documents/vat-ii_const_19651207_gaudium-et-spes_en.html.

———. *Populorum Progressio*. 1976. https://www.vatican.va/content/paul-vi/en/encyclicals/documents/hf_p-vi_enc_26031967_populorum.html.

———. "Speech to the United Nations, October 4, 1965." https://www.vatican.va/content/paul-vi/en/speeches/1965/documents/hf_p-vi_spe_19651004_united-nations.html.

Pontifical Council of Justice and Peace. *Compendium of the Social Doctrine of the Church*, 2004. https://www.vatican.va/roman_curia/pontifical_councils/justpeace/documents/rc_pc_justpeace_doc_20060526_compendio-dott-soc_en.html.

Sobrino, Jon. "The Significance of Puebla for the Catholic Church in Latin America." In *Puebla and Beyond*, edited by John Eagleson and Philip Scharper and translated by John Drury, 289–311. New York: Orbis, 1979.

Suman, Joel, and Keith Meador. *Heal Thyself: Spirituality, Medicine, and the Distortion of Christianity*. Oxford: Oxford University Press, 2003.

Tognato, Carlo. "In the Name of Money: Central Banking as a Secular Religion." Bogota, Universidad Nacional, October 30, 2004, unpublished manuscript.

Chapter 5

The Specter of Capitalism

Dorothy Day and the Catholic Worker Movement as Response to Magisterial Financial Trends

MARTIN TOMSZAK

Smuggling $26 million in cash on a private jet from Switzerland to Rome sounds like the plot of a blockbuster action film rather than something attempted by a Catholic priest. And yet, in June 2013, Monsignor Nunzio Scarano was arrested in the wake of such an attempt. The Vatican's lead accountant had spent years laundering money through the Vatican Bank and its real estate holdings, amassing close to $10 million for himself (including a $2 million villa in Salerno) and countless millions for the Catholic Church. Due to loosened restrictions on money flow in and out of the sovereign territory of the Vatican, Scarano was able to take on the business of some less than desirable figures to the church's financial benefit. Throughout Scarano's trial, reminiscent of the Banco Ambrosiano scandal that plagued the Vatican in the early eighties, it became evident that such practices were not uncommon for the church nor was Scarano the only source of fiscal misconduct for the Vatican.

The scandal led to a drastic restructuring of Vatican financial rules and unprecedented cooperation with the European Union's fiscal watchdogs, but the effectiveness of this restructuring has faced recent scrutiny. In July 2022, Pope Francis was forced to once again revisit investment policies as it was embarrassingly revealed that Monsignor Alberto Perlasca, a man with no background in finance, had virtually sole control over the $600 million

Vatican Secretariat of State account and was investing in everything from oil speculation in war torn countries to arms deals and poor real estate investments. The most recent example, and the one that drew attention to Perlasca, was a bad luxury rental property deal in London that cost the church tens of millions.

These two cases pose important existential questions for an institution that is meant to worship God, preach the gospel, serve the poor, and be a light to the world rather than be co-opted by the ways of the unjust system proliferating throughout that world. The words of an itinerant preacher from Nazareth—words that spoke of equity and equality, of a preferential option for the poor, of giving rather than garnering, and of self-sacrifice rather than self-aggrandizement—have little to do with the aforementioned trends. More explicitly, the accumulation of wealth and financial misdeeds of the Vatican should be labeled as antithetical to the message of someone who once overturned the tables of vendors charging a premium for access to temple rituals. Much like the vendors in this exemplar from Christ's ministry, those who are charged with the upkeep of the sacraments—literal signs pointing to the presence of the Divine—have seemingly turned their priorities elsewhere. However, as with Jesus's response in the temple, a glimmer of hope is evident for those who understand the vitality of resistance.

The following chapter will examine alternate approaches to what this volume has labeled the Church Industrial Complex from within the Catholic tradition itself. On the surface, the history-rich denomination may seem to be immune from the trends of younger and more modern denominations that acquiesce to the blurring of lines between business and faith, but the reality is far removed from such an assumption. In addition to the aforementioned trends of fiscal impropriety, the Catholic Church mirrors other aspects of the business realm that could be considered less than savory. With around 177 million acres of land around the globe across over 5,100 registered properties, the Catholic Church is the single largest landholder outside of government entities in the world.[1] While there is tremendous potential for good in such a reality (houses of hospitality, environmental conservation, parish upkeep, etc.), the scale of this wealth offers a stark reminder of just how vast is the potential for further impropriety. When you add other trends like the 2021 US Conference of Catholic Bishops U-turn on investment (moving from a centuries-long ban on usury and speculation to outlining the bounds for ethically responsible investment guided by Catholic Social Teaching itself); a growing utilization of church property in the US for rental to both other religious organizations and secular ones

---

1. "Church Properties Initiative."

for profit; and a widespread wave of Diocesan financial mismanagement, that although far more boring than our action flick-esque example above, is nonetheless worrisome; the presence of the Catholic Church within the bounds of the Church Industrial Complex seems firm indeed.

Utilizing a methodology that traverses scripture, mines the documents of Catholic Social Teaching (CST), and uplifts radical lay communities, an alternate approach to gospel witness will be offered as we collectively attempt to move such resistance from the periphery of ecclesiology to its center. A revisitation of Matt 20:1–16, commonly referred to as the parable of the vineyard, will provide a scriptural basis for discussing an aversion to capitalist endeavor as a distinct prerequisite for ministry. Following this, a brief overview of CST documents related to the dangers of neo-liberalism and its ties to free market capitalism will provide a catalyst for re-thinking the Church Industrial Complex by utilizing the hierarchy's own understanding. Excerpts from Pope Paul VI's *Populorum Progressio* will serve to highlight a continuous thread of anti-capitalist rhetoric from within the tradition and serve as the litmus paper with which the magisterium might test itself. Most extensively, an examination of Dorothy Day and the Catholic Worker Movement will provide an example of Catholic identity harbored in mutual aid, voluntary poverty, self-sacrifice, and anarcho-pacifism dedicated to authentic gospel living. Archival material from the *Catholic Worker Newspaper*, Day's *Long Loneliness*, and Peter Maurin's *Easy Essays* will demonstrate the possibility of living otherwise in a church entrenched in the ways of the world. The Catholic Worker model of radical community can reinvigorate modes of resistance to the power structures blemishing the gospel message and serve as a dialogue partner in unlocking the true potential of the church in the world.

"A Denarius for a Day": Scriptural Economics for the Magisterium

As we begin to reimagine—or perhaps return to—an ecclesial model that might avoid the types of near fantastical occurrences of worldly corruption cataloged above, I would like to present the Matthean parable of the workers in the vineyard for discussion.[2] Typically interpreted as an allegory that illus-

---

2. Matt 20:1–16 NASV: "For the kingdom of heaven is like a landowner who went out early in the morning to hire laborers for his vineyard. After agreeing with the laborers for a *denarius*, he sent them into his vineyard. When he went out about nine o'clock, he saw others standing idle in the marketplace; and he said to them, 'You also go into the vineyard, and I will pay you whatever is right.' So they went. When he went out again about noon and about three o'clock, he did the same. And about five o'clock he

trates God's unbounding generosity and grace, I propose that such a reading ignores the basic principles of how parables function as narratives rooted in particular experiences and contexts. When read considering Jesus's original audience of hearers rather than Matthew's reinterpretation of the parable (influenced by conflicts arising between the gentile and Jewish members of the early church community), an allegorical understanding of the owner of the vineyard as a stand in for the benevolence of God makes little sense. Moreover, for our purposes here, the parable is placed within a pericope that not only describes the kingdom, but also provides a direct response to Peter and the disciples' inquiry into their role in that kingdom, which further negates such an interpretation. Instead, I will show the parable to be an indictment of the vineyard owner as exploitative and as a model for what leadership in the coming kingdom *should not* look like. The juxtaposition of ideal leadership as presented by scripture with the distinct shortcomings of current institutional realities ought to create a serious occasion for reflection on this volume's exploration of the Church Industrial Complex.

In order to avoid an overly exhaustive exercise in biblical criticism in what is meant to be an ethically rooted chapter, I will immediately highlight my exegetical presupposition of scriptural interpretation yielding liberative praxis. Again, I am well aware of the ways in which the parable has been interpreted classically[3] and one need only perform a Google search of the "Parable of the Vineyard" to see those interpretations carry over to our contemporary sphere.[4] When we interpret the text via a distinct liberative her-

---

went out and found others standing around; and he said to them, 'Why are you standing here idle all day?' They said to him, 'Because no one has hired us.' He said to them, 'You also go into the vineyard.' When evening came, the owner of the vineyard said to his manager, 'Call the laborers and give them their pay, beginning with the last and then going to the first.' When those hired about five o'clock came, each of them received the usual daily wage. Now when the first came, they thought they would receive more; but each of them also received the usual daily wage. And when they received it, they grumbled against the landowner, saying, 'These last worked only one hour, and you have made them equal to us who have borne the burden of the day and the scorching heat.' But he replied to one of them, 'Friend, I am doing you no wrong; did you not agree with me for the usual daily wage? Take what belongs to you and go; I choose to give to this last the same as I give to you. Am I not allowed to do what I choose with what belongs to me? Or are you envious because I am generous?' So the last will be first, and the first will be last."

3. For an extensive genealogical mapping of these commentaries/approaches please see the following: Caponi, "Thomas Aquinas on the Parable of the Late-Come Workers"; Carter, *Households and Discipleship*; Donahue, *Gospel in Parable*; and Goud, *Encountering the Parables in Contexts Old and New*.

4. Each of the top fifty hits include discussions of Grace, Sovereignty, and Generosity, not to mention that they all assume the vineyard owner to be God. As an interesting aside, when I workshopped this passage with my introductory courses as I authored

meneutical principle, the problem that I see in these classic approaches is twofold. First, they ignore the general trajectory of Jesus's parabolic speech as words of practical hope in his own context (i.e., the sensitivities of the original hearers), and second, they offer no programmatic possibilities for praxis for contemporary hearers, both in the laity and hierarchy, particularly when read in light of the pericope pointing to behavior befitting the apostles and their successors.

Helping along the way in this re-reading of the parable are two crucial texts authored by biblical scholars that will hopefully lend credence to the claims I make from the position of a theo-ethicist: Shinji Takagi's "The Boundary of Distributive Justice: An Economics Reading of Matthew 20:1–16"[5] and William R. Herzog II's *Parables as Subversive Speech: Jesus as Pedagogue of the Oppressed*. From the former, the guiding principle that an allegorical reading of this parable ignores the vast majority of details present in Jesus's narration will be garnered; this includes adopting the assumption that the parable itself is a gloss of Christ's answer to the rich man in the preceding verses. Though I differ significantly with Takagi's conclusions that the parable does not condemn excess in material wealth but rather offers an avenue for distributive justice as a foundational Christian economic ethic, his work is vital in displacing commonly held assumptions about the parable. The latter source, an exquisite argument for parables as social analysis and theo-ethical formation, will be utilized to draw out the codification of an economically liberative praxis and a shaming of oppressive class structures.

By way of brevity, the classic interpretations of the parable of the vineyard—stretching from Origen's allegorical interpretation through to Augustine and Aquinas who follow in his footsteps—go something like this: the landowner, lord of the vineyard, or master of the house (*oikodespotes*) serves as a stand in for God; the vineyard itself is seen as a metaphor for some combination of the kingdom of Israel *and* its successor, the *ekklesia*; the *denarius* or "daily wage" becomes a stand in for salvation; and the perceived payment discrepancy between the first hired and the last hired workers becomes understood as God's boundless grace.

Herzog argues that Matthew himself invests theological value into such allegorical assumptions and the Gospel author's emphases would set the course for subsequent interpretations, solidifying a chasm between Jesus's parable and Matthew's presentation of it.[6] Both interlocutors caution

---

this chapter, not a single one of my ninety-six students submitted an initial reflection that included an atypical interpretation. All of that is to say, these classical assumptions are very much the popular norm today.

5. Takagi, "Boundary of Distributive Justice," 207–15.
6. Herzog, *Parables as Subversive Speech*, 80.

against such conclusions about the parable's meaning as they severely lack firm rooting in the context of first-century Judea. The two following missteps are made by continuing the trajectory of allegorical interpretations of a genre that is meant to have visceral connotations for its original audience—the lower classes of an agrarian society under Roman occupation.

First, both Herzog and Takagi argue that a hasty alignment of the vineyard owner with God warps the potential the narrative has to serve as a commentary on the socioeconomic context surrounding Jesus's ministry that he himself points to extensively throughout the parable. Instead, Takagi utilizes a lexicon overlay to point out that the Synoptic Gospels tend to utilize *oikodespotes* (householder) as a parallel for a faithful follower of God—thus shifting the interpretative setting from an eschatological one to an economic one where the righteous actions of the householder are juxtaposed with the failures of the rich man in the preceding passages.[7]

Herzog, on the other hand, points not to a righteous *oikodespotes* but an oppressive one that serves as a secondary example to that of the rich man as antithetical to the ideals of the kingdom. The utilization of land for a luxury product, the employment of a steward, and the need to return to the agora multiple times to handle the extent of the harvest (indicating a large estate) all point to a landholder with exorbitant amounts of wealth—an all too familiar reality for many of the peasant class that lost its landholdings to such figures via loan defaults.[8] Herzog's point here is that Jesus's parable deliberately pits two social strata against one another: the expendables against the elite.

This hypothesis is furthered by following several of the vineyard owner's actions closely, something Herzog insists Jesus motions toward via deliberate details included in the parable. The repeated visits to the town center indicate both that the unemployment rate is high during this time of harvest (laborers are present throughout the day) and that the vineyard owner is attempting to get the most value out of his labor costs by hiring the minimum number of laborers required to get the job done. Additionally, the lack of bargaining power exhibited by each group of laborers called after the initial men agree to a denarius for a day's labor (even this is seen by Herzog as a take it or leave it proposition) is evidence of the socioeconomic instability present for the lowest class of an agrarian society. They trudge off to work with no distinct contract for wages as the nine, noon, and three o'clock groups are told they will be paid what the landowner thinks is a "fair" wage, and the five o'clock group is merely just told to go work after being accused

---

7. Takagi, "Boundary of Distributive Justice," 210.
8. Herzog, *Parables as Subversive Speech*, 85.

of being lazy ("why have you been standing here all day doing nothing?") without any mention of payment.

The pinnacle of the vineyard owner's character is revealed in the moment of equal payment to all who had worked regardless of time and production. Rather than connotations of generosity, Jesus's parable insinuates that this is a moment of embarrassment and shunning of the day laborers. The man that dares speak up for the unfairness of what has occurred is insulted and blacklisted by the vineyard owner as he is told to "take what is his and go."[9] In fact, I would point to the use of *hypage* by Matthew here as no mere farewell but more of a "get out" considering Matthew used the same imperative to describe Jesus's response to Satan in the temptation narrative ("Be Gone Satan!"). More bluntly put, the vineyard owner has belittled the workers while elevating his own status as honorable patron amid a dichotomous and skewed socioeconomic context of extremes. All of this of course revolves around the elephant in the room and the second common misinterpretation according to both Takagi and Herzog, the value of a denarius.

This second stumbling block for a soteriological reading of the parable revolves fundamentally around the fact that we really have no way to translate the value of a denarius unequivocally, and most indications are that this certainly was not an amount that alludes to abundant generosity.[10] Though translations of Matt 20:2 also include a footnote that alludes to a denarius being the daily wage for a day laborer, given the dire situation alluded to in the agora, I would argue that this was nothing more than the amount needed for a bare minimum subsistence at the bottom social rung. Takagi and Herzog take the reality of an incalculable value of the denarius in two separate directions within their economic re-readings of the parable, offering both a positive and condemning conclusion to the mystery of the denarius and the character of the landowner respectively.

For Takagi, the equal payment of a *denarius* provides an ethical imperative of distributive justice for those of significant economic means. His gloss of the rich man from Matt 19 is accompanied by the conclusion that

---

9. Herzog, *Parables as Subversive Speech*, 92. Herzog provides an etymological breakdown which explains that friend (*hetaire*) is used facetiously to highlight their different strata. Had the term meant to indicate a positive connotation, he would have used the more informal *phile*. To this I would add that even without an extensive linguistic analysis, the tone of the scenario can be read to indicate a speaking down to the workers and de-valuing the worth of their labor while reminding them of who has the power in this particular scenario.

10. For an explanation of both the general contours of Roman coinage of this period and the added uncertainty surrounding value by the fact that the Herodians were given their own dispensation for coining *denarii* in their region, see Gitler, "Roman Coinages of Palestine."

the rich must go beyond traditional understandings of economic justice to ensure that the basic needs of others are met even in instances where they might not necessarily be able to contribute to the labor force. He thus sees the landholder as establishing an economic principle of justice reflective of the kingdom as opposed to the complaining laborer's understanding of justice as reflective of the world.[11] Though admirable in essence, I find such a conclusion incongruent with Takagi's own assumptions of the parable of the vineyard as a response to the story of the rich man, given the declarative, "go and sell your possessions" as well as the weeping of the man as he departs. Takagi does not go far enough in his sketch of economic justice.

Herzog's interpretation of the denarius and his conclusion follow the trajectory of the landholder's exploitative nature alluded to above. Extracting the most value from his labor force indicates for him that the subsistence level wages paid during the harvest are certainly not something to be proud of and the way in which the payment is made is a moment aimed at dividing the workers further and to solidify a favorable labor/cost ratio. The denarius, then, serves as a lynchpin for asserting neither a salvific motif nor some economic imperative of faux generosity for the rich; rather, it signals a complete incongruence between the kingdom of God—in its most visceral sense as inaugurated by the ministry of Jesus of Nazareth—and the earthly systems of oppression codified in first-century Palestine.[12] Ultimately, the landowner is not meant to be emulated but vilified.

For my part, as I often tell my students, Jesus of Nazareth was not executed by the state via a method reserved for seditionists because he promised people heavenly rewards alone. The socioeconomic, political, and religious foundations of his ministry were fundamentally dangerous to the orders of the day. In this sense, the presentation of a distinctly economic reading for the parable is not only warranted but necessitated. Thus, the utilization of Takagi as the baseline minimum of what Jesus's lesson may have been and the utilization of Herzog as my preferred understanding of the liberative *kerygma* of the kingdom serve to highlight the intricacies of the parable genre generally and the specific econo-ethic reflected in the narrative of the vineyard owner. Moreover, without losing sight of the trajectory of my contribution to this volume, I would like to follow this reading to its limit by moving beyond the isolation of the parable by Herzog and Takagi's gloss relating to the story of the rich man to emphasize that this lesson was not simply a guiding principle for the rich or a condemnation of the oppressive structures present in Jesus's context. My unique addition

---

11. Takagi, "Boundary of Distributive Justice," 214.
12. Herzog, *Parables as Subversive Speech*, 97.

here is that when taken together as a dual-block, the story of the rich man and the parable of the vineyard have a distinct bearing on the ways in which institutional facets of the church are to function, and fundamentally that its stewards are not to rely on the broken processes of the world around them.

If the assumption can be made that the lesson of the parable was aimed at the disciples, as is inferable given that it comes in the wake of their astonishment to Jesus's response to the rich man, then it behooves those that lay claim to that heritage via apostolic succession to listen carefully to those words as well. Furthermore, the addition of the rebuking of the sons of Zebedee and their mother lends credence not just to this assumption but to the distinction between leaders of the kingdom and leaders of the Hellenistic realm. ("You know that the rulers of the Gentiles lord it over them, and the great ones make their authority over them felt. But it shall not be so among you. Rather, whoever wishes to be great among you shall be your servant, whoever wishes to be first among you shall be your slave."[13])

In this way, the repetition of the last shall be first and the first shall be last mantra to end the parable is a distinct warning to the disciples not to act according to the ways of the world (like the vineyard owner) but to act in a manner contrary to them. Concurrently, the socioeconomic standing of those participating in the kingdom community is to be anything but that of the plight experienced by the day laborers. The stewards of the structures in the "already not yet" dichotomy ought to forcefully reject those economic practices that lead to the blemishing of the *imago Dei* highlighted in the parable, or at the very least, not participate in those practices themselves. With such damning evidence of the Magisterium's economic impropriety highlighted by my presentation of the parable of the vineyard, I now turn to those texts authored by the hierarchy itself, which seem to align with such condemnation.

Revisiting the Canon of Catholic Social Teaching: The Third Way's Rejection of the Ethos of Capitalism

As I shift to examining the way in which CST's own understandings and implementations of the equity and equality exhibited in the aforementioned scriptural passages have worked themselves out, I must be sure to approach with caution and an appropriate delineation of terms, categories, time period, and genealogical context. Several points of clarification must be made before moving to the documents themselves. First, discussing singular, uniform trends within the entirety of the corpus is nearly impossible due to the

---

13. Matt 20:26–7 NABRE.

leanings of each papal figure, the particular cultural trends of each context, and the growing emphasis on the role of the church in the wider world as we move closer to our own time period. However, commonalities of approach do exist as do distinct rebuttals of the mechanisms that function within the Church Industrial Complex.

Second, though there are distinct allusions to a Third Way that rejects the ideals of economic trends on the right and the left of the political spectrum in favor of the ideals presented by CST, like with most papal declarations within these documents, there is no programmatic outlining of what this might look like. There are no explicit cataphatic claims made about economic systems; there is no favoring of distinct actions or models; and there is certainly no compulsory support of initiatives required for the faithful. Instead, the hierarchy pursues apophatic critique of the socioeconomic and political realms while leaving the Catholic emphasis on individual conscience intact. These gaps leave us with a lack of distinct guidance on the one hand, but the potential to think, hope, and act on the other hand.

Lastly, and perhaps a way of pointing out the elephant in the room, the encyclicals form a doctrinal ideal of what CST might look like, and they are spoken carefully and clearly, and according to the Magisterium, they are indicative of moral normativity. These categories do not necessarily apply to the persons tasked with running the operations of an earthly institution. The divide here is evident between CST and the aforementioned misconduct on the part of Scarano, Perlasca, and any other individual guilty of ingraining the ways of the world into the ecclesiological realm. In a modern exemplar of *non ex opere operantis*, we are faced with the brokenness of humankind within the economic realm. These clarifiers made, I venture forward with an analysis of a document at the heart of what the church holds as ideal economic concepts that focus on the flourishing of persons.

With regards to a singular document dealing with questions of the relationship between the church and the world that focuses extensively on economic norms, we come to Pope Paul VI's encyclical released in the wake of Vatican II: *Populorum Progressio* (*PP*). Though its relevance to this chapter on the Church Industrial Complex will soon be expounded upon further, the adoption of praxis-oriented language from the Council is evidenced immediately in the opening lines as the encyclical rejects the accumulation of temporal power on the part of the Magisterium.

The progressive development of people is an object of deep interest and concern to the church. This is particularly true in the case of those people who are trying to escape the ravages of hunger, poverty, endemic disease and ignorance, of those who are seeking a larger share in the benefits of civilization and a more active improvement of their human qualities, and of those who are consciously striving for fuller growth. With an even clearer awareness since the Second Vatican Council of the demands imposed by Christ's gospel in this area, the church judges it her duty to help all human beings explore this serious problem in all its dimensions and to impress upon them the need for concerted action at this critical juncture.[14]

Instead of focusing on the ways of the world that are antithetical to human flourishing, *PP* stresses the destiny of the goods of creation to serve the needs of all, the growing gap between the rich nations and poor nations, and the need for social justice to govern economic platforms. Paul VI also confirms the fact that social justice is a worldwide concern and one that is ever more important in the developing world as distinctly impacted by the neo-liberal order.

While those trends are seen as generalizations reflecting CST on human flourishing, *PP* also makes one of the most clear and succinct statements on the proper use of material wealth in the church's social corpus. The Holy Father harkens back to the Patristic period to reflect an ethos of communal goods being utilized for the good of all. Specifically:

> He who has the goods of this world and sees his brother in need and closes his heart to him, how does the love of God abide in him? Everyone knows that the Fathers of the Church laid down the duty of the rich toward the poor in no uncertain terms. As St. Ambrose put it: "You are not making a gift of what is yours to the poor man, but you are giving him back what is his. You have been appropriating things that are meant to be for the common use of everyone. The earth belongs to everyone, not to the rich."[15]

The ethical imperative for giving rather than amassing is clear. This statement is further clarified by Pope Paul VI's explicit delineation that private wealth is to function with express limits, mainly that no one is to accumulate surplus goods for private use when there are those that lack the basic necessities of life. The extent to which such conditions exist around the globe is noted not just in the encyclical, but *PP* directly links the existence of such conditions to "unbridled liberalism." Much like the original critique of industrial capitalism in *Rerum Novarum*, the follow-up presented by Paul VI reiterated that capitalism gives rise to hardship, unjust practices, and fratricidal conflict. Instead, he champions the continuing CST trend of the economy being in the service of humanity rather than vice versa.[16]

---

14. Paul VI, *Populorum Progressio*, no. 1.

15. Paul VI, *Populorum Progressio*, no. 23.

16. Though perhaps beyond the scope of this chapter, this encyclical subtly makes one of the most controversial economic claims in the doctrine of CST by introducing

Though the lack of distinct programmatic responses within the encyclical genre has been noted, *PP* offers some general contours for addressing the inequalities caused by the misuse of wealth. A focus on education, investment in cultural institutions rather than economic ones, divestment from the weapons race to make funding of such initiatives possible (Paul VI's "World Fund"), and an adoption of the ethos of "Welcoming the Stranger" all serve as the building blocks for a just and equitable society. In the spirit of Vatican II, the encyclical not only turns part of the responsibility over to the Catholic laity, but it also addresses "All People of Good Will" for the first time in CST history.

With that being said, like all letters authored by the papacy, the primary audience is Paul VI's brother bishops, which raises the question as to why the Secretariat for the Economy has an investment fund to begin with. The very acts of economic speculation, of real estate investment, and of control over natural resources are counterintuitive to proper economic functions of CST as expressed over and over again in the corpus. *PP* extensively highlights the inability of such economic practices to reflect the ideal of love that should be present in all of our endeavors. The very mechanisms responsible for blemishing human dignity throughout the globe described by Pope Paul VI would go on to be adopted as ecclesial norms for handling the surplus wealth of the Vatican, something that according to the church itself should not exist. In light of this, perhaps an exploration of a radically different ecclesial approach is warranted for reflection.

Dorothy Day, Peter Maurin, and the Catholic Worker: A Mirror for the Church

In this final segment of the chapter, I turn to the Catholic Worker Movement, a community model in which we continue to see the vitality of concepts presented by Catholic Social Teaching translated into the realm of the Real. Through its fivefold program of encountering the Divine in the world and in the Other—specifically through Works of Mercy, Houses of Hospitality, *The Catholic Worker* newspaper, Round Table Discussion, and a Return to the Land—Dorothy Day, Peter Maurin, and the Catholic Worker Movement embodied many of the anti-capitalist theoretical trends present

---

the concept of "expropriation" with regard to nationally held lands and natural resources. The concept was not revisited in future documents, probably due to the context of Latin American Liberation movements implementing concepts of expropriation, but its inclusion in *PP* could bear fruit for the support of more radical economic platforms on the part of the faithful.

in the canon of social teaching and the scriptural passages mentioned above. In doing so, they offer a dissenting voice, or rather a dissenting ethic, to that of the Church Industrial model exemplified by the Catholic hierarchy. Moreover, I will argue that how this firm commitment to a true ecclesiology of poverty functioned might serve as a mirror for the current problem of the Church Industrial Complex that we are addressing. The concept of a "Third Way" beyond Marxist influenced ideologies and an unrestricted neo-liberal capital order championed by CST was lived out by Day, Maurin, and, most relevantly for the context at hand, by the communities they continue to influence.

To begin, perhaps it is best to allow Day to introduce the Catholic Workers basic program in her own words as it not only situates our conversation but also provides insight into the Movement being birthed directly from the CST corpus itself. The very first issue printed in May of 1933 laid out Maurin and Day's plan for this understanding of the gospel message. Day dedicated that issue, and the paper in general to:

> Those who think that there is no hope for the future, no recognition of their plight—this little paper is addressed. It is printed to call their attention to the fact that the Catholic Church has a social program—to let them know that there are men of God who are working not only for their spiritual, but for their material welfare.... In an attempt to popularize and make known the encyclicals of the Popes in regard to social justice and the program put forth by the Church for the "reconstruction of the social order," this news sheet, *The Catholic Worker*, is started.[17]

A few issues later she clarified this ethic as well as its relation to ecclesiology:

> Together with the Works of Mercy, feeding, clothing, and sheltering our brothers and sisters, we must indoctrinate. We must "give reason for the faith that is in us." Otherwise we are scattered members of the Body of Christ, we are not "all members of one another." Otherwise our religion is an opiate, for ourselves alone, for our comfort or for our individual safety or indifferent custom.[18]

In these two brief passages, we have moved beyond just the aforementioned five traditional facets of the Catholic Worker Movement and have pointed out that voluntary poverty, solidarity rather than charity, and a commitment to the unity of the body of Christ also undergirded the work that Day and

17. Day, *Catholic Worker*, May 1933.
18. Day, *Catholic Worker*, February 1940.

Maurin undertook. Moreover, they saw dignity in that poverty, undertook solidarity in visceral ways, and reminded themselves of the commitment to the body of Christ through the daily observance of the liturgy and partaking in Mass. In this way, it is through the elevation of the Other via works of mercy that we understand and effect the gospel more clearly. This is also where their distinctly anti-capitalist ethos comes into play.

Through their ministry and its undergirding anarcho-pacifist and anti-capitalist values, Day and Maurin butted heads with the institutional church, which on more than one occasion threatened to censor the duo and asked them not to use the descriptor "Catholic." Qualms with their solidarity with labor movements, their unapologetic stance on usury, and an emphasis on a lived-in community of shared goods rather than simple charity led to at least two summonses for Day to the Chancery of the Archdiocese of New York to clarify her positions before the archbishop. Perhaps it is no surprise then that in a letter to friend and fellow pacifist Gordon Zahn Day stated, "I never expected much of the bishops. In all history, popes and bishops and abbots seem to have been blind and power-loving and greedy. I never expected leadership from them. It is the saints that keep appearing all through history who keep things going."[19]

It is with this portrait of the fundamental ethical relation within the gospel tradition as understood by Dorothy Day and Peter Maurin along with their anti-capitalist action that I must now evaluate how that ethic has been implemented, or at least structured, within the institutional church's central understandings of social concerns. If I am going to continue to argue that pursuing the practical program of the Catholic Worker on a wider scale and as a primary mode of being church is worthwhile—as opposed to the model of the Church Industrial Complex—then I must juxtapose it with how the tradition of social teaching has functioned. More specifically, I will need to clarify why and how Day's and Maurin's functional economic ethic differs from the CST tradition that helped birth their movement, continues to serve as a sound board for its contemporary iterations, and to some extent claims the program as its own as the church undergoes the process of canonizing its founder.

Though often charged with accusations of communism, or at least Marxist-influenced understandings of property, *The Catholic Worker* actually mirrored what would come to be described by CST as a "Third Way." Similar to Pope Leo XIII's weariness toward elements of both systems, Maurin's foundational rhetoric on property and labor was more akin to a description of its necessity but non-ultimacy. Several exemplars of this elevation

---

19. Day, "Letter to Gordon," 1968.

of labor and rejection of Marxist implications are offered within Maurin's *Easy Essays* and, lest capitalists get too excited, are paired with equally poignant critiques of an economic system that has become an all-encapsulating death-dealing ethos. For Maurin, Catholic Action, a neologism coined to express the works of mercy, acts of hospitality, and the agro-revolution Maurin sought, was itself an expression of labor at its core, and it functioned on a level beyond what either contemporary alternative could offer. In *On Marxism*, Maurin succinctly outlined how Marxist critique fell into the common traps of dystopic materialism, ignoring the fundamental principle of selfhood expressed by what CST calls "human flourishing" and what the Catholic Worker defined as spirituality. In his rejection of Marxist conceptions, Maurin introduces Catholic Action as follows:

> We Catholics have a better criticism
> of bourgeois society
> than Victor Considerant's criticism
> used by Karl Marx.
> Our criticism of bourgeois society
> is the criticism of St. Thomas More.
> We Catholics have a better
> conception of Communism
> than the conception of Proudhon.
> Our conception of Communism
> is the conception of St. Thomas Aquinas
> in his doctrine of the "Common Good."
> We Catholics have better means
> than the means proposed by Karl Marx.
> Our means to realize the "Common Good"
> are embodied in Catholic Action.
> Catholic Action is action by Catholics
> for Catholics and non-Catholics.
> We don't want to take over the control
> of political and economic life.
> We want to reconstruct the social order
> through Catholic Action
> exercised in Catholic
> institutions.[20]

The rejections of Marx are clear, but what did Maurin have in mind on labor specifically? He shares a concise definition elsewhere in his *Easy Essays*, in the form of a response to questions on Catholic Labor guilds from a reader of *The Catholic Worker* newspaper early in 1934. Though winding and

20. Maurin, "On Marxism," 15.

formulated on rhyming and word play, Maurin is concise in his definition of labor:

> When the worker sells his labor to a capitalist or accumulator of labor he allows the capitalist or accumulator of labor to accumulate his labor. And when the capitalist or accumulator of the worker's labor has accumulated so much of the worker's labor that he no longer finds it profitable to buy the worker's labor then the worker can no longer sell his labor to the capitalist or accumulator of labor. And when the worker can no longer sell his labor to the capitalist or accumulator of labor he can no longer buy the products of his labor. And that is what the worker gets for selling his labor to the capitalist or accumulator of labor. He just gets left and he gets what is coming to him. Labor is not a commodity to be bought and sold. Labor is a means of self-expression, the worker's gift to the common good.[21]

Although the inherent communal understanding so typical of the Catholic Worker shines through, a parallel with CST's understanding of labor as a tool of self-formation is also clear. Labor, at its core, is not a commodity, nor is it inconsequential to the realm of human flourishing. The failures of misunderstanding this are evident for Maurin in a way reminiscent of the encyclicals' portrayal of the lack of self-expression inherent in a commodification of labor, which leads to the paradigm of depression, anxiety, and hopelessness evident in Maurin's post-industrial context. Alleviating such blemishes of the *imago Dei* were a contributing factor to the spread of the Catholic Worker ethos.

Maurin's harsh critique of misunderstanding labor is rooted in the ability for commodification to be death-dealing. His economic program combatting lending at interest, championing guild-like mechanisms for ensuring both quality and self-expression as well as living wages, and a focus on living off of the land were all tied to labor—and the property it creates *for the laborer*. However, the purpose of labor was for elevating the spiritual component of the human person. It is both the human person as a specific exemplar and the human community as a general category that the Catholic Worker saw as left behind by the systems and institutions of its context—not just the two streams of economic thought but by a significant segment of the Catholic Church itself—and it aimed to reintroduce a program that included this particular understanding of labor to combat a rampant spread of inhumane conditions. Day's memoirs illustrate the function of Maurin's

---

21. Maurin, "On Marxism," 31.

program of labor within both the Houses of Hospitality and the Agro-Universities (farming retreats) of the Movement.

The foundational aspects of Maurin's labor theory were well articulated by Day,[22] but the subtlety of its implementation (from the consoling of guests through conversation around cooking a communal pot of soup, to the ease with which nervous visitors or first time volunteers were integrated through the act of being handed a mop or a peeling knife) was equally as pivotal to personal and communal formation as it was to satiating the basic needs of subsistence.

The life-giving nature of physical labor sparked both the farming retreats of the Catholic Worker as well as the assignment of volunteer tasks and responsibilities around the urban houses of hospitality, but Day was also clear in labor's wider applications. She clarifies, "*The Catholic Worker*, as the name implied, was directed to the worker, but we used the word in its broadest sense, meaning those who worked with hand or brain, those who did physical, mental or spiritual work. But we thought primarily of the poor, the dispossessed, the exploited."[23] The gospel category of "the least of these" became intertwined with an ever-expanding definition of "laborers" for Day and Maurin. Cataloging not just the violations of dignity present in practices that crippled the core of labor, the newspaper also made it a point to highlight the success of individual labor actions, picketing, strikes, etc., and to elevate the dignity of laborers far from the mind of mainstream coverage. Ultimately, the paper served as an outlet for the tangible expression of living *with* the worker.

The centrality of labor for self-expression, communal formation, and flourishing was expressed by Day through a sense of solidarity reminiscent of a prime ethical relation elevating the Other above the self in a way that takes CST's understanding of economics to new heights. It was in and through labor that hospitality functioned at its core, a core that pointed to the transcendent ability present in the Other, and one that shattered subjectivity. In the wake of visiting with the founder of an attempted Ford union, including conversations with the severely beaten workers reprimanded for handing out literature, Day shared:

---

22. See for example her discussion of the program in various places within the *Long Loneliness*, specific to labor concerns in her observations that "Peter the 'green' revolutionist, had a long-term program which called for hospices, or houses of hospitality, where the works of mercy could be practiced to combat the taking over by the state of all those services which could be built up by mutual aid; and farming communes to provide land and hoes for the unemployed, whom increasing technology was piling up in the millions." Day, *Long Loneliness*, 185.

23. Day, *Long Loneliness*, 204.

> Going around and seeing such sights is not enough. To help the organizers, to give what you have for relief, to pledge yourself to voluntary poverty for life so that you can share with your brothers is not enough. One must live with them, share with them in their suffering too. Give up one's privacy, and mental and spiritual comforts as well as physical.[24]

Though many of *The Catholic Worker's* initial publications, one might even say the entirety of its first decade, were focused on articles discussing capital and labor, it took a turn more and more toward a concise elevation of human dignity present in labor rather than the category itself as time went on. Or, as Day would say retrospectively, "there was so much more to the Catholic Worker Movement than labor and capital. It is the people who are important, not the masses."[25] It was the understanding, the relationships, and the community that came about through the labor and the production of what she might label "capital" that mattered, it was the people that mattered. Moreover, this ethic was not simply argued for, it was lived within the communities of the Catholic Worker Movement.

Through the multifaceted process of analysis, agitation, and action, *The Catholic Worker* was able to step beyond a monotonous performance of works of mercy for their own sake, and move toward what the social encyclicals called for: an engaged theo-economic ethic. This theo-economic ethic, called for by Pope Leo XIII in the paradigmatic shift of *Rerum Novarum* (which impacted the Catholic Worker Movement extensively) and exemplified by *Populorum Progressio*, was one that could not quite be realized by an institution in transition, or perhaps not even by any institution at all. It wasn't just that Day attempted to pinpoint the causes for social inequality or to offer those things which provide a baseline of human dignity; rather, she and her community did them both in conjunction.

Analysis of anti-union laws was coupled with both joining the picket line and cataloging violence against strikers, breaking down the ways in which the unrestricted free-market capitalism warned against by the Vatican was impacting Day's own community. This impact was caused by the correlation between J. P. Morgan's success and the growing number of evictions in the Bowery. In response, Day's work was coupled with food collections and clothing drives as well as securing people available co-op housing. Finally, the homeless crisis was not spoken of in abstract terms, but rather culminated in the founding of the first Catholic Worker House of Hospitality—St. Joseph's House. It is perhaps not a coincidence that Houses

24. Day, *Long Loneliness*, 214.
25. Day, *Long Loneliness*, 221.

of Hospitality sprung up not from the commands of the bishops, as they had in the Patristic period, but through the persistence of someone who would reject the ability of institutions and bureaucracy to reflect loving economics. This type of radicality should be encouraged, adopted, and uplifted as central to how economics might function within the kingdom in the here and now. It is my hope that the juxtaposition of differing economic models offered here via the parable of the vineyard, the encyclical tradition, and the ministry of the Catholic Worker Movement may spark a conversation on how to avoid the continued misappropriation of finances and reinvestment in broken systems, as highlighted in the introduction. Moreover, the radical alternatives offered by Dorothy Day, specifically, ought to provide encouragement of distinct ways of being otherwise in a world that desperately needs such examples, as well as encouragement to a church that has continually lost relevance in offering authoritative moral norms. Lest the spiral of the Church Industrial Complex continue, may we pray and work toward systems that are becoming of our faith. Amen.

Bibliography

Caponi, Francis J. "Thomas Aquinas on the Parable of the Late-Come Workers (Matthew 20:1–16)." *Journal of Theological Interpretation* 12 (2018) 90–109.

Carter, Warren. *Households and Discipleship: A Study of Matthew 19–20*. Sheffield: Sheffield Academic, 1994.

"Church Properties Initiative: Fitzgerald Institute for Real Estate Report on Church Properties." University of Notre Dame. https://churchproperties.nd.edu.

Day, Dorothy. *The Catholic Worker*. May 1933. https://thecatholicnewsarchive.org/?a=d&d=CW19330501-01.1.1&e=-------en-20--1--txt-txIN--------.

———. *The Catholic Worker*. February 1940. https://thecatholicnewsarchive.org/?a=d&d=CW19400201-01&e=-------en-20--1--txt-txIN--------.

———. "Letter to Gordon." 1968. Dorothy Day Papers, Marquette Archives (DDCWL, #423a), Marquette University.

———. *The Long Loneliness*. New York: Harper One, 1952.

Donahue, John R. *The Gospel in Parable: Metaphor, Narrative, and Theology in the Synoptic Gospels*. Philadelphia: Fortress, 1988.

Gitler, Haim. "Roman Coinages of Palestine." In *The Oxford Handbook of Greek and Roman Coinage*, edited by William E. Metcalf. Oxford: Oxford University Press, 2012.

Goud, T. E., ed. *Encountering the Parables in Contexts Old and New*. London: Bloomsbury, 2022.

Herzog, William, II. *Parables as Subversive Speech: Jesus as Pedagogue of the Oppressed*. Louisville, KY: Westminster John Knox, 1994.

Maurin, Peter. "On Marxism." In *Easy Essays*. Eugene, OR: Wipf & Stock, 2003.

Paul VI. *Populorum Progressio*. 1967. https://www.vatican.va/content/paul-vi/en/encyclicals/documents/hf_p-vi_enc_26031967_populorum.html.

Takagi, Shinji. "The Boundary of Distributive Justice: An Economics Reading of Matthew 20:1–16." *Biblical Theology Bulletin* (2020) 207–15.

SECTION 3

Theological Reflections on Church Practices

Chapter 6

Challenging the Metrics of Ministry

DARRYL W. STEPHENS

Christendom, nation, and market function as competing and colluding expressions of empire in the United States of America. *Empire*, as defined by Joerg Rieger, consists of "large and ever-changing conglomerates of power that are aimed at controlling all aspects of our lives."[1] These powers compete for loyalty within this religious, political, and economic context. To witness the rivalry between these sectors, a church member need only suggest removing the Stars and Stripes from the sanctuary or paying the staff according to need rather than status. The inevitably strong pushback reveals that patriotism and capitalism do not yield authority so easily. Rather than challenge these expressions of empire, US Christendom aligns with these principalities and powers against which Christian faith is called to defend itself (Eph 6:12). The resulting Church Industrial Complex mirrors a society suffused with the values of US patriotism and assumptions of market capitalism.

The powerful trinity of church, country, and mammon collude through religiously garbed market logic and nationalism. Currency emblazoned "In God We Trust" attests to the religious nature of this connection. The beliefs that "bigger is better" and "growth equates with success" exemplify a US capitalistic mindset in which quantification yields value: what cannot be measured cannot be valued. Furthermore, a pervasive ethos of American exceptionalism interprets wealth and prosperity as signs of divine favor. Thus, the economic and political success of the United States serves as its

---

1. Rieger, *Christ and Empire*, vii.

own doctrinal warrant, offering justification, means, and ends for the activities of this country and the institutions within it, including the church. Growth and exceptionalism feed an Industrial Complex in which churches focus on self-perpetuation and social legitimacy to the neglect of transcendent purpose and meaning.

Empire, however, cannot prevent solidarity among those marginalized by its power. Rieger observes "a potential for alternative relationships among people who are brought together by the economic system, often against their will."[2] The market forces that produce winners and losers also create communities of resistance among those who do not benefit from the structures of empire. Despite adverse circumstances, people can engage in constructive cooperative action. "These relationships," claims Rieger, "can lead to new kinds of solidarity," creating a "surplus" that cannot be measured by capitalist logic.[3] The same potential exists within the empire church and its market-driven programs.[4] Rieger's notion of surplus, "anything that points beyond the status quo," provides glimpses of grace beyond the structures of empire.[5] The kin-dom of God irrupts, overturning hierarchies of politics and wealth (Mark 10:31; Luke 1:46–55; Luke 4:18–21). By challenging the metrics of ministry, this chapter seeks such a surplus within the Church Industrial Complex.

In this chapter, I illustrate how the business of predominantly White US mainline churches is both beholden to and a challenge to the capitalistic doctrines of US society.[6] I begin with the widespread use of quantitative measures for assessing congregational vitality, an approach that prioritizes easily quantifiable practices, such as membership and average worship attendance, over other values, such as love of neighbor and racial reconciliation. Shorn of missional purpose, the statistically driven congregation exists primarily for itself rather than for others or for God. Then, I offer an immanent critique of the metrics of vitality from a standpoint of economic theory, drawing on the work of Herman E. Daly and John B. Cobb Jr. The problems of externalities and misplaced concreteness expose fundamental flaws in a free market approach. Finally, I present multivocational ministry

---

2. Rieger, *No Rising Tide*, 162.
3. Rieger, *No Rising Tide*, 162.
4. On empire church, see Edington, *Bivocational*, 8–12.
5. Rieger, *Christ and Empire*, 9.
6. I use the term *mainline* loosely to refer to the historically influential group of predominantly White Protestant denominations of the Federal Council of the Churches of Christ in America and, later, the National Council of the Churches of Christ in the USA. I capitalize White and Black when referring to race or ethnicity, in accordance with the University of Chicago Press Editorial Staff, "Black and White."

as a practice arising from and counter to the Church Industrial Complex. Multivocational ministry is often interpreted as a market-driven adaptation to scarcity, signifying a lack of congregational vitality. However, *intentional* multivocational ministry is inherently counter to the logic of capitalism. Thus, this form of ministry reveals deficiencies in the business of the market-driven church, offering a surplus beyond the control of empire.

Vital Congregations Initiatives[7]

Since the 1970s, predominantly White mainline churches in the United States and Canada have grappled with an existential crisis: shrinking membership rolls and waning cultural influence. Methodists, Presbyterians, Lutherans, Anglicans, Congregationalists—all pillars of a bygone North American Christendom—have seen their mainline prominence become sidelined within US society. While diagnoses have varied, the solution has garnered surprising consensus: increase congregational vitality by measuring and monitoring key attributes correlated with success. When the metrics overtake the mission, though, the church becomes overly focused on its own perpetuation.

In the Church Industrial Complex, declining membership statistics are self-evidently problematic. In 1972, Dean M. Kelley diagnosed the mainline church's problem as an accommodation to culture. In his book *Why Conservative Churches Are Growing*, Kelley argued that liberal churches were losing members because they had lowered their expectations of membership: neglect of doctrine and personal morality were to blame for the mainline's decline. Kelley's thesis was immediately contested by those on the receiving end of his critique. By the late 1970s, interdisciplinary researchers countered that mainline membership decline was due primarily to external social and demographic changes, such as the declining birthrate of the White middle class.[8] More recently, David Hollinger turned Kelley's thesis on its head: mainline churches lost membership due to their higher (not lower) social expectations, engaging members in difficult conversations about race, poverty, and other structures of oppression.[9] Conservative evangelical churches grew by proffering a gospel that largely ignored questions of civil rights and inequality. Growth-based congregational vitality initiatives are subject to the same critique.

---

7. This section draws on Stephens, *Reckoning Methodism*, chapter 3.
8. Hoge and Roozen, "Some Sociological Conclusions," 326, 329.
9. Hollinger, *Christianity's American Fate*, 5.

When the problem is perceived as declining numbers, the obvious solution is to increase the numbers. Seeking new tools, mainline judicatory leaders and their advisors borrowed from their evangelical competitors. The evangelical church growth movement equates fecundity with fidelity, providing a theological veneer to the capitalistic value of growth. While measurement is nothing new for mainline churches—Methodists, Presbyterians, and others have kept careful statistical records throughout their histories, accounting for their adherents as carefully as their dollars—the church growth model tapped into a capitalistic mindset. The expansion of US evangelicalism, both in numbers and cultural influence through the 1970s and 1980s, lent legitimacy to the homogeneous unit principle and the missiological model behind it.[10] This model tracked closely the path of US industrialization and corporate growth, paralleling the Fordism and post-Fordism of the national economy. It is but a small step to interpret growth as a sign of divine blessing and decrease as divine punishment.

Church growth offered an antidote to the existential fear of decline. However, tools designed for planting new communities of faith had to be adapted for use in mainline denominations.[11] Mainline denominations already had an abundance of congregations. The United Methodist Church (UMC), for example, was present in nearly every county of the United States, claiming more local outposts than the US post office. Applying the church growth model to an established congregation meant learning how to measure its numerical success, understood as vitality.

The concept of congregational vitality caught on quickly. Alternatively labeled healthy, fruitful, faithful, or even missional, the *vital congregation* represented an ideal for churches seeking to guarantee their future through empirically validated measures. In 1990, church consultant Herb Miller declared, "The vision of vital congregations and the need for more churches to live up to that term is washing across the beaches of all denominations."[12] By the first decade of the new millennium, nearly every White-majority mainline denomination in North America, including those as varied as the Anglican Church of Canada and the Evangelical Covenant Church, had launched initiatives on congregational vitality.

For example, on the two-hundredth anniversary of independent Methodism in the United States, the UMC audaciously resolved to double

10. The homogeneous unit principle, developed by Donald McGavran, postulated that it is easier for people to convert to Christianity when they have fewer social barriers to cross. Stated positively, people are more likely to join a congregation of persons who share their race, ethnicity, class, education level, language, and other characteristics.

11. McGavran, "Church Growth and the Conciliar Movement," 16.

12. Miller, *Vital Congregation*, 12.

its membership within eight years.[13] The year was 1984, and Methodists were still buoyed by the patriotic zeal of the nation's bicentennial eight years prior. This church and its nation seemed to share a sense of exceptionalism and divine favor, inspired by the great commission (Matt 28:19). United Methodists embarked on an extensive study of membership, average worship attendance, annual giving, hours of involvement, and other easily measurable characteristics of congregational life. Consultants and church leaders alike identified these "vital signs" as indicators of congregational health and vitality. However, actual membership in the UMC decreased between 1984 and 1992.

Membership decline across all denominations continued unabated for decades. By 2014, the percentage of the US population identifying as White and Christian dipped below 50 percent for the first time in the nation's history, prompting Robert P. Jones to declare the "end of white Christian America."[14] Furthermore, conservative churches were also shrinking. In 2021, the Southern Baptist Convention reported its fourteenth consecutive year of membership decline.[15] These trends were cause for alarm: the logic of capitalism dictates that less is worse, and more is better. As with the national economy, health in the Church Industrial Complex is linked to growth, not stasis or decline.

Missiologists and theologians in mainline traditions contested this statistics-driven approach to mission and ministry from the start. In the early 1980s, the Institute for World Evangelism at Candler School of Theology sponsored a five-day consultation of one hundred delegates from Canada, the United States, and Mexico to discuss "challenges and issues regarding the revitalization of existing congregations and the development of new ones."[16] George Morris, the Institute's director, acknowledged the cultural pressures at work and warned that the "passion for numerical success and power" must not supplant the priority of authentic witness.[17] Several years later, William J. Abraham critiqued the church growth movement along the same lines. In *The Logic of Evangelism*, he argued that a focus on numerical growth was a theologically inadequate approach to evangelism. According to Abraham, the church growth movement and, by extension, metrics-driven vital congregations initiatives failed to address cultural diversity,

---

13. The United Methodist Church, *Journal of the 1984 General Conference*, 1:445, 2:1166.
14. Jones, *End of White Christian America*, 47.
15. Meyer, "Southern Baptist Convention Membership Drops."
16. Morris, "Introduction."
17. Morris, "Theological Bases," 31–32.

social and corporate sin, inclusiveness, racism, social action, injustice, and oppression.[18] However, Abraham's logic of evangelism was no match for the logic of capitalism.

The idea that growth equates to success resonated with capitalism in a way that qualitative approaches could not. For example, in 1990, the United Methodist Council of Bishops published a qualitative study based on two years of research involving hundreds of United Methodists. This document, "Vital Congregations—Faithful Disciples: Vision for the Church," described vital practices of congregational life: worship calling people to conversion, celebrating the sacraments regularly, forming disciples, practicing care and hospitality, seeking moral discernment, raising up new leaders, equipping persons for witness and announcing the good news of Christ, and joining in ministries of justice, hope, and peace.[19] While attention to practices over products is a theologically promising alternative to metrics, it proved no match within the Church Industrial Complex.[20] In 2007, Robert Schnase named five practices that he and other bishops identified as shaping and sustaining a "vital" or "fruitful" congregation: radical hospitality, passionate worship, intentional faith development, risk-taking mission and service, and extravagant generosity.[21] Implementation of Schnase's model, however, was reduced to data collection. Fruitful congregations were measured by numbers of new visitors, worship attendance, small group participation, missional service opportunities and participation, and per capita giving.

The United Methodist Council of Bishops soon dispensed with the language of practices to focus directly on numerical data. They issued a "Call to Action" in 2009, engaging the services of a consulting firm to measure vitality in United Methodist congregations.[22] Towers Watson, the hired consultancy, used a process of "data mining" to correlate certain characteristics with the most successful congregations. They defined a vital congregation as having high levels of the following: membership growth, persons involved in ministry, engagement in the community, and financial giving.[23] They found that only 15 percent of United Methodist congregations in the

---

18. Abraham, *Logic of Evangelism*, 85–86.

19. The United Methodist Church, Council of Bishops, "Vital Congregations—Faithful Disciples," 113–23.

20. On a practices approach, see Bass, *Practicing Congregation*; Bass, *Practicing Our Faith*; Drummond, *Holy Clarity*.

21. Schnase, *Five Practices of Fruitful Congregations*.

22. de Wetter et al., "UMC Call to Action."

23. "Implementing the 16 Drivers of Vital Congregations." See also The United Methodist Church, Council of Bishops, "Call to Action Study Guide."

United States showed high levels of these "signs of vitality."[24] Towers Watson then statistically correlated the available data on these vital congregations to discover sixteen common characteristics, which they termed "drivers of vitality." Thousands of United Methodist congregations were then encouraged or required by their bishops to report weekly measures of their "signs of vitality" through a "VitalSigns Dashboard." Leaders in the Episcopal Church (US) and other mainline denominations report similar experiences of metric-driven growth strategies for vitality.

The dashboard approach continued to overshadow qualitative and contextual approaches to missional health. A concurrent, qualitative study of United Methodist congregations by the General Board of Discipleship in 2012 garnered scant attention.[25] This study of the dynamics of congregational change could not gain footing against the unrelenting undertow of metrics-driven programmatic fixes promising to reverse mainline membership decline. In 2014, Gil Rendle, a prominent church consultant, offered a defense of the Towers Watson approach, seeking to "advance the conversation about, and the use of, metrics as a tool for ministry."[26] Declaring the vitality index "an invaluable tool of health for all congregations," he described the metrics of vitality an "absolutely essential" and "necessary" tool: "a standard" for measuring "all congregations."[27] Measurement can indeed be a valuable tool. However, uniform data collection denies attention to distinct congregational contexts and the stories they tell. The mission and vocation of small rural churches, for example, are not valued within this rubric.[28]

The metrics of vitality are not inherently connected to any missional purpose—other than growth as an end in itself. The Towers Watson's study did not account for congregational context and purpose "because reliable data was not available."[29] In the science of vitality, that which cannot be measured cannot be valued. Measurement becomes its own purpose when vitality is understood as growth. Thus, Episcopalian bishop Mark Edington asserted, "Data, as information, can be helpful. Data as purpose is deeply problematic."[30] Rendle also observed that vitality is distinct from purpose, and in a later publication, argued for a countercultural church valuing

---

24. de Wetter et al., "UMC Call to Action," 61.
25. The United Methodist Church, General Board of Discipleship, "Toward Vitality."
26. Rendle, *Doing the Math of Mission*, 2.
27. Rendle, *Doing the Math of Mission*, 42–44.
28. Stanton, *Reclaiming Rural*, 27–30.
29. Acevedo, *Vital*, 20.
30. Edington, personal communication, July 24, 2023. For a theologically grounded approach to ministry assessment, see Drummond, *Holy Clarity*.

narrative and complex discipleship, leaning into congregational practices that contribute to the common good.[31] However, in the Church Industrial Complex, increasing numbers represent divine favor and faithfulness—exceptionalism in a marketplace of ministry.

An Economic Analysis

While "vital congregations" discourse seems to equip churches to compete in the marketplace of ministry, the values and assumptions of free market capitalism upon which this theory is based are problematic for reasons both theological and economic. Methodists Herman E. Daly and John B. Cobb Jr. offer a relevant critique from the standpoint of economic theory in their book, *For the Common Good*. They illustrate the false underpinnings of capitalism as growth, citing the failure of common economic indicators to promote sustainability and to account for environmental costs. Their discussions of the problems of growth and "the fallacy of misplaced concreteness" are particularly relevant to the discourse of vital congregations.[32]

Daly and Cobb amend economic theory to value community and environment over growth. They identify several fundamental problems with market capitalism, including the facts that self-interest erodes the moral context of community and that public goods and externalities are not well accounted for.[33] Flawed moral assumptions about persons and communities contribute to these problems. Thus, in contrast to the autonomous rational private individual normally assumed by market economists, they posit the "person-in-community" as the relevant moral actor.[34] This shift in perspective recognizes a different economic value: rather than maximizing individual choice, "the purpose of the economy [is] the service of community."[35] Since communities have histories, contexts, and cultures that make them unique, the economy must also value these particularities rather than prioritizing abstractions, such as growth.

Traditional market economics fails communities when the abstractions of theory are mistaken for the actual circumstances and people involved. Daly and Cobb observe, "The very existence of a measure invites the fallacy of misplaced concreteness."[36] Church metrics contribute to the

---

31. Rendle, *Doing the Math of Mission*, 42–44; Rendle, *Countercultural*.
32. Daly and Cobb, *For the Common Good*, 36.
33. Daly and Cobb, *For the Common Good*, 49.
34. Daly and Cobb, *For the Common Good*, 7.
35. Daly and Cobb, *For the Common Good*, 19.
36. Daly and Cobb, *For the Common Good*, 84.

problem of abstraction. The attempt to turn congregational vitality into a science problematically confuses "what is universal and necessary" with "what is particular and contingent"; in other words, the measure itself becomes the value rather than being recognized as a representation of what is truly valued.[37] In the discourse of vitality, congregational metrics are abstracted from the communities and practices that give them meaning.[38] Furthermore, overreliance on theory and abstraction results in an inability to see what cannot be measured: "Those facts not correlated to the theories have been largely ignored."[39] For example, an economic index measuring growth does not necessarily indicate anything about well-being.[40] The same is true of church statistics. Simply increasing numbers says nothing about the quality of faith or discipleship represented by those numbers.

When churches attempt to apply statistical correlations beyond their meaningful context, the discourse of vital congregations is subject to Daly and Cobb's critique of externalities in market capitalism. In economic terms, that which cannot be measured is labeled an externality. For example, environmental degradation is generally considered an externality in market economics; the environmental effects of production are often not measured and accounted for when determining cost. Externalities can be localized, requiring adjustments in certain contexts, or pervasive, requiring widespread reassessment of the economic model. Daly and Cobb note, "All conclusions in economic theory about the social efficacy of pure competition and the free market are explicitly premised on the absence of externalities."[41] However, there is much about economics and religion that cannot be measured.

Vital congregations discourse includes many externalities—qualities for which a vitality index cannot account. For example, the unique narratives of individuals and communities, which give specificity to members of the body of Christ and historicity to people and places, become externalities in the science of congregational vitality. Thus, the value of a convert becomes the statistical impact on a vitality dashboard rather than the witness of that person's conversion narrative and experience of the Holy Spirit. These features of faith are considered ancillary to numerical increase. Daly and Cobb argue that externalities should be accounted for and costs internalized.[42] For vital congregations, the tangible yet unmeasurable aspects

---

37. Compare to Daly and Cobb, *For the Common Good*, 28.
38. Compare to Daly and Cobb, *For the Common Good*, 43.
39. Daly and Cobb, *For the Common Good*, 31.
40. Daly and Cobb, *For the Common Good*, 62–63.
41. Daly and Cobb, *For the Common Good*, 52–55.
42. Daly and Cobb, *For the Common Good*, 56–57.

of church life must be valued and nurtured. For example, Allen T. Stanton argued for the centrality of community and asset-based community development, rejecting the convergent metrics abstracted by Towers Watson, as primary indicators of congregational health in small rural congregations.[43] However, the metrics of vital congregations cannot be redeemed simply by accounting more accurately for externalities.

The problem is more deeply rooted, having to do with the animating motivation for seeking vitality. "Survival," Lovett H. Weems Jr. acknowledged, should not be "an end in itself" for the church.[44] Vitality is not a goal to be accomplished but rather a journey of faithfulness, involving a qualitative assessment of unquantifiable features:

> The task for each generation is to help the faithful discern an appropriate engagement to meet changed circumstances, new realities, and emerging needs. To do so, they must have an accurate assessment of those circumstances, realities, and needs. To the extent that leaders are able to accomplish these tasks, there are vitality and renewal within the religious tradition.[45]

Vitality and renewal emerge from faithful engagement within one's particular time and place. To resist the forces of empire, church leaders need to let go of anxiety-provoking metrics and focus instead on the life-giving narrative of faith.[46] According to Weems, "the most vital congregations seem always to do two things. They connect with their communities, and they connect people with God."[47]

These connections, these life-giving relationships, cannot be reduced to numbers, and even those features that can be quantified must be interpreted with care. For example, Weems recommended paying attention to gross numbers rather than net numbers when examining changes in church membership: "Looking only to the net numbers will not only lead to discouragement but may tell a false story of the spiritual energy of the congregation."[48] Underneath a net zero change in membership from one year to the next, for example, may be hidden stories of multiple baptisms, deaths, departures, and arrivals. The life of the faith community is the surplus of stories and relationships not accounted for by a growth model in the Church Industrial Complex.

43. Stanton, *Reclaiming Rural*, 64.
44. Weems, *Focus*, 11.
45. Weems, *Focus*, 11.
46. See Rendle, *Countercultural*, xxii and 130.
47. Weems, *Focus*, 66.
48. Weems, *Focus*, 13.

Multivocational Ministry

One of the faithful stories obfuscated by the doctrines of growth and exceptionalism is that of bivocational or multivocational ministry. *Multivocational* generally describes someone who holds more than one job, paid or volunteer, when one of those jobs is pastoring a congregation. *Multivocational* can also refer to pastors who are not paid at all, who volunteer in ministry, or someone who works two ministries, for example, combining a part-time pastorate with part-time hospital chaplaincy. Intentional multivocational ministry, though, is a feature of the entire congregation, not just the pastor.[49] Every member shares responsibility for ministry, complicating a straightforward economic narrative of part-time versus full-time employment. Multivocational ministry arrangements illustrate both the way capitalistic logic governs the work of the church and how it fails to capture the essence of this form of ministry.

The connection between multivocationality and economics seems self-evident. Typically, a multivocational pastor receives partial (or no) compensation for the work of ministry, necessitating other employment to make ends meet. Economic challenges facing multivocational pastors include: less pay; fewer, if any, medical or retirement benefits; similar congregational expectations to full funded pastors; and less support for training, education, and ongoing skills development. Likewise, congregations hiring a multivocational pastor are typically motivated by an insufficiency of funds to pay a full-time pastor. These realities construct an incomplete picture, though, hiding many features external to the market.

Multivocational ministry can also connote creativity and surplus rather than scarcity, particularly when ministry is understood as the activity of the entire congregation, not just the pastoral leader. Multivocational ministry is the most common form of pastoral leadership throughout Christian history and in churches across the globe today. Paul was a leatherworker or tentmaker. Medieval monks brewed beer and baked bread, and many religious communities still combine work and prayer today. Worldwide, the typical person in pastoral leadership relies on multiple employments; for example, the farmer-priest is not an uncommon identity in developing countries. In North America, the Black Church, Latinx congregations, and immigrant communities rely heavily on part time, partially compensated, and volunteer leaders. These collaborative ministries are not viewed as deficient by these communities. When ministry is shared, it resists the boundaries of federal employment classifications, such as full-time or part-time.

49. Stephens, "Bivocational Ministry as the Congregation's Curriculum."

The description *multivocational* references a larger context in which fully compensated ministry is the standard. Multivocational ministry is often contrasted to full-time, fully compensated, seminary trained, professionalized ministry, which is the norm within predominantly White, mainline churches. The context of Christendom necessitates a special term for ministries that do not fit this "Standard Model."[50] In fact, the words *bivocational* and *multivocational* are only necessary in contexts in which this form of ministry is considered anomalous, such as the North American Church Industrial Complex. For example, the term is not used in Black churches with a tradition of partially compensated leaders. One colleague in the Missionary Baptist tradition told me, "We don't call it bivocational. We just call it ministry." Thus, the term *bivocational* exposes a corporatist mindset that implicitly undermines the legitimacy of partially funded pastorates by measuring them against economically successful corporation-style congregations that can afford to hire a full-time CEO.

Within a capitalistic mindset, this comparison renders the partially funded pastorate as less than and less desirable. So-called part-time pastors are stigmatized for being paid less, though all ministry is, in a sense, full time. Even in traditions in which multivocational and volunteer ministry are common, fully compensated ministry functions as an implicit norm, against which other forms of ministry are measured as inferior. This economic measure of faithfulness as numerical success registered clearly among students at Lancaster Theological Seminary: 75 percent agreed that bivocational ministry is the future of pastoral ministry; yet, barely 30 percent agreed that bivocational ministry is preferable to fully funded ministry.[51] These attitudes reveal capitalistic assumptions based on market values—an understandable concern given the large amount of student debt accumulated by the average seminarian. For pastors and communities conditioned to value or aspire to fully compensated, professionalized pastorates, a multivocational ministry arrangement reeks of scarcity and want, implying a failure to thrive.

Actually, it is the capitalist logic, not alternative arrangements, that is failing to thrive. In market terms, multivocationality results from the insufficiency of full-time ministry arrangements to meet current economic challenges. Thus, the existence of multivocational ministry reveals the inadequacy of the standard model, not the other way around. Faith communities exploring intentional multivocational ministry must learn to think and act in ways that challenge the values of empire.

50. Edington, *Bivocational*, 5.
51. Stephens, "Preparing to Educate," 231–32.

Choosing to enter multivocational ministry goes against market logic. For example, multivocational pastors in Canada revealed that "money and time were not necessarily their primary concern."[52] Researchers learned that multivocationality provides a unique fit for each person,[53] eschewing the abstractive tendency of market capitalism. Multivocational pastors understand their calls to ministry and financial stewardship in diverse ways, resulting in many different employment and ministry arrangements. Furthermore, many persons claim a single vocation or call to ministry, supported financially in multiple ways.[54] Thus, it is often more accurate to speak of one vocation expressed through multiple jobs rather than multiple vocations. The balance depends on individual and contextual factors, including personality, financial status, employment opportunities, previous work experience and job skills, congregational needs, and cultural milieu. The Canadian researchers discovered several sustainable patterns, which they described as *integrative*, *complementary*, and *lucrative*, and a fourth category of unsustainable or unsatisfying arrangements for the pastor, which they called *conflicted*.[55] Through a market lens, however, multivocational arrangements can only be seen as conflicted.

The full-time bias of capitalism prevents people from seeing the advantages and successes of multivocational ministry. For example, when Jeffrey MacDonald embarked on research to study vital congregations with part-time clergy, judicatory leaders responded, "We don't have any."[56] MacDonald quickly realized he "wasn't facing a dearth of empirical data but rather a habitual way of thinking that simply equated healthy with having full-time clergy."[57] Equating part-time with deficiency is common in communities of privilege or aspiring privilege, such as majority White congregations. MacDonald recognized that the common presumptions that part-time clergy are less dedicated, skilled, or effective arise from an "inherently classist" attitude that "reinforced a premise equating wealth with moral wholeness."[58] These are the values of the Church Industrial Complex.

By challenging traditional structures of power, multivocationality becomes stigmatized within the mindsets shaped by those structures. The "empire church" and its "Standard Model" of fully funded ministry are

---

52. Watson et al., "Canadian Multivocational Ministry Project," 10.
53. Watson et al., "Canadian Multivocational Ministry Project," 11.
54. Deasy, "Multivocational Plans," 261.
55. Watson et al., "Canadian Multivocational Ministry Project," 16–17.
56. MacDonald, *Part-Time Is Plenty*, 5.
57. MacDonald, *Part-Time Is Plenty*, 6.
58. MacDonald, *Part-Time Is Plenty*, 27.

rooted in North American Christendom and its market logic.[59] Edington observed that bivocational ministry can seem counter to the received wisdom of what counts as "church" and "ministry" in many White, mainline congregations.[60] In a study of Canadian bivocational clergy, Ross Bartlett interrogated "a market-based approach to congregational survival," in which "the numerical size of a congregation" is judged to be a primary factor "in considering vitality, vibrancy, and faithfulness."[61] Understanding the full potential of multivocational ministry requires shifting our perspective from a hiring arrangement to match shrinking budgets to a vision for mutually shared ministry and mission that values particularity over uniformity.

Multivocational ministry is a creative adaptation to the failure of the model of fully compensated ministry to meet current economic challenges in a fading culture of Christendom. For example, across all denominations, women and minorities find fewer opportunities for fully compensated ministry, and plans by seminary graduates, for example, show distinct patterns by race and ethnicity.[62] It is also well documented that Black pastors and women pastors earn less than their White male counterparts. In a study of US bivocational clergy, researchers found that White, married men in the Southeastern United States were more likely to be fully compensated for pastoral ministry; pastors in every other demographic—women, persons of color, immigrants, single persons—were more likely to be partially funded in ministry.[63] Thus, structures of power make multivocationality necessary for those with fewer resources by retaining the normative status of fully funded, professionalized ministry for the privileged and as a mark of privilege. Yet, multivocational ministry also serves as a means of resistance to these oppressions. For example, Black women reported access to partially funded pastorates when encountering barriers to fully funded positions, thus subverting patriarchal structures that would have kept them out of the pulpit.[64] To be clear, the use of workarounds does not validate these unjust situations. We should not expect women and BIPOC pastors to work multiple jobs to support themselves. Rather, their creativity in the face of hardship is an example of a surplus of divine energy that resists the control of empire.

---

59. Edington, *Bivocational*, 8.

60. Edington, *Bivocational*, 6.

61. Bartlett and Jones, *It's Real Ministry*, 43.

62. Deasy, "Multivocational Plans," 258–59, 266, 269; Young Brown, "Black and Bivocational," 77.

63. Perry and Schleifer, "Are Bivocational Clergy Becoming the New Normal?"

64. Young Brown, "Black and Bivocational," 74.

When approached equitably, multivocational ministry can shape congregations in practices of resistance to the Church Industrial Complex and its overpowering logic of capitalistic growth. Multivocational ministry should not be the pastor's onus; rather, it must become the congregation's curriculum. Intentional multivocationality requires a re-negotiation of leadership involving all the laity as active ministers. What counts as ministry and leadership may not be quantifiable in the ways that the market dictates. As an intentional missional strategy, multivocational ministry can subvert systems of discrimination and oppression; it can allow pastors to serve low wealth communities and lessen dependency on the church for a pastor's livelihood; and it can provide economic flexibility for congregations. Multivocational ministry, without stigma, shapes the imagination beyond a capitalistic preoccupation with size and growth. Furthermore, multivocational ministry is better suited to most congregational contexts, replacing a mindset of economic scarcity with an awareness of theological abundance. As an intentional form of ministry, multivocationality provides a surplus of meaning beyond the power of empire.

Seeking a Theological Surplus

Market-driven ministry, characterized by growth and numerical success, is an inherent feature of the Church Industrial Complex of North American Christendom. Vital congregations initiatives and multivocational ministry operate inescapably within this context. Both feed on a fear of scarcity and a motivation to survive when abstracted from the lives of real people and places. The measures of congregational vitality prioritize efficiency and growth over interpersonal relationships. The material challenges of multivocational ministry reflect the same systems of privilege and power in US society. Yet, neither vitality nor multivocationality can be fully appreciated through statistics. The unquantifiable surplus of meaning within thriving churches and multivocational congregations challenges the metrics of ministry, revealing the inadequacy of the business of God when reduced to numbers and growth.

Christendom, nation, and market—these three remain within a context of empire. Yet, so do the externalities of the market—the practices, contexts, persons, and relationships defying abstraction through their particularity. Within this surplus, ministry finds meaning.

Multivocational ministry reveals the limits of the empire church and its standards of success, providing a surplus of relationships and meaning that cannot be accounted for within the market's valuation. Intentional multivocational ministry, chosen for reasons that defy the logics of capitalism and empire, reveals glimpses of the kin-dom, in which "the last will be first, and the first will be last" (Matt 20:16 NRSV). This is a true measure of vitality in the church. The intensity with which the Church Industrial Complex tries to limit, define, belittle, and control multivocational ministry reveals the extent to which partially compensated and volunteer ministry threatens the capitalistic ideology underlying contemporary church practices.

The stories and practices of real congregations exude vitality beyond the value of growth. The unique relationships and circumstances of each moment of ministry, not abstract data, reveal the true vitality of the Spirit to which the church as the body of Christ makes its witness. Relationships discounted by a market-mentality generate a kind of subversive solidarity. These externalities resist quantification. The Church Industrial Complex, bent on accumulating adherents for the sake of growth, cannot measure up to the reckless generosity of the Holy Spirit.

Bibliography

Abraham, William J. *The Logic of Evangelism*. Grand Rapids: Eerdmans, 1989.
Acevedo, Jorge. *Vital: Churches Changing Communities and the World*. Nashville: Abingdon, 2012.
Bartlett, I. Ross, and Kate Jones. *It's Real Ministry: How Part-Time and Bi-Vocational Clergy Are Challenging and Empowering the Church*. Altona, Manitoba: Friesen, 2022.
Bass, Diana Butler. *The Practicing Congregation: Imagining a New Old Church*. Herndon, VA: Alban, 2004.
Bass, Dorothy C., ed. *Practicing Our Faith: A Way of Life for a Searching People*. San Francisco: Jossey-Bass, 1997.
Chaves, Mark, et al. *National Congregations Study: Waves I-IV Summary Tables*. Durham, NC: Duke University Department of Sociology, 2021. https://sites.duke.edu/ncsweb/files/2021/01/NCS-IV_Summary-Tables_For-Posting.pdf.
Daly, Herman E., and John B. Cobb Jr. *For the Common Good: Redirecting the Economy Toward Community, the Environment, and a Sustainable Future*. 2nd ed. With contributions by Clifford W. Cobb. Boston: Beacon Press, 1994.
Deasy, Jo Ann. "The Multivocational Plans of Students in Graduate Theological Education." In *Bivocational and Beyond: Educating for Thriving Multivocational Ministry*, edited by Darryl W. Stephens, 253–75. Teaching Religion and Theology series. Chicago: Books @Atla Open Press, Scholarly Editions, 2022.
de Wetter, David, et al. "UMC Call to Action: Vital Congregations Research Project." Findings Report for Steering Team. Towers Watson, June 28, 2010. http://umccalltoaction.org/files/CTA_TOWERS-WATSON_RPTS_45-126.pdf.
Drummond, Sarah B. *Holy Clarity: The Practice of Planning and Evaluation*. Herndon, VA: Rowman & Littlefield, 2009.

Edington, Mark D. W. *Bivocational: Returning to the Roots of Ministry*. New York: Church Publishing, 2018. http://www.bivocational.church/.

Faith Communities Today. "Twenty Years of Congregational Change: The 2020 Faith Communities Today Overview." Hartford, CT: Hartford Institute for Religion Research, 2021. https://faithcommunitiestoday.org/fact-2020-survey/.

Hoge, Dean R., and David A. Roozen. "Some Sociological Conclusions About Church Trends." In *Understanding Church Growth and Decline, 1950–1978*, edited by Dean R. Hoge and David A. Roozen, 315–33. New York: Pilgrim, 1979.

Hollinger, David A. *Christianity's American Fate: How Religion Became More Conservative and Society More Secular*. Princeton: Princeton University Press, 2022.

"Implementing the 16 Drivers of Vital Congregations." https://s3.amazonaws.com/Website_Properties/how-we-serve/documents/vital-congregations-implementing-the-16-drivers-of-vitality.pdf.

Jones, Robert P. *The End of White Christian America*. New York: Simon & Schuster, 2016.

Kelley, Dean M. *Why Conservative Churches Are Growing: A Study in Sociology of Religion*. New York: Harper & Row, 1972.

MacDonald, G. Jeffrey. *Part-Time Is Plenty: Thriving Without Full-Time Clergy*. Louisville, KY: Westminster John Knox, 2020.

McGavran, Donald. "Church Growth and the Conciliar Movement." *The Asbury Seminarian* 33 (1978) 11–18.

Meyer, Holley. "Southern Baptist Convention Membership Drops for 14th Year in a Row." *Nashville Tennessean*, May 28, 2021, updated June 14, 2021. https://www.tennessean.com/story/news/religion/2021/05/28/southern-baptist-convention-membership-drops-14th-year-row/7419455002/.

Miller, Herb. *The Vital Congregation*. Effective Church Series 1. Nashville: Abingdon, 1990.

Morris, George E. "Introduction." In *Rethinking Congregational Development*, edited by George E. Morris, vii–viii. World Evangelism Library 3. Nashville: Discipleship Resources, 1984.

———. "Theological Bases for Congregational Development." In *Rethinking Congregational Development*, edited by George E. Morris, 20–33. World Evangelism Library 3. Nashville: Discipleship Resources, 1984.

Perry, Samuel L., and Cyrus Schleifer. "Are Bivocational Clergy Becoming the New Normal? An Analysis of the Current Population Survey, 1996–2017." *Journal for the Scientific Study of Religion* 58 (2019) 513–25.

Rendle, Gil. *Countercultural: Subversive Resistance and the Neighborhood Congregation*. Lanham, MD: Rowman & Littlefield, 2023.

———. *Doing the Math of Mission: Fruits, Faithfulness, and Metrics*. Lanham, MD: Rowman & Littlefield, 2014.

Rieger, Joerg. *Christ and Empire: From Paul to Postcolonial Times*. Minneapolis: Fortress, 2007.

———. *No Rising Tide: Theology, Economics, and the Future*. Minneapolis: Fortress, 2009.

Schnase, Robert. *Five Practices of Fruitful Congregations*. Nashville: Abingdon, 2007.

Stanton, Allen T. *Reclaiming Rural: Building Thriving Rural Congregations*. Lanham, MD: Rowman & Littlefield, 2020.

Stephens, Darryl W. "Bivocational Ministry as the Congregation's Curriculum." In *Bivocational and Beyond: Educating for Thriving Multivocational Ministry*, edited by Darryl W. Stephens, 17–35. Teaching Religion and Theology series. Chicago: Books @Atla Open, 2022.

———. "Preparing to Educate for a Thriving Bivocational Ministry." In *Bivocational and Beyond: Educating for Thriving Multivocational Ministry*, edited by Darryl W. Stephens, 225–52. Teaching Religion and Theology series. Chicago: Books @Atla Open, 2022.

———. *Reckoning Methodism: Mission and Division in the Public Church*. Eugene, OR: Cascade, 2024.

The United Methodist Church. *The Journal of the 1984 General Conference of The United Methodist Church*. 2 vols. Edited by John L. Schreiber. Nashville: UMPH, 1984.

The United Methodist Church, Council of Bishops. "Call to Action Study Guide." 2011. http://umccalltoaction.org/files/CallToActionSG.pdf.

———. "Vital Congregations—Faithful Disciples: Vision for the Church. Foundation Document." Nashville: Graded, 1990.

The United Methodist Church, General Board of Discipleship, The United Methodist Church. "Toward Vitality Research Project: Final Report." 2012. http://gbod.org.s3.amazonaws.com/legacy/kintera-files/Toward_Vitality_Research_Project_FINAL.pdf.

University of Chicago Press Editorial Staff. "Black and White: A Matter of Capitalization." June 22, 2020. https://cmosshoptalk.com/2020/06/22/black-and-white-a-matter-of-capitalization/.

Watson, James W., et al. "Canadian Multivocational Ministry Project: Research Report." 2020. https://www.canadianmultivocationalministry.ca/master-report.

Weems, Lovett H., Jr. *Focus: The Real Challenges That Face the United Methodist Church*. Adaptive Leadership Series. Nashville: Abingdon, 2011.

Young Brown, Jessica. "Black and Bivocational." In *Bivocational and Beyond: Educating for Thriving Multivocational Ministry*, edited by Darryl W. Stephens, 65–80. Chicago: Books @Atla Open, 2022.

Chapter 7

Curiosity Killed the Cat(echism)
The Managerial Church and the Intellectual Appetites

MATTHEW J. DODRILL

> Reality is what is revealed to the patient eye of love.
>
> —Iris Murdoch

There's a story in the Gospel of Mark where Jesus, his disciples, and a large crowd encounter a blind beggar named Bartimaeus. As the caravan draws near, Bartimaeus entreats the Lord's help with a loud shout: "Jesus, Son of David, have mercy on me!" (Mark 10:47).

But the disciples have places to go and things to do. They are on a crusade, marching toward Jerusalem to accomplish a mission they do not understand. They have problems to solve, agendas to push, crises to manage, and goals to achieve. So, they reprimand the beggar for interrupting their journey, and they try to silence him.

But then, in a move that's uncharacteristic in Mark's Gospel, famous for its hurried pace, the evangelist says that Jesus *stood still* (Mark 10:49).

While it would be impossible for the evangelist to operate with modern mental health categories, I want to pause here to consider the relationship between the refusal (or inability) to "stand still" and the psychiatric disorder known as depression. Indeed, the Parisian sociologist Alain Ehrenberg makes the provocative claim that depression is an ailment of speed. Depression, he argues, became a psychiatric diagnosis around the time when Western society became increasingly optimistic about the limitless boundaries of human potential. This anthropological optimism was wedded to the logic of the free market, subjecting the plastic, moldable "self" to the metrics of free enterprise, which reduces the human to an "identity" that's curated over time. The problem, of course, is that markets are inherently volatile, such that one's marketability is relative to the demands of consumers, requiring a constant state of flux in the curation of one's identity. The human self is thus consigned to the economic principle of creative destruction, undergoing a process of creation, improvement, destruction, re-creation, *ad infinitum*, until the speed of the process and the demoralizing loss of "value" push the subject to the brink of mental and spiritual fatigue if not a diagnosis of clinical depression.

Depression, argues Ehrenberg, simply *is* the fatigue of becoming oneself.[1] To put it in Mark's terms, it's the inability to *stand still* amid the speedy crusade of efficiency and self-production, rendering us numb to the world's unity and interiority, which are perceived only when we attend to them through the stillness of contemplation. Due to this frenetic pace, we become deadened to the things that beckon our attention in the immediate vicinity of our bodies, unmoored from the flora and fauna that give coherence to our lives. Indeed, in the process of "becoming" ourselves, we become alienated from ourselves.

While depression is primarily a psychiatric diagnosis assigned to individual persons, I will argue in this chapter that the collective body of Christ is currently experiencing the same ailment of speed that Ehrenberg identifies in his work. In the American context in particular, I attribute this ailment to the church's unwitting adoption of technique and innovation—the primary *modi operandi* under the governing rationality of neoliberalism, in which all areas of life are treated like markets that are aimed toward maximizing productivity.[2] In this way, the church becomes its own Industrial Complex, not just in the sense of yielding profits, but in the sense of reproducing and expanding a metaphysical imagination in which all aspects of life, including ministry, are conceived in terms of the free market. The Fresh Expressions movement is especially noteworthy in this regard, as I will lay out shortly.

The central claim of this essay is that our technocratic paradigm betrays an epistemological crisis. Technique is not primarily a method, nor is technology simply an assortment of instruments. Rather, they represent

---

1. Ehrenberg, *Weariness of the Self*.
2. Brown, *Undoing the Demos*, 9–10.

an epistemological regime in which knowledge is conflated with utility. As an epistemological paradigm, technique involves a certain (dis)ordering of the intellectual appetites known as *curiositas*—a vice that seeks to possess, control, and manipulate the objects of knowledge. Truth, in this paradigm, is not conceived as a divine transcendental that invites our participation. Rather, it is conceived as a product of human innovation. Truth is what you get when a problem is solved or a desire is fulfilled, which is why the Manager and Entrepreneur are seen as modernity's custodians of truth. They conjure new truths through the whims of power until those truths are no longer marketable, which affords them the opportunity to "problem solve"—that is, to facilitate the process of creative destruction, which is driven by consumer demand. When applied to the church, the result is novelty that breeds more novelty, until the body of Christ is exhausted and demoralized—which is to say, fatigued of becoming itself.

After providing a brief history of the Fresh Expressions movement, I will offer a more detailed account of the epistemological crisis that ails the church, which is rooted in modernity's malformation of the intellectual appetites, resulting in *curiositas*. This account will be followed by a critical appraisal of the "managed body" ecclesiology, which hails innovation as its chief virtue. I will then offer a corrective to the church's technocratic paradigm, suggesting that we recover what Albert Borgmann calls "focal practices."

Fresh Expressions: The Needs-Based Church

In 2003, the General Assembly of the Church of England produced a report called "The Mission Shaped Church." Cognizant of gradual church decline in the West, the goal of the report was to offer evidence of new ecclesial initiatives that were attracting "particular networks of people."[3] According to the report, such networks included "workplace churches" and "school-based churches" that cater to the demographics, interests, and stations-in-life of the people in a given context, yielding a variety of ecclesial forms known as the "Fresh Expressions" movement.[4] The goal was to take the preexisting networks of unchurched people and allow the church to express itself through the cultural idioms of those networks. In some cases, these churches consist of mothers who gather for breakfast at their kids' schools. In other cases, they revolve around a common interest in, for example, board games, yoga, bagels, or kayaking. Quite literally, the goal is to meet

3. Church of England, "Mission-Shaped Church," 43.
4. Church of England, "Mission-Shaped Church," 43.

people where they are, where the gospel can be translated through the idiosyncrasies of these particular contexts.

But while the Fresh Expressions movement champions a contextual approach to ministry, the meaning of the word "contextual" here seems to be framed by consumer preferences, where one's context is a matter of lifestyles or hobbies or politico-ideological leanings. How many poor people can afford to buy a kayak? Do they often find themselves in spaces where kayaking networks are formed? How diverse, really, is a church consisting mainly of yoga moms or Backgammon players? A context, in this view, is untethered from a local *place*, which draws people together across various demographics and interests, and is defined instead by the disparate *networks* that are presumed to transcend that place.[5] As Ben Quash aptly notes, "The risk of some Fresh Expressions is that they are communities which people have opted into rather than found themselves present to. Place is not their starting point, and if you take *place* out of the equation it is prone to being replaced by a more naked sort of *choice*."[6]

The socioeconomic consequences of this approach are noteworthy, as each respective "context" or "network" inadvertently excludes people who lack the money and resources that make consumer choice possible. For example, I serve a church that is situated in a hip, artistic neighborhood in central Arkansas. The median household income is relatively high, the average age is relatively young, and the various skillsets are reflective of an educated populace. But my church is also positioned on a main thoroughfare that connects downtown to various neighborhoods and interstates, resulting in lots of foot traffic that puts our congregation in the pathway of people experiencing poverty and homelessness. When it comes to identifying the various "contexts" of our neighborhood, these people lack the resources necessary to curate their lifestyles, pay for hobbies, or consistently access reading materials and social clubs that cultivate robust ideological leanings, so it's difficult to determine which "networks" they belong to. Bereft of the consumer choices that everyone else in the neighborhood is privileged to exercise, our impoverished neighbors are excluded from the marketplace and factored out of the process of determining what counts as a "fresh expression," even though they inhabit the same local place.

---

5. It's important to note, however, that not all networks are defined by consumer preferences. Some networks are formed out of necessity, as in the case of disabled persons who are actively excluded from their places, including their churches. It's also worth acknowledging that places can become siloed by income, race, and other such factors that corrupt the inherent goodness of place.

6. Quash, *Abiding*, 20.

In many ways, the Fresh Expressions movement has ceased being a discrete *trend* and has become a ubiquitous *ethos* within Protestant Christianity. The crisis of decline has prompted an uptick in church-growth strategies that glean insight from the corporate world: An organizational rationale generates an ecclesial culture that identifies the needs, wants, and desires of a particular target audience (a "network") and caters to the demands of said audience, aiming at innovation and "fresh" expressions that give way to fresher expressions, until the church is fatigued of its own perpetual novelty. The goal of the church, therefore, is now conceived in terms of meeting the needs of religious consumers, trading an incarnational logic—a divine *Logos*, which is tied to *place*—for an instrumental logos, which is tied to *networks*. The church in the West is possessed by the demons of efficiency and innovation, taking every thought captive to instrumental reason and its Pelagian imperative: Seek the most effective means to achieve the most marketable ends. This imperative, which can be characterized in terms of optimizing for efficiency, is what philosophers and social critics have called *technique*. It is not merely a strategy for growth and production; it is a malformed epistemology that was spawned by the disordering of our intellectual appetites.

The Epistemological Crisis: Technique and *Curiositas*

That the Fresh Expressions movement became a Protestant ethos is quite predictable. As the philosopher Charles Taylor has shown, the prominence of efficient causation and instrumental reason was partly the result of the Protestant impulse to safeguard the sovereign will of God. According to this reasoning, if a creature's goodness is determined by its nature, that would seem to limit God's ability to determine what is good. As the Reformers saw it, the goodness of a creature's nature should be determined by the divine will, not by its nature. The result of this move was an evacuation of creaturely "essences" with value-laden "natures," effectively reducing creatures to what God *names* them. This nominalist revolution and its logical corollary, divine voluntarism, made possible the view that moral and ontological realities are products of divine volition.[7]

With the eclipse of essences came the demise of teleology and final causation. To illustrate the point, Brad Kallenberg gives the example of a wristwatch: "If we ask, 'What is the wristwatch for?' the usual answer is that watches are for timekeeping. To put it more technically, we could say that

---

7. Taylor, *Secular Age*, 97.

the purpose or *telos* of the watch is timekeeping.... Knowledge of this *telos* enables us to render judgment against a grossly inaccurate watch as a 'bad' watch."[8] The essence of the watch is determined by its *telos*, which ascribes a certain "oughtness" to the watch's nature: It *ought* to keep time well, and it *ought not* keep time badly or juggle bowling pins on a unicycle. But if we evacuate the intrinsic *telos* of the watch, we are left saying that the purpose of the wristwatch is extrinsic to the watch itself, reducible to external "causes" that produce a desired effect—namely, the mechanistic process that produces the thing in question. Thus, when someone asks, "Why do wristwatches keep time?" the answer is no longer, "Because that's what watches *do*, by virtue of their nature." Rather, the answer is, "Because a watchmaker sets in motion a process of kinetic energy that moves various gears, springs, and balance wheels." According to Taylor, we are left with "a new understanding of being, according to which, all intrinsic purposes have been expelled, final causation drops out, and efficient causation alone remains."[9]

The consequences of this metaphysical revolution are profound. When the world is stripped of its essences and intrinsic *teloi*, it becomes a formless piece of clay that can be manipulated and managed. According to Alasdair MacIntyre, this bleak state of affairs gives rise to modern character-types, including the bureaucratic manager: "The manager represents in his *character* the obliteration of the distinction between manipulative and nonmanipulative social relations.... The manager treats ends as given, as outside his scope; his concern is with technique, with effectiveness in transforming raw materials into final products, unskilled labor into skilled labor, investment into profits."[10]

Ends are outside the manager's scope because, with the rise of nominalism and the eclipse of teleology, there are no ends to consider at all. The manager is thus under no moral obligation to consider questions regarding human nature or the good life because there are no moral ends that determine what human life is *for*. Hence, managers "conceive of themselves as morally neutral characters whose skills enable them to devise the most efficient means of achieving whatever end is proposed."[11] When it comes to Fresh Expressions, the proposed end is church growth via network formation, and the manager who implements the efficient means is called "pastor."

The foregoing genealogy, which takes us back to the Late Middle Ages and the Protestant Reformation, tells part of the story of how we got here.

---

8. Kallenberg, "Master Argument of MacIntyre's *After Virtue*," 26.
9. Taylor, *Secular Age*, 98.
10. MacIntyre, *After Virtue*, 30.
11. MacIntyre, *After Virtue*, 74.

But interrogating the metaphysical underpinnings of our current ecclesial reality is not enough. We must also give an account of the epistemological paradigm that coincided with the nominalist revolution. It all starts with the inversion of *curiositas* from vice to virtue.

For the first sixteen hundred years of Christian history, *curiositas* (often translated as "curiosity") was thought to be an intellectual vice. Almost all Christians were happy to concede Aristotle's dictum that "all men by nature desire to know," but this appetite for knowledge was by no means considered morally neutral. Before the earliest Christians began to formulate their critical attitudes toward *curiositas*, we already find deep reservations about it in the writings of Cicero, Plutarch, and Seneca. The Christians took up the mantle during their contest with the Gnostics, attempting to differentiate their form of catechesis from the latter's possessive mode of knowledge acquisition. According to Paul Griffiths, the purpose of censuring *curiositas* was to "distinguish a rightly ordered appetite for knowledge from a wrongly ordered one, and to attempt to institute programs of catechesis that would order the intellectual appetites of Christians in the right way."[12] Christians almost never equivocated in their opposition to *curiositas*, and we find a wealth of polemics against it in the writings of Tertullian, Cyprian, Basil the Great, Ambrose, Augustine, St. Jerome, Bernard of Clairvaux, Aquinas, and many others.

When *curiositas* first appeared in the writings of Cicero, it was defined as intellectual intemperance. Simply put, it is the failure to exercise restraint and moderation in the pursuit of knowledge. Early Christian writings on the vices refer to 1 John 2:16 as the clearest prooftext condemning *curiositas*, where the "concupiscence of the eyes" is said to be one of the three powers that constitute "the world." Concupiscence of the eyes is likened to intellectual gluttony or an excessive hunger for the acquisition of knowledge, and Aquinas writes that such intemperance yields several consequences: It produces knowledge that distracts from one's obligations; it fails to discriminate between credible and dubious sources; it "puffs up" or induces pride; and it produces knowledge that is presumed to be non-sacramental in character—which is to say, knowledge that is untethered from the God in whom it participates ontologically, losing its ability to point beyond itself to the glory of God.[13] It is my estimation that *technique* and instrumental reason are insidious forms of *curiositas*.

As we have discussed already, the nominalist revolution gave us a world deprived of intrinsic essences, and the concomitant loss of teleology

12. Griffiths, *Intellectual Appetite*, 12.
13. Aquinas, *Summa Theologiae* II.II, q.167.

gave us a world that is governed by efficient causation alone. As a result, naked volition takes precedence over stable natures, such that even *God's* will is no longer thought to be constrained by his nature.[14] Now that the world is vacated of all that once gave it coherence, modern character types (managers, entrepreneurs, etc.) can fill the vacuum and subject the world to the tyranny of efficient causation, which is activated by their autonomous will. Indeed, the world becomes something that is *made* rather than something that is *encountered*, which is why technology has become the governing regime of modernity. We can begin to see this shift with the inception of the word itself: The merging of the words *technê* and *logos*, making and knowing, intimates the emergence of a new epistemological paradigm—a knowing-by-making. This epistemological shift was heralded by Francis Bacon, who famously conflated truth with utility when he announced that "knowledge is power." As Michael Hanby argues:

> [The meaning of this famous maxim] is not simply that we now know the phenomena of nature *for the sake of controlling them*; it is, rather, that we know natural phenomena *by means of* controlling them. This is ultimately why Bacon says that truth and usefulness come to the same thing: because the "truth" of this kind of knowledge is precisely identical to our power . . . . To put the matter crudely, if nature is essentially a machine or a mechanical process, then the knowledge of nature is essentially engineering. And if knowledge is essentially engineering, then *truth* is essentially whatever is technically possible.[15]

Here we arrive at the crux of the matter. Due to the conflation of truth and possibility, innovation becomes the chief virtue of our technocratic regime. Within a market economy, innovation is steered by an infinite number of consumer desires, rendering a limitless set of possibilities. Given the limitless scope of these possibilities, all innovations are destined for obsolescence, quickly replaced by a new possibility, which in turn is replaced by yet another one. Taking us back to where we started, Ehrenberg argues that depression derives from the "confrontation between the notion of limitless possibilities and the notion of the uncontrolled."[16] That is to say, depression is the internal conflict between a ceaseless movement-into-becoming

---

14. The nominalist revolution undercuts the meaning of the divine name in Exodus 3:14 where God's existence is identical with his *essence*. God's name, I AM, tells us that God is *maximally* stable, such that his being and volition can never be divided into disparate "parts." Given divine simplicity, God's will can never deviate from the love that he *is*, contra divine voluntarism.

15. Hanby, "Questioning the Science and Religion Question," 160.

16. Ehrenberg, *Weariness of the Self*, 230.

and a stable participation-in-being that was forfeited during the nominalist revolution, giving rise to a sense of self-alienation. The depressed ecclesial body has an acute sense of this conflict, which is why the church is fatigued of innovating herself into oblivion by offering an endless array of "fresh expressions." Indeed, she is fatigued of becoming herself.

So, to reiterate: The nominalist revolution produced the conditions of possibility for the emergence of modern technology, which cannot be reduced to technological *artifacts* but must instead be construed in terms of what Heidegger called *Gestell*, or enframing—a way of seeing and *knowing* the world as standing reserve, as raw material that is known *by means of* control; hence "knowledge is power." This instrumental knowledge—a knowing-by-making—is at the root of modern society's incessant hunger for innovation, the speed of which produces the conditions of clinical and corporate depression, which the church is currently experiencing in the West.

If the essence of technology is *Gestell*—a way of knowing—then Pope Francis is right in suggesting that our technocratic paradigm is also an epistemological paradigm.[17] As such, it is integrally related to the intellectual appetites, particularly to the vice of *curiositas*. Specifically, it bears the rotten fruit of *curiositas* in two ways: it seeks knowledge by means of control, and it pursues novelty for its own sake.

Regarding control, Paul Griffiths writes that curiosity seeks to "control, dominate, or make a private possession" of new knowledge, and its principal method is "enclosure by sequestration."[18] Whereas the virtue of *studiositas* (or studiousness) inhabits a world of gifts and participates in what is known, the vice of curiosity "inhabits a world of objects, which can be sequestered and possessed."[19] For the curious, the world becomes what Harmut Rosa calls a "point of aggression." In this orientation to the world, "everything that appears to us must be known, mastered, conquered, made useful," which is reinforced "by the demands for optimization and growth produced by financial market capitalism."[20] This is where MacIntyre's modern character types swoop in and fill the *telos*-deprived vacuum. When we eliminate intrinsic purposes and final causes, managers and entrepreneurs are given license to optimize for efficiency without any regard for proper ends. In the church, for example, questions about the good life and the kingdom of God are replaced by questions about growth and maximizing outputs;

17. Francis, *Laudato Si'*, §107.
18. Griffiths, *Intellectual Appetite*, 20.
19. Griffiths, *Intellectual Appetite*, 22.
20. Rosa, *Uncontrollability of the World*, 6–7.

hence the need for *entrepreneurial* pastors. For this reason, Andrew Root writes that churches now operate with an equation of M + P = M2, members plus programs equals members prime.[21] His use of a mathematical equation is apt. As Griffiths argues, curiosity is formed by a "mathetic catechesis," which is "aimed at knowledge of its chosen objects that would be exhaustive and certain in something like the same way that a mathematician's proof of a theorem is exhaustive and demonstrative."[22] This is precisely the kind of catechesis that Hannah Arendt worried about in the mid-twentieth century, as she recognized that the whole of nature was becoming an object for applied mathematics, foreclosing the ability to ask profound questions about human nature and the good life.[23] After all, with the eclipse of teleology, questions like "What is man?" or "What is justice?" or "What is beauty?" are rendered unintelligible, inducing the kind of thoughtlessness that makes totalitarianism possible.[24] All that matters is "priming" growth and maximizing outputs, which do not take moral ends into consideration.

Applied to the church, then, pastors are no longer expected to ask profound questions as part of the vocation of the cure of souls, which would be the way of *studiositas*. Rather, they are expected to "solve problems" by means of various managerial and technical methods, which is the way of *curiositas*.[25] Any Christologically rooted ecclesiology is thus ruled out of court since a Christological doctrine of the church would involve an account

21. Root, *Congregation in a Secular Age*, 16.
22. Griffiths, *Intellectual Appetite*, 144–45.
23. Arendt, *Human Condition*, 257–73.
24. Cultures that are under the tutelage of mathetic catechesis are more likely to get swept away by the agendas of repressive regimes. When efficient causes supersede final causes, we lose our aptitude for moral appraisal. It is no coincidence that the German philosopher Josef Pieper wrote *Leisure: The Basis of Culture* soon after the Nazi regime came to an end. Whereas the total work ideology of mid-century Germany induced thoughtlessness that led to bureaucratic passivity, contemplative leisure (engendered by *studiositas*) seeks the truth about formal and teleological realities, inducing questions about the proper ends of humanity. When such questions are obscured by matters of efficiency and mathesis, we lose the moral criteria by which to judge political actions. The *via contemplativa*, therefore, should not be held in opposition to the *via activa*. After all, contemplation is not apolitical. On the contrary, true wisdom unites contemplation with action, rendering a *truly* political disposition whereby, in the words of Arendt, we can "*think* what we are doing" (Arendt, *Human Condition*, 5; emphasis mine).
25. According to Griffiths, the "magical key" to knowledge in the mathetic catechism is *method*. See Griffiths, *Intellectual Appetite*, 148. Peter Harrison likewise suggests that when *curiositas* was transformed from a vice into a virtue, it was due in part to Bacon's objectification of scientific knowledge, which "shifted focus away from the moral qualities of investigators and the propriety of particular objects of knowledge to specific procedures and methods." See Harrison, "Curiosity, Forbidden Knowledge, and the Reformation of Natural Philosophy," 265–90.

of the final and formal cause of the *ekklesia*—namely, Jesus Christ. Again, as MacIntyre helps us to understand, final causes, or *teloi*, are outside the scope of the managerial pastor, freeing him to impose form on the church by reducing its purpose to *external* causes that he sets in motion. Just as we trade final causes for efficient causes when assessing the excellence of a wristwatch, we exchange the final cause of the church—Jesus Christ— for the efficient causes that produce the desired effects predetermined by consumer "networks." The Fresh Expressions church, therefore, can only be known by means of control, a knowing-by-making that is reduced to engineering. And you can only *make* what you possess and dominate at the point of aggression.

As to novelty, John Webster writes that "curiosity is manifest as a kind of restlessness or instability, where discriminations about what must and what must not be objects of attention do not operate. In acute form, this becomes a species of intellectual promiscuity, driven by addiction to novelty and a compulsion to repeat the experience of discovery."[26] If, as Hanby argues, our modern technological paradigm reduces knowledge to technical *possibilities*, then the pursuit of knowledge is defined as the technocratic actualization of those possibilities, which immediately lend themselves to further possibilities *ad infinitum*. Applied to the church, managerial and entrepreneurial pastors are given the task of actualizing the church's possibilities, which are quickly outdated and replaced by new—or *novel*—possibilities that emerge from the ecclesial marketplace, fostering an eternal cycle of creative destruction. The intellectual analogue of creative destruction is novelty engendered by *curiositas*, where, according to Griffiths, "once the new thing is known . . . it is, at once, no longer new, and therefore no longer satisfying to the curious. Something new, some new object, must at once be sought. The curious gaze is endlessly restless, insanely so, in fact."[27] Innovation thus never ends, and the perpetual curation (and *re*-curation) of the church's "identity" has the ironic effect of making the church feel adrift, unsettled, and fatigued of becoming itself. That is why Webster maintains that curiosity's addiction to novelty leads to restlessness and instability, or to what Aquinas calls the "roaming unrest of the spirit"—a sign, according to Josef Pieper, "of complete rootlessness."[28]

---

26. Webster, *Domain of the Word*, 198.

27. Griffiths, "Vice of Curiosity," 52. For a biblical example of *curiositas* as the pursuit of new knowledge, or novelty, consider Acts 17:21: "Now all the Athenians and the foreigners living there would spend their time in nothing but telling or hearing something new."

28. Pieper, *Josef Pieper: An Anthology*, 86.

This frenetic pace of novel innovation—or, in Griffiths's parlance, the rapid penetration of an object that turns the long gaze into a quick glance before moving on—is why *curiositas* "precludes contemplation, which requires time and repeated attention to sameness, the constant return of the gaze to an object understood not quickly or easily to yield itself."[29] Churches that preoccupy themselves with (re)creating mission statements, (re)conducting visioning processes, and overhauling programs for the sake of "priming membership" and creating "fresh expressions" are like the caravan in Mark's Gospel, marching toward Jerusalem at such a hurried pace that they incur a spiritual ailment—a "roaming unrest of the spirit"—of which Bartimaeus's physical condition is a sign.

We would do well to mimic the posture of Jesus, who *stands still* and allows his gaze to rest on the poor beggar and who comports himself in a way that requires time and repeated attention to sameness. The philosopher Byung-Chul Han calls it a posture of "lingering," the ability to "be at home in the world" (*einhausung*) by discovering the intensity of life in the objects of perception, which requires a repetitive, sustained gaze that "stabilizes and deepens attention."[30] This lingering is only possible if we are committed to a *place* of lingering, a place wherein the objects of perception are *given* to us, which is forfeited when churches define themselves as networks. When the church sees itself as a local place, it fosters the deep attention necessary to see what is given—the people, the traditions, the liturgy—as a gift of reality. But when it sees itself as a collection of networks, it perceives reality as something to be engineered, and it creates an attention *deficit*, moving us from one "fresh" expression to another, until we are completely unmoored and fatigued of becoming ourselves. As Han puts it, "The person who expects something new and exciting all the time . . . overlooks what is already there."[31] Indeed, to recognize what is "already there" is to recognize the givenness of creation and its sacramental character, hitherto eclipsed by the nominalist revolution and its intellectual modality, *curiositas*. If the church is to cultivate the virtue of lingering, she must relinquish the pursuit of efficiency and innovation and recover the *via contemplativa*. Such a recovery will entail a paradigm shift in the way we think about the church as a social body.

---

29. Griffiths, "Vice of Curiosity," 53.
30. Han, *Disappearance of Rituals*, 7–10.
31. Han, *Disappearance of Rituals*, 10. See also Han, *Scent of Time*.

The Managed Body: *Corpus Mortuum*

In the 1970s, cultural anthropologist Mary Douglas argued that a dialectical tension exists between the physical body and social body. That is, they are both symbolic of each other: The physical serves as a microcosm of the social, and the social provides the web of existence that individuates the physical. Douglas was simply putting in social-scientific terms what the apostle Paul had already put in theological terms. As Dale Martin writes in *The Corinthian Body*, "No ontological dichotomy between the individual and the social can be located in Paul's logic . . . , [which] depends on the breaking down of any possible boundary between the individual body and the social body."[32] For the ancients, "the differentiation between inner and outer body was fluid and permeable," such that a physical body could be infiltrated by a social body, and vice versa.[33] For Paul, individual bodies, or "members," are either incorporated into the social body of Christ (and, concomitantly, the social body of Christ infiltrates and individuates the physical body of the believer), or they are incorporated into the social body of Adam, which likewise has the ability to infiltrate and individuate the physical body.

This dialectical tension opens two pathways of further analysis: First, it supports the idea of a *real* relationship between the depressed individual and the depressed church. That is, it can help problematize the reductive account of clinical depression, which ascribes the diagnosis only to individual bodies as if they exist in a vacuum. Given the permeable relationship between physical and social bodies, it is perfectly plausible to suggest that a social body, such as the church, can suffer the depressive ailment of speed that emerges from our post-nominalist and technocratic age. Moreover, this ailment can be causal in both directions: the depressed individual can affect the social body, and the depressed social body can affect the individual.

Second, it establishes an *analogical* relationship between the depressed individual and the depressed church, each constraining the way the other is perceived.[34] In order to understand this connection, we must first consider the resemblance between a physicalist account of the human body—that is, the view that humans are entirely physical, lacking an immaterial soul—and a managerial account of the social body.

As Lyndon Shakespeare has argued, a physicalist understanding of the individual body is analogically correlated with a managerial understanding of the social body. Just as the reductive physicalist maintains that individual bodies lack the formal principle of the soul, the managerial body is likewise

32. Martin, *Corinthian Body*, 173.
33. Martin, *Corinthian Body*, 20.
34. Douglas, *Natural Symbols*, 74.

bereft of any intrinsic form, due in large part to its nominalist metaphysics. And note well: For Aquinas, all forms are necessarily inclined toward a *telos*. "On the basis of its form," he writes, "fire . . . is inclined toward a higher place and toward generating its like."[35] Without an account of fire's proper inclination, we cannot give an account of its form, just as we cannot understand the essence of a wristwatch without ascertaining its *telos*. Such is true of physical and social bodies: Without an account of their proper ends, we cannot give an account of their true form, rendering an amorphous piece of clay that can be manipulated at will. As Shakespeare writes, the body of reductive physicalism lacks "human purposefulness . . . , which sets human inclinations adrift from the attributes and capacities that are particular to human bodily life, thereby requiring purpose to be imposed through various physical enhancements."[36] Likewise, managers and entrepreneurs (and in this case, many pastors) impose form and purpose on the managed social body through various technical methods that were learned through mathetic catechesis. When pastors operate managerially, then, the result is a church whose form is not given but *made*—a knowing-by-making.

Shakespeare goes on to say that physicalism cannot give an account of the body as a *unified* thing. Without the soul, there is no overarching structure that unifies the material components, no principle of actuality that makes the body *what it is*. The soul, as the substantial form of the body, allows us to say that the body possesses a certain nature. But with physicalism, we get an "ordered aggregate, a set of parts put into external relations by some ordering principle (e.g., the laws of efficient causation within 'nature') to form a whole."[37] On this account, the operations of the body are not activated by the formal cause of the soul; instead, they are activated by the *efficient* causes of other disparate parts that are "organized" and "coordinated" in ways that are measurable and predictable. The analogical correlate is the bureaucratic social body, which is primarily concerned with the organization and coordination of disparate parts "in the service of the goals of efficiency, effectiveness, predictability, and control."[38] Again: $M + P = M_2$.

And this is where depression comes into play. If a physical or social body lacks an animating principle (or substantial form), it is effectively *dead*. As Shakespeare rightly argues, "the body of reductive physicalism is a *corpse*, animated by a metaphysic of efficient causation."[39] Likewise, "an

---

35. Aquinas, *Summa Theologiae* 1a.80.1.
36. Shakespeare, *Body of Christ in the Age of Management*, 143.
37. Shakespeare, *Body of Christ in the Age of Management*, 106.
38. Shakespeare, *Body of Christ in the Age of Management*, 107.
39. Shakespeare, *Body of Christ in the Age of Management*, 143.

over-reliance on a managerial logic reduces the life of the church to that of a mechanized corpse," leaving it susceptible to technocratic manipulation just as a cadaver is susceptible to medical manipulation.[40] Devoid of a formal principle, the managerial church lacks a discernible *telos* internal to its nature. As a result, its purpose is defined by the shifting winds of consumer desire, curating its identity at the frenetic pace of a volatile market until it grows weary of innovation, suffering the "roaming unrest of the spirit" that comes with a failure to linger. Indeed, the managerial church is depressed because she is walking dead, a body without an animating principle: *a corpse.*

The Body of Christ: A Focal Community

If the managed body is bereft of concrete form because it lacks a principle of actuality, the opposite is true of the church *qua* church. This is demonstrated in the grammar of the church's description as the "body of Christ." The church is not just *any* body. It is the body *of Christ*. As such, it possesses a unifying principle (or a unifying *person*) that yields a particular *whatness*, a concrete existence that cannot be reconfigured by managers and entrepreneurs. Just as the living body has no concrete existence apart from the soul, the church has no concrete existence apart from the Word of God—an insight that derives from Karl Barth's ecclesiological appropriation of Chalcedon's anhypostasis/enhypostasis formula.[41] So, while the church is not identical with Jesus Christ (analogous to the body not being identical with the soul, or to Christ's human nature not being identical with his divine nature), she is nonetheless "actualized" by the agency of Christ through an inseparable union that historicizes the ascended Lord. Jesus Christ, in other words, both activates the church and is manifested *through* the church, which is why we can declare that he is Lord of his church even while acknowledging that the church is his body.[42]

Continuing the theme of the church's concrete nature, Christopher R. J. Holmes states the following:

> The church's concreteness is tied up with the person of Jesus Christ, One who cannot be said to be himself without the

---

40. Shakespeare, *Body of Christ in the Age of Management*, 183.

41. Barth, *Church Dogmatics* 1/2:163–65; and *CD* 4/2:49–51; 90–91. See also Bender, *Karl Barth's Christological Ecclesiology*.

42. Kimlyn Bender describes this tension as the "dialectical relation between the divine constitution and historical manifestation of the church." See Bender, *Karl Barth's Christological Ecclesiology*, 78.

apostles and us in them. His reconstitution of the people Israel around himself is peculiar to his unique identity as One whose person creates a people, is generative of a people whose witness takes up space in the world.[43]

Holmes is pointing to the dialectical relation between the church's concreteness as a divinely constituted reality on the one hand, and Jesus Christ's concreteness in the historically situated reality of the church on the other. The people of God are thus "*ingredient in*" the identity of Jesus Christ, who in turn is "never without concrete form, that is without the apostles."[44] The concreteness of the church and the concreteness of the Lord's presence are predicated on each other, enabling us to say of Christ that "his form is never without [the church]: Christ and Christians."[45]

We see this dialectic play out in Luke's account of the Emmaus Road journey, where the risen Lord "disappears" immediately after Cleopas and his companion break bread. But the point is not that Jesus vanishes in the sense of withdrawing his presence. The point, rather, is that through the breaking of the eucharistic body, the historical body of Christ is re-instantiated in the *ecclesial* body of Christ. He does not disappear in the strict sense; he is simply made visible (or concrete!) in a new way—through the communion of believers.

The Eucharist, then, as the sacrament that makes the church a concrete reality, safeguards the integrity of the church against the impulses of entrepreneurialism, which presumes that the church is deprived of concrete form and therefore needs management. To be clear, I am not suggesting that the Eucharist is a magic pill, nor am I naive to the fact that churches with managerial pastors also devote themselves to the Eucharist. My goal is rather modest: I merely want to raise attention to the incoherence of a church that receives concrete form in the Eucharist while employing missional strategies that assume the *absence* of form, simultaneously a living body and a dead corpse. Becoming cognizant of this contradiction might elicit a renewed emphasis on eucharistic theology within congregations.

Indeed, the Eucharist *qua* practice embodies a form of life that recovers a sense of "being at home" (*einhausung*). As a mode of lingering, it calms the roaming unrest of the spirit that ails the entrepreneurial church. This kind of practice is what Albert Borgmann calls a focal practice. Deriving from the Latin, the word *focus* literally means "hearth" or "fireplace." Until recently, the hearth was the center of the household, not just in the sense of

---

43. Holmes, "Church and the Presence of Christ," 269.
44. Holmes, "Church and the Presence of Christ," 269.
45. Holmes, "Church and the Presence of Christ," 280.

being a feature of the household, but in the sense of constituting the household by facilitating a culture. Concerning the hearth, Borgmann writes:

> It assigned to the different family members tasks that defined their place in the household. The mother built the fire, the children kept the firebox filled, and the father cut the firewood. It provided for the entire family a regular and bodily engagement with the rhythm of the seasons that was woven together of the threat of cold and the solace of warmth, the smell of wood smoke, the exertion of sawing and of carrying, the teaching of skills, and the fidelity of daily tasks.[46]

On this account, the hearth does two things: First, it provides friction by fostering bodily engagement; and second, it facilitates community.

Regarding friction, the hearth requires everyone in the family to chip in and use some elbow grease. The wood needs chopped, the embers need stirred, and the chimney needs swept. None of these tasks are "efficient," which is why they require some physical effort. But in modern homes, those who can afford them have gas fireplaces that can be powered by remote control, making the process "easier" for everyone involved. The question, however, is whether convenience and efficiency rob us of our agency. According to Ivan Illich, we exercise agency only when we exert mastery over our tools through the cultivation of skill.[47] By contrast, we lose our agency when our tools work *for* us. For example, manually sweeping the floor can be a convivial exercise of agency whereas letting the Roomba do it for us can atrophy our sense of being-in-the-world. In the former case, friction provides some *traction* in life, like a tire that sticks to the road. By "grounding" us in the world, it provides a sense of being-at-home. But in the latter case, convenience and efficiency leave us feeling adrift.

Regarding community, the hearth was once the family's primary gathering place. It was used for preparing food, and it's where the family would gather to stay warm. In this way, it facilitated the bonds of the family, which is the meaning of the word *religion*—"to bind." But with the rise of central heating units, family members can now stay warm in their own bedrooms without congregating. The heating device, which is primed for efficiency, provides the same warmth as the fireplace, but it deprives us of the "*world* of the fireplace."[48] Not only does it leave us adrift by robbing us of our embodied agency; it leaves us adrift by dissolving the bonds of the *oikos*.

46. Borgmann, *Technology and the Character of Contemporary Life*, 42.

47. Illich, *Tools for Conviviality*.

48. Borgmann, *Technology and the Character of Contemporary Life* 42; emphasis added.

Thus, for Borgmann, focal practices structure our attention in a way that resembles the hearth. They generate agency through the inculcation of a skill, which stimulates our conscious awareness of ourselves as living beings, and they train us to attend deeply to focal things (like fireplaces) and the communities they create. Put differently, focal practices cultivate the posture of lingering—a disposition that we lose when we seek novel innovation, which is the goal of the curious.[49]

As stated already, the Eucharist is one such focal practice, which Borgmann himself acknowledges.[50] It provides the friction of preparation and ritual, which gives the community a sense of embodied agency; and it facilitates the bonds of community, which is why we call it communion. Moreover, it trains us to attend deeply to the focal things of bread and wine (the eucharistic body), which in turn points our attention to the ecclesial body it creates. While he does not make the eucharistic connection explicit, Borgmann often talks about the "culture of the table," where the family meal, much like the hearth, facilitates deep bonds and rapt attention: "The great meal of the day, be it at noon or in the evening, is a focal event par excellence. It gathers the scattered family around the table."[51] The culture of the table is a culture of encounter, a culture of lingering that stabilizes and deepens attention. Recalling Han, the culture of the table re-anchors the church in time and space, enabling the body of Christ to be "at home" (*einhausung*) after a long season of unmooring itself and curating its identity.

As the Emmaus Road story illustrates, the ecclesial culture of the table is not merely a sociological reality. It is the concrete manifestation of Christ's body on earth, receiving its form and *telos* from the risen Lord. Thus, the church's identity is stable, leaving no vacuums to be filled by modern character types who would otherwise impose form and purpose extrinsically. Moreover, the culture of the table is tied to *place*, eschewing the technical methods that cater to *networks* and their consumer desires. That's because the church's focal orientation keeps it anchored to the "hearth"—that is, to the place of communion.

---

49. Kevin Hood Gary puts it well when he asserts that focal practices overcome "the temptation to move from one thing to the next." See Gary, *Why Boredom Matters*, 91. Compare this to Griffith's claim that *curiositas* turns the long gaze into a quick glance before moving to the next thing.

50. Wood, "Prime Time."

51. Borgmann, *Technology and the Character of Contemporary Life*, 204.

Conclusion: *Studiositas* and the Church Industrial Complex

I have argued that the Fresh Expressions paradigm is part and parcel of a technocratic regime in which pastors become modern character types (managers, entrepreneurs, innovators) who impose form on the church extrinsically. I provided a genealogical account of this paradigm, proposing that the managerial church is the spawn of nominalism, which made conceivable an account of the church that lacks intrinsic form, rendering it a corpse that's vulnerable to managerial manipulation, allowing pastors to mold and shape it according to the whims of consumer preference—an essential component of the Church Industrial Complex. In the case of Fresh Expressions, those consumer preferences are manifested in the formation of networks, which then constitute the church *qua* church. The church, then, is not known by virtue of its formal and final cause (Jesus Christ); rather, it is known by means of control—a knowing-by-making that characterizes a technological epistemology. I have argued that this mode of knowing characterizes *curiositas* in two ways: it dominates the object of knowledge (the church) as a point of aggression, and it cultivates a "roaming unrest of the spirit" that comes with novel (or "fresh") innovation, which repeats itself infinitely as consumer preferences shift over time. This eternal cycle of creative destruction—the perpetual curation of the church's identity—makes the church feel rootless, depressed, and fatigued of becoming itself. Finally, I made the modest proposal that pastors recover a eucharistic theology that sees the Supper as a focal practice, which provides the balm of lingering for a rootless church. As a focal community, the church is a stable *place*, not a transient network.

Drawing on the work of Albert Borgmann, Brent Waters makes the compelling claim that focal communities are "leisurely receptive rather than frenetically creative."[52] This contrast neatly maps onto the theological distinction between *studiositas* and *curiositas*. As we have now seen, *curiositas* seeks "nothing other than the ownership of new knowledge."[53] In our modern age, this intellectual vice manifests itself as a technological knowing-by-making, a frenetic creativity that requires efficient methods to achieve desired ends: $M + P = M_2$. More members, more programs, more growth, more production: these are the hallmarks of a church that operates according to the governing rationality of neoliberalism, which is the main ingredient of the Church Industrial Complex. In order to maximize outputs and achieve these ends, the church has to become a managed body that reinvents itself by curating its identity at the frenetic pace of the spiritual

---

52. Waters, *Christian Moral Theology in the Emerging Technoculture*, 220.
53. Griffiths, "Vice of Curiosity," 50.

marketplace. As I have argued, this frenetic creativity is the source of the church's depression.

But *studiositas*, on the other hand, recognizes that all knowledge is already known to God. Novelty, therefore, is an illusion because there is no such thing as new knowledge, no knowledge that is not already divinely apprehended. Thus, whereas *curiositas* clutches at knowledge as a technological achievement, *studiositas* receives knowledge as a divine gift.[54] It attends deeply to the givenness of things, a givenness that is intensified around the hearth and table, where focal practices tune our senses to the gift of being. In this way, the focal practice of the Eucharist creates an ecosystem—a culture of the table—wherein our intellectual appetites can be properly formed in a way that disabuses us of mathetic catechesis, which cultivates a hunger for novel innovation and overlooks what is "already there"—the gifts of God in Jesus Christ. Indeed, just as the hearth intensifies our focus and gives us the ability to *see* what is already there, the Lord's table cultivates a studious disposition whereby the stillness of leisure—or the virtue of lingering—opens the eyes of the church, just as it did long ago for the blind beggar in Jericho.

Bibliography

Aquinas, Thomas. *Summa Theologiae*. Translated by the Fathers of the English Dominican Province. London: Burns, Oates and Washbourne, 1920–22.

Arendt, Hannah. *The Human Condition*. 2nd ed. Chicago: The University of Chicago Press, 1998.

Barth, Karl. *Church Dogmatics: The Doctrine of the Word of God, Part 2*, edited by Thomas F. Torrance and Geoffrey W. Bromiley. Edinburgh: T. & T. Clark, 1957.

Bender, Kimlyn J. *Karl Barth's Christological Ecclesiology*. Eugene, OR: Cascade, 2013.

Borgmann, Albert. *Technology and the Character of Contemporary Life*. Chicago: University of Chicago Press, 1984.

Brown, Wendy. *Undoing the Demos: Neoliberalism's Stealth Revolution*. New York: Zone, 2017.

Church of England, Mission and Public Affairs Council. "Mission-Shaped Church." London: Church House, 2003.

Douglas, Mary. *Natural Symbols: Explorations in Cosmology*. New York: Routledge, 2003.

Ehrenberg, Alain. *The Weariness of the Self: Diagnosing the History of Depression in the Contemporary Age*. Montreal: McGill-Queen's University Press, 2016.

Francis. *Laudato Si'*. Encyclical Letter of the Holy Father on the Care for Our Common Home. May 24, 2015. https://www.vatican.va/content/francesco/en/encyclicals/documents/papa-francesco_20150524_enciclica-laudato-si.html.

Gary, Kevin Hood. *Why Boredom Matters: Education, Leisure, and the Quest for a Meaningful Life*. New York: Cambridge University Press, 2022.

---

54. Griffiths, *Intellectual Appetite*, 21–22.

Griffiths, Paul. *Intellectual Appetite: A Theological Grammar*. Washington, DC: The Catholic University of America Press, 2009.

———. "The Vice of Curiosity." *Pro Ecclesia* 15 (2006) 47–63.

Han, Byung-Chul. *The Disappearance of Rituals: A Topology of the Present*. Medford, MA: Polity, 2020.

———. *The Scent of Time: A Philosophical Essay on the Art of Lingering*. Medford, MA: Polity, 2017.

Hanby, Michael. "Questioning the Science and Religion Question." In *After Science and Religion: Fresh Perspectives from Philosophy and Theology*, edited by Peter Harrison and John Milbank, 155–70. Cambridge: Cambridge University Press, 2022.

Harrison, Peter. "Curiosity, Forbidden Knowledge, and the Reformation of Natural Philosophy in Early Modern England." *Isis* 92 (2001) 265–90.

Holmes, Christopher R. J. "The Church and the Presence of Christ: Defending Actualist Ecclesiology." *Pro Ecclesia* 21 (2012) 269.

Illich, Ivan. *Tools for Conviviality*. San Francisco: Harper & Row, 1973.

Kallenberg, Brad J. "The Master Argument of MacIntyre's *After Virtue*." In *Virtues and Practices in the Christian Tradition*, edited by Nancey Murphy et al., 7–29. Harrisburg, PA: Trinity International, 1997.

MacIntyre, Alasdair. *After Virtue: A Study in Moral Theory*. 3rd ed. South Bend, IN: University of Notre Dame Press, 2007.

Martin, Dale B. *The Corinthian Body*. New Haven, CT: Yale University Press, 1999.

Pieper, Josef. *Josef Pieper: An Anthology*. San Francisco: Ignatius, 1989.

Quash, Ben. *Abiding: The Archbishop of Canterbury's Lent Book 2013*. London: Bloomsbury, 2013.

Root, Andrew. *The Congregation in a Secular Age*. Grand Rapids: Baker Academic, 2021.

Rosa, Harmut. *The Uncontrollability of the World*. Medford, MA: Polity, 2020.

Shakespeare, Lyndon. *The Body of Christ in the Age of Management*. Eugene, OR: Wipf & Stock, 2016.

Taylor, Charles. *A Secular Age*. Cambridge, MA: Belknap, 2007.

Waters, Brent. *Christian Moral Theology in the Emerging Technoculture: From Posthuman Back to Human*. New York: Routledge, 2016.

Webster, John. *The Domain of the Word: Scripture and Theological Reason*. New York: T. & T. Clark, 2012.

Wood, David J. "Prime Time: Albert Borgmann on Taming Technology." *Christian Century*, April 23, 2003. https://www.christiancentury.org/article/2003-08/prime-time.

Chapter 8

Neoliberal Homesteading in the Life of Churches

CHRISTY M. NEWTON

The Church Industrial Complex distorts the work of deepening spirituality, serving others, and working for justice by focusing a church's collective energy and resources, instead, on the accumulation of wealth, power, and prestige. This chapter describes the blueprint of neoliberalism and how it uses colonizing, homesteading tools to build, develop, and collude with the Church Industrial Complex to service these priorities. It shows how neoliberalism has become so ingrained in the life and work of churches that it takes on a life of its own. In what I argue can be understood as spiritual "homesteading," neoliberalism stakes a claim on the thoughts, decisions, and meaning-making of individuals and groups. It takes up residence in—*it homesteads*—the life of churches, assuming ownership of the ways people behave and limiting their ability to imagine alternatives to its priorities and values. Yet, rather than being viewed as a corrupting influence, these neoliberal ideals are often accepted as inevitable and necessary, which ultimately reinforce the continuation and dominance of the Church Industrial Complex, leading church communities further away from inclusive ministries focused on "the least of these" and toward work focused on their own institutional survival and dominance. By describing responses and ramifications of neoliberal homesteading in the life of churches, this chapter asserts that focused spiritual awareness, intentional partnership-building, and determined community organization are required to counteract and resist the neoliberal mentality and the structures it works so hard to build in our lives.

The Blueprint of Neoliberalism

Neoliberalism is an economic philosophy that contributes to the Church Industrial Complex by distorting life-affirming theological and ethical commitments to the common good in favor of profit-centered behaviors and beliefs. The basic myth of neoliberalism is that ever-increasing consumption is the goal of life, and neoliberal policies work to eliminate anything that inhibits that goal. Neoliberalism emphasizes privatized, deregulated, individualized economic freedoms without the responsibilities of social accountability or social responsibility. It promotes market exchange as its own supreme ethic, advocates for markets to dictate major social and political decisions, reshapes government to support profit accumulation, backs greater freedoms for corporations, resists trade unions, and asserts that citizens should be given less, rather than more, social protections. Essentially, neoliberalism rewards, protects, and restores power to those who possess financial capital and punishes those without it. It functions as a form of economic Darwinism—ensuring the survival of the richest, even at the expense of the most vulnerable segments of the population. And it increases the allocation of freedom and power to the richest citizens, guaranteeing their continued dominance. Social inequality, therefore, is a structural consequence of neoliberalism's overall project.[1] Beyond prioritizing economic strength over the needs of individuals and communities, this belief system also requires a comprehensive process of commodifying relationships, convictions, values, and behaviors that determine every level of social life.

When neoliberalism stakes a claim, assumes ownership, and refuses to relinquish control over thoughts and beliefs, it successfully homesteads the lives of ordinary people. When this happens, critical questions, opposition, and resistance fall away, and individuals and communities begin to believe they have no power over it. The familiar refrain is TINA: There Is No Alternative.[2] This acquiescence allows neoliberalism to function freely as a largely unrecognized, unnamed, overpowering, invisible force that seems to be beyond anyone's control, and which consequently shapes individual desires and drives without challenge. Yet, no matter how strongly it manipulates beliefs and behaviors, when it is named and identified, it carries neutral (if not positive) connotations. Despite the apathy and denial that accompany it, which often result in complicity with everyday forms of injustice and violence, it is often understood as a form of progress and a source of opportunity since it contributes to the wealth accumulation of an elite few.

---

1. Harvey, *Brief History of Neoliberalism*, 3–19.
2. Harvey, *Brief History of Neoliberalism*, 39–63.

When people begin to believe there is no alternative, and subsequently are unable to envision an alternative, little opposition can come.

The Tools of Homesteading

Homesteading is a powerful metaphor for the way neoliberalism stakes claims in the lives of people and churches. Historically, homesteading expanded private land ownership to (primarily white) pioneers and settlers under President Abraham Lincoln's 1862 Homestead Act, which liberalized the Preemption Act of 1841. Under the auspices of "improving the land," Native American communities were dispossessed of their homes, and their land was granted to individuals who squatted on the land and claimed it through a biased legal process. The Homestead Act required potential landowners to follow three steps: File an application for ownership of "government land," improve the land by cultivating it in some way, and file for the land deed. Homesteading was legal practice until 1976, except in Alaska, where it lasted until 1986. Homesteading was a primary way some people were able to embody the ideological doctrine of Manifest Destiny, the belief, first coined in 1845, that the United States was destined by God to expand its dominion across the entire North American continent, spreading democracy and capitalism with it and removing Native Americans and any other "obstacles" in its way.

Today, neoliberalism not only homesteads people's lives economically, politically, culturally, and geographically but also homesteads the life and ministry of churches by setting up shop in the ways people think, decide, make meaning, and relate to others. Then and now, homesteading is a form of colonization. By staking its claim and homesteading people's theological beliefs and lived spiritualities, neoliberalism colonizes the ways people understand ministry, property, service, outreach, and consumption, and it thereby contributes to the Church Industrial Complex. It prioritizes numeric size and growth of congregations over the quality of relationships and the felt sense of belonging. It prioritizes the amount and visibility of program output over deep engagement with community needs. It prioritizes the level of financial income and growth of investments and savings over the generation of justice and care for the most vulnerable. And it points toward prioritizing the needs and wishes of those who financially contribute more over and above others who contribute less. Relationships with other human beings and the rest of creation are important only as far as they serve these priorities. This instrumentalization of relationships can cause people to become ever more apathetic and unaffected by the profound needs and tragedies both around the corner and around the world.³ The extent to which people feel indifferent and resign their abilities to think critically and act compassionately—even when faced with suffering and injustice—signals the extent to which neoliberal homesteading has ensconced the Church Industrial Complex and succeeded in using economics to normalize idolatrous beliefs and behaviors that harm vulnerable human populations while empowering the interests of elite individuals.

Constructing the Neoliberal Homestead

The consumerism promoted by neoliberal ideals often takes the form of an individualistic pursuit of life, liberty, and property, shaped by cultural producers who work to create desire and demands in consumers.⁴ Neoliberalism, however, refers not only to individuals' positive rights to possess life, liberty, and property; equally important—and equally devastating—it advocates for the *negative counterparts* of those rights, which obligates no one to take the life, liberty, property, freedoms, happiness, needs, desires, or concerns of others into account when making their own consumer, or producer, decisions. Consequently, each individual and congregation has the right to pursue their own self-interest, regardless of the ways it might affect the needs and realities of anyone else. In other words, the economy is not put to work to support human beings; instead, human beings are put to work to support the economy. As a result, human agency diminishes and the greatest human costs—including safety risks, health risks, environmental risks, loss of rights and privileges—must be endured, primarily by the most vulnerable human populations.⁵ Deviating from the views of "the father of modern economics," Adam Smith, who understood economics to be a branch of ethics concerned deeply about the ways economic decisions affect people's actual lives, neoliberalism grants individuals and congregations the *right*, perhaps even obligation, to be selfish. Neoliberalism's understanding of freedom includes the freedom to exploit others, to make inordinate gains without commensurable service to the community, to keep technological inventions from being used for the public benefit, and to profit from public calamities secretly engineered for private advantage.⁶ The relational

---

3. Delgado, *Shaking the Gates of Hell*, 93–117.

4. Drawing on John Locke's 1689 *Second Treatise of Government*, Thomas Jefferson ironically equates property to the pursuit of happiness in the US Constitution.

5. Delgado, *Shaking the Gates of Hell*, 70–77.

6. Harvey, *Brief History of Neoliberalism*, 34–36; Sen, *Ethics and Economics*, 1–3; Polanyi, *Great Transformation*, 257–68.

foundations of social responsibility and social accountability are effectively eroded by these beliefs. In this way, neoliberalism's insistence upon negative rights and its myopic understandings of freedom have the potential to stunt and shutter the generosity, outreach, cooperation, and mission of churches.

The problem with this kind of thinking is not only the development of skewed values that incline people to build up their own comfort at the expense of other people's basic well-being. The problem is actually much larger: By structuring the economy and society according to neoliberalism, people become largely detached from the process of material production, the things they consume, the ways economic decisions are made, and the needs and concerns of other people.[7] Quite plainly, neoliberal values and beliefs train people to isolate themselves and to sever vital connections from the people and things that surround them that can potentially contribute significant meaning to their lives. This abstraction radically decreases awareness and engagement with the wider community. It obscures the environmental and human costs of people's actions, including their production and consumption, while also insulating people from the consequences of their beliefs and behaviors and limiting the transformative possibilities of relationships. Theologian John Cobb argues that "to organize the whole world to serve ends that degrade life, human and natural, is strictly and literally insane," and yet, the world's most powerful governments collude with corporate wealth and manipulate global institutions to do just that.[8] We can never be fully human if we live in isolation, oblivious to the realities and needs of others around us. Relationships are necessary for human survival, but neoliberal homesteading strips us of these life-giving relationships, isolates us from others, and produces feelings of scarcity and desperation. Neoliberalism is structured to serve its own self-interest and leaves many people, and entire communities, floundering in its wake.

Residing in the Neoliberal Homestead

Congregations can succumb to the Church Industrial Complex, or they can resist it. Below, I will present brief descriptions of two, vastly different, churches I know well, along with a discussion of the implications and possibilities that arises from those descriptions. The first has been staked and claimed by neoliberal ideology.

The church stands in grand fashion with its imposing columns and ornate façade. Carefully swept steps lead up to a polished door handle and a

---

7. Cavanaugh, *Being Consumed*, 36–37.
8. Cobb, *Resistance*, xi–xii.

locked door. A prominent sign on the door indicates that a well-known security company alarms the door. The church has methodically bought all the surrounding property for parking and possible expansion. Most of the people who attend the church drive in from outside the community, which is experiencing a great deal of transition. No one from within the church knows its neighbors, who are highly transient, but they are considering hiring someone to do outreach to the people who live close by—possibly asking them to contribute to the church's building fund. Occasionally, someone parks in one of the church's lots overnight and sleeps in their car. This is troubling to some people in the church, and they have hired an overnight security guard to keep things like that from happening. . . .

As this depiction shows, churches are certainly not immune from neoliberal homesteading. Christian communities organize their churches to meet definite and distinct human needs, and churches rise to prominence based on how well they meet those needs. However, like any institution, without careful and intentional attention to its mission, churches can take on lives of their own, seemingly beyond the control of the people they are created and intended to serve. Neoliberal thinking contributes to these happenings. Neoliberal ideals can be casually introduced and then effortlessly enforced, almost without conscious thought. They can then direct the church along, offering what seems like common sense goals and decisions, until after some time, church members realize it has stopped serving the needs of the community altogether and has accumulated a huge savings account with no plans to spend it. They start accumulating money and resources just for the sake of accumulating them. Neoliberalism shifts the thinking of church members enough to enable situations like this to happen, and then it can be extremely difficult for them to reverse course.

When a church shifts its focus away from the pressing needs present in its community, the deep spiritual longings of its members, and the relationships that are so greatly needed and instead moves toward increasing its own size and the sources of its own income and power, the church effectively has been homesteaded by neoliberalism. The genuine needs of the community, at that point, have become distorted, and the church's vision has grown cloudy. When a church then acts and makes decisions based upon this distortion—primarily prioritizing its own growth and development over community needs and spiritual growth—it reinforces this neoliberal ideology, which is not only deeply formative; it actually begins to stand in for the church's operative theology, communicating and reflecting understandings of what is ultimately important and what holds sacred significance within that church community. The boundaries between sacred and secular blur, and neoliberalism not only provides the central *context* for the church's theology but also begins to shape the theological *content* and priorities of the church: what gives life, what abundance looks like, how to work for the kin-dom of God, what offers salvation, how one should relate to others, and why the institution should be preserved over everything else. In neoliberalism, consumption, accumulation, prestige, growth, and affluence are primary concerns and form the touchstones of moral agency. Everything and everyone else are afterthoughts, if they are thought of at all. Freedom, development, and the common good in neoliberalism are defined exclusively through the lens of wealth and power accumulation.[9] As a basis for theology, of course, wealth and power accumulation will always distort the ways we see and understand those in need. This focus leaves little room for empathy, altruism, and concern for others. It squeezes all compassion out.

Pastor and activist Sharon Delgado claims that the rules of neoliberalism "are not designed to provide a just distribution of the world's goods, but to protect and multiply wealth. They are not designed to preserve the earth, but to turn its gifts, such as forests and water, into money. They are not designed to improve the lives of the majority of human beings, but to bring financial benefits to the few."[10] When neoliberalism homesteads a church, church members are likely to capitalize on these opportunities and resources with little thought for the consequences. Neoliberalism distorts the deeply relational qualities of human beings by transforming individuals into opportunistic consumers programmed to protect the profits and financial well-being of the institutions they are a part of, including churches. These congregant-consumers are supplied with a steady stream of taken-for-granted, common sense assumptions about what they need to live meaningful lives as well as the accepted norms and routines that reinforce decisions and behaviors. These people wonder "what's in it for me?!" Neoliberal homesteading distorts theological understandings of liberation, abundance, and grace by equating freedom with the means to consume, accumulate, discard, and consume some more. This cycle, no matter how it might be framed theologically, depends primarily on convincing people that they never have enough; they never do enough; they never are enough. Delgado notes, ironically, "To be free and happy, our church must have . . . a new gym, more property, bigger signs." Ironically, it is as if to be free and happy, churches feel like they must have a new gym, more property, bigger signs. This would make us look better, stronger, more desirable, and ultimately able to accumulate even more. Neoliberal homesteading also distorts

9. Harvey, *Brief History of Neoliberalism*, 34–35.
10. Delgado, *Shaking the Gates of Hell*, 168.

the connection between beliefs and behaviors. Money is spent to communicate identity, to demonstrate prominence, to express values, to contend for social status, to vie for power, and to assert intangible values and ideals, such as success, righteousness, sophistication. These actions all reinforce the Church Industrial Complex. And no matter what the rationale, consumption is always still consumption; it takes much and yields little lasting spiritual value.

Because of the way neoliberalism trains individuals and communities, consumers today buy, own, and throw away more stuff than at any other time in history, but they know less about the origins and implications of that stuff, largely because the origins and implications are intentionally opaque. Many people simply do not care about where that chicken breast on their salad came from, or those strawberries, or those roses. Others are so inundated with things that they cannot feasibly muster the mental energy it would take even to consider where and how all their stuff originated, much less how it made its way to them. They consume what producers supply. Prepared foods, ready-made clothes, factory-made furniture, and paper towels are taken for granted. Not only do people no longer make their own clothes; they have no idea who does. Vincent Miller, professor of culture and theology, describes how "commodities appear on the scene, as if descended from heaven, cloaked in an aura of self-evident value, saying nothing about how, where, and by whom they were produced."[11] All of these things are thoroughly abstracted, isolated, and removed from their vital connections: circumstances and relationships surrounding production, distribution, and consumption. Thus, consumers use toothpaste that materializes at the store, wear shoes made by no one, turn on heat that originates from a dial on the wall, and believe watermelons grow year-round. But these abstracted practices have lasting theological significance. They significantly form church consumers' identities, dispositions, beliefs, and values—all while they make dinner, wear clothes, use computers, drive cars, go to work, and watch YouTube.

Consumers, then, take those neoliberal dispositions to church, and just like they do not have the capacity to consider where their paper towels come from, they do not question how their money is invested—as long as it yields a healthy return. When neoliberalism homesteads church life, church members begin to believe that their real worth and purpose are reflected in their property values, the amount of their income, the depth of their endowment, and the size of their building. Bigger is better, and true freedom is the ability to consume in greater quantities, no matter what the actual

---

11. Miller, *Consuming Religion*, 3.

cost. When neoliberalism homesteads church life, each singular church starts believing that they are alone in ministry and must do all their work independently and separately from others. Partnerships indicate possible areas of weakness; true strength is demonstrated in what one can accomplish alone. When neoliberalism homesteads church life, the hard work of mission and ministry can be outsourced, rather than accomplished by engaging church members in that work. The church no longer depends on the time, commitment, and voluntary, hands-on work of its church members. There is a belief that we can "pay people to do church for us (which is why megachurches are on a meteoric rise and small churches are dying)."[12] With enough money, every aspect of church life can be outsourced—even if those who are hired tend to be paid poorly and precariously. What is lost when this happens, however, is spending time in relationship, building up and depending upon church members to do ministry together for the common good, the kin-dom of God, and the good news that each person and all of creation is worthy of love and belongs to God.

Neoliberal homesteading prioritizes a church's money, power, and size. It perpetuates and encourages cycles of desensitizing consumption disconnected from human experience, genuine community needs, and life-giving sources of connectedness, meaning, and value. And although neoliberalism insidiously homesteads many aspects of church and society, by unmasking its tendencies and anchoring to Christian practices of living justly, the church has the power to resist and withstand its force. By intentionally resisting neoliberalism's focus on wealth accumulation and its maintenance of dehumanizing power relationships, the church can focus on truly life-giving work: expanding God's abundant welcome to others, creating places of belonging for diverse people, deepening relationships and spirituality, and serving those in need both within and outside the church community. Focusing attention on these spiritual touchstones has the capacity to counteract and transform the alienating, distorted, and profit-driven priorities of neoliberalism; it may also allow new possibilities of thriving and flourishing to emerge. Breaking free from the confines of neoliberal ideology makes room for church communities to build partnerships, develop crucial awareness of the sacred in everyday life, and identify the distinct places where hope and grace crystallize. These are the places where people most desire to hang their hearts. These are the places where people most desire to belong.

---

12. Florer-Bixler, "Capitalism Is Killing the Small Church," para. 13.

Resisting the Neoliberal Homestead

The second church I invite us to consider is quite different than the first. It demonstrates everyday ways it is possible to resist neoliberalism and the Church Industrial Complex.

The church has invested time, labor, and resources in the community garden that wraps all the way around the church building, utilizing all its extra outdoor space to grow fresh food for the local food bank. It also has a Free Little Pantry right outside the church doors with a sign that reads "Take what you need. Leave what you can." in both English and Spanish. In this cabinet, people are invited to share canned goods, toiletries, and other essential items with neighbors who are in need. The congregation also invests considerable time advocating for social change and a larger safety net to support people at risk of falling through the cracks. A giant banner above the church entrance reads "You are welcome here." Other bulletin boards share that the church is an Open and Affirming Congregation—embracing all people regardless of sexual orientation, gender identity, education, income, or ability level—and shares communion every week where ALL are welcome. There is no designated parking lot or fancy architecture, but members of the church are present every week helping people in and out of cars, opening doors, and welcoming anyone who comes by . . . .

A church does not need to have a large membership to be significant or to do important work. Bigger is not necessarily better. And certainly, no church needs to do ministry alone. The strongest church movements today are often coalitions of small churches and interfaith groups banding together, organizing their communities, and addressing community needs. One example of these types of coalitions includes the Industrial Areas Foundation (IAF) community organizing efforts in local communities in the United States.[13] These partnerships demonstrate great strength, resilience, and power—not weakness. Individual church members are frequently eager to join in and participate in work that is meaningful and connects them

---

13. The Industrial Areas Foundation (IAF) was founded in 1940 and is currently the largest and longest-standing network of local faith and community-based organizations in the United States. It partners with local interfaith religious congregations and civic organizations to build broad-based organizing projects that cross lines that traditionally divide communities and work toward addressing pressing community needs: "The measure of IAF's success is the extent to which its organizations contribute to human flourishing in communities where human development is often devalued and human dignity trampled. These successes, when they occur, take the form of imaginative responses to seemingly intractable problems, new relationships overcoming racial, religious and socioeconomic divisions and immediate, concrete victories that change communities for the better and inspire hope in the future." https://www.industrialareasfoundation.org.

with others in authentic, potentially life-changing ways. These efforts demonstrate that there is no need to outsource all the ministry a church does. Professionalizing every component of a church's ministry does not necessarily demonstrate better quality; instead, it might genuinely disenfranchise church members who would be willing to step into leadership but who are overlooked and not invited (or trusted?) to participate in the church's ministry. An important exception, however, is the justice issue of compensating women and other marginalized groups who, too often throughout history, have been unpaid and unrecognized for their work in ministry. Their significant contributions have frequently been taken for granted rather than acknowledged and celebrated as ways to widen the circle of leadership and increase engagement in the church's ministry.

Members of church communities, after all, are never completely passive consumers. Even people who have been greatly influenced by neoliberal ideology have the ability and agency to express alternatives to ideas and actions that they have often taken for granted. No part of life is on an inevitable course; there are always ways to challenge the status quo, to confront oppressive structures, to expand opportunities, to invest in new ways for diverse communities to thrive, to separate church culture from neoliberal culture, and to distinguish the true value of spirituality from its calculable economic value. And all this work is necessary. It is deeply spiritual work with great social possibilities and ramifications. Only hegemony desires to remain silent and still. Neoliberalism would greedily conscript the church and the entirety of Christianity as capitalist commodities and use them to further its own interests. However, aware of the damage caused by unrestrained and deregulated capitalism and committed to the vast possibilities of human connectedness and meaningful community, people demonstrate the capacities to rise and resist and counteract this neoliberal homesteading in the lives of individuals and churches. For example, from 2020 to 2023, Common Ground, a California IAF community organizing effort in Solano County, which includes various unions and interfaith groups, successfully worked to pass an eviction moratorium that provided a pathway for tenants to pay back rent gradually without the threat of eviction. Additionally, the organization successfully advocated for significant rental assistance and mobilized a massive volunteer effort to distribute the funds. People of faith with an intentional focus on the church's mission to love and serve "the least of these" challenged the inertia of TINA (There Is No Alternative). They understood that the separation and isolation demanded by neoliberalism has diminished the great possibilities of human relationships and human communities, and they insisted on something different.

Beyond Neoliberalism and the Church Industrial Complex

Neoliberalism reduces vulnerability to a liability, as a weakness to be exploited. But this is never truly the case. The church exists to offer an alternative. The church exists to embrace the most vulnerable, weak, and broken. It exists to provide a refuge and place of welcome and belonging for any and all. It exists to shine a beacon of hospitality and justice for all people in a world that seems to exist only for the rich and powerful. To do this, the church must confront the idolatries of neoliberalism, subvert the seemingly inescapable forces that colonize collective consciousness and behavior, lift the veil from dehumanizing power structures, empower the moral-spiritual agency of diverse communities, cultivate socially just and ecologically sustainable economic life,[14] convert economic relations to support the needs of all people, and live in life-giving relationships with all of God's creation. These spiritual practices of just living counteract the temptations of neoliberalism and the Church Industrial Complex. They challenge the ways neoliberalism sets up residence in our beliefs and behaviors and point us toward other, more life-giving and more life-affirming possibilities. And although confronting and dismantling the reified structures of neoliberalism may be difficult, it is necessary work.

Evidence of this work can be found in places where individuals and churches build partnerships to resist the colonizing force of strictly self-interested, profit-driven, neoliberal behavior and claim an alternative. It can be experienced when people join their individual efforts, organizing coalitions of churches and other community members, working together to create spaces of safety and hospitality, fighting for just laws that protect the disenfranchised, tending community gardens, and using their resources to provide food, housing, school supplies, and other needs to members of their communities. It can be witnessed when the social safety net is made strong and capable of supporting whatever, whenever, and wherever is necessary. As difficult and counter-cultural as this work may be, it is necessary work if the church is to be a place of liberation, abundance, and grace for all, including "the least of these." Living and serving in ways contrary to neoliberalism points us toward the hope of sharing in meaningful community where true value does not lie in stockpiles of power-fortified wealth but in the profound riches of deep connectedness.

---

14. Moe-Lobeda, *Healing a Broken World*, 172.

Bibliography

Cavanaugh, William T. *Being Consumed: Economics and Christian Desire*. Grand Rapids: Eerdmans, 2008.

Cobb, John B., Jr., ed. *Resistance: The New Role of Progressive Christians, Progressive Christians Uniting*. Louisville, KY: Westminster John Knox, 2008.

Delgado, Sharon. *Shaking the Gates of Hell: Faith-Led Resistance to Corporate Globalization*. 2nd ed. Minneapolis: Fortress, 2020.

Florer-Bixler, Melissa. "Capitalism Is Killing the Small Church." *Faith and Leadership*, April 30, 2019. https://faithandleadership.com/melissa-florer-bixler-capitalism-killing-the-small-church.

Harvey, David. *A Brief History of Neoliberalism*. New York: Oxford University Press, 2005.

Miller, Vincent J. *Consuming Religion: Christian Faith and Practice in a Consumer Culture*. New York: Continuum, 2003.

Moe-Lobeda, Cynthia D. *Healing a Broken World: Globalization and God*. Minneapolis: Fortress, 2002.

Polanyi, Karl. *The Great Transformation: The Political and Economic Origins of Our Time*. Boston: Beacon Press, 2001.

Sen, Amartya. *On Ethics and Economics*. The Royer Lectures, edited by John M. Letiche. Cambridge, MA: Blackwell, 1988.

Chapter 9

COVID-19 Pandemic, Technology, and the Church Industrial Complex

KELLY COLWELL

The COVID-19 pandemic both raised and challenged important identity markers for churches around the world, as restrictions on physical gathering caused churches to rethink and redefine what it means to gather for worship. This chapter will draw on qualitative research conducted for my 2022 dissertation, which focused on the experience of congregations in the United Church of Christ located in the San Francisco Bay Area during the first few months of the COVID-19 pandemic. This research incorporates twenty-one semi-structured interviews with pastors and church leaders between April 15 and July 5, 2020, which focused on their experiences of moving worship online and specifically what they learned about their churches' senses of identity and mission through that experience. Those interviews illuminated a complex and challenging season of rapid change, much of which intersected with various forms of technology, both those created for churches and those repurposed from other main roles. I will argue in this chapter that the pandemic both revealed and intensified the ways that technology reinforces the Church Industrial Complex.

Although at the time of writing (winter 2023), the experience of the early pandemic still feels recent, I will provide an overview of events relevant to the churches in my study population to provide context for future readers who need a reminder. In early 2020, news began to arrive in the United States about a novel coronavirus wreaking havoc in China. By January 2, 2020, the World Health Organization had mobilized incident management teams to

Wuhan, China.[1] On January 20, 2020, the first laboratory-confirmed case of COVID-19 was confirmed in the United States with a sample taken from an American recently returned from China. By the end of January, Wuhan was under a strict lockdown, and one case had been identified in California.

Churches remember moving quickly from praying for Wuhan to praying for the world to praying for the safety and health of their own members,[2] the anxiety moving closer and closer to home. Over the course of the month of February, case numbers increased in the United States, and the first death from COVID-19 in the United States was reported on February 29, 2020, of a man in his fifties. Late February also found the Bay Area watching the spectacle of the Diamond Princess cruise ship sitting off the Port of Oakland under forced quarantine. The passengers, many of whom would test positive for COVID-19, were eventually evacuated to Travis Air Force Base to finish their quarantine before being allowed to return home on March 2. Most of the Bay Area counties had declared a State of Emergency by the end of February.

On March 6, a Sunday, several Bay Area counties recommended postponing or cancelling mass events, and San Francisco recommended that people over sixty years of age avoid public outings. Churches in the Bay Area certainly took note of this: One church in my study reported the volunteers "dropping off the Coffee Hour snacks but unwilling to stay for the service, for their safety."[3] Mass gatherings of one thousand people or more were banned on March 10 in most Bay Area counties. By March 12, San Francisco Unified School District announced a three-week school closure, and sports seasons were suspended for hockey, soccer, basketball, and baseball. On March 15, California's Governor Gavin Newsom ordered bars, nightclubs, wineries, and brewpubs to close, but allowed restaurants to stay open at limited capacity. And finally, on March 16, six Bay Area counties issued a shelter-in-place order, fully requiring people to stay at home outside of essential activities.

For the churches in my study, this meant that gathering in person for worship would not be allowed for at least two weeks. Many churches experienced this as a profound challenge to their identity and mission—who are we if we cannot gather in our sanctuary for worship? I will discuss details of their response below, but by way of introduction, it is important to highlight what a profound rupture the experience of the pandemic was on church

---

1. This material and following details of dates and timelines are sourced from a comprehensive local news timeline of the pandemic. See Eby, "Coronavirus Timeline."
2. Subject 5, interview by author, Berkeley, CA, via Zoom, May 15, 2020.
3. Subject 5, interview by author, Berkeley, CA, via Zoom, May 15, 2020.

practices. Almost nothing could be done the way it had been done just a few weeks before. It became vitally important to maintain a sense of connection and continuity with prior practices. Technology was a vital link to reduce isolation, share information and best practices for staying safe and healthy, learn about and address crucial needs in communities, and stay informed. However, the need to move so quickly to new and technologically facilitated ecclesial practices may have prevented a more thorough consideration of what technologies and practices were consonant with churches' values.

Industrial Complexes

As previous chapters have detailed, some aspects of church practices may be described using the framework of Industrial Complex, which originated in analyses of the United States military and the ways in which it tended to seek its own self-perpetuation, rather than responding solely to events outside influence. In other words, rather than a structure focused on the primary stated goals, the structure became its own goal, and decisions were (and are) made to sustain the structure. The American carceral system has also been described as an Industrial Complex, an entity that seeks to perpetuate itself—and even grow—by incarcerating more people. Payments from the government for each incarcerated person, payments from incarcerated people and their families for incidentals, phone calls, and other needs, and even the labor from incarcerated people themselves generates profit for the shareholders of private corporations running America's prisons. The prison system provides a clear example of an Industrial Complex whose profit motive stands directly against the stated goal of rehabilitating individuals and reducing crime. More crime and more law enforcement leads directly to more profit.

One important characteristic of Industrial Complexes is the proliferation of an ecosystem of adjacent businesses serving (and profiting from) the needs of the system. In the prison system, adjacent businesses include companies that supply phone connection and internet service to prisons, providers of cafeteria food and of concession items available, as well as suppliers of uniforms, cleaning supplies, building materials, and many other things. In that system, those companies influence, and are influenced by, their relationship with the prisons themselves as well as the government entities and private companies that directly administer them. But when we speak in this volume about the Church Industrial Complex, we must also examine the corresponding church-adjacent businesses that influence and are influenced by their relationship with churches. This chapter will focus specifically on technologies that are utilized by churches to explore the ways that those technologies (and the companies that sell them) are part of what shapes practices of churches, in some cases contrary to churches' own self-understandings of identity and mission.

Online Meeting Platforms

The first specific form of technology we will examine in this chapter is online meeting applications, the popularity of which grew rapidly in the last several years during the COVID-19 pandemic. In interviews I conducted in the first few months of the pandemic, most churches represented in my study[4] were not subscribers of any online meeting platform and had not conducted meetings online in any regular way. Three congregations were already conducting a few meetings over either Zoom, GoToMeeting, or Microsoft Teams prior to the shelter-in-place order in the San Francisco Bay Area, but while most of my interview subjects had used these technologies in other settings, most congregations were conducting meetings and holding worship services exclusively in person prior to the pandemic.

In the hectic early days of the pandemic, as changes in recommended gathering sizes and activities were coming fast and furious, churches (and especially their ministers and leaders) were scrambling to find new solutions to carry on practices[5] that would be unsafe or even illegal under pandemic restrictions. In the Bay Area, many of my interview subjects attended the same webinar with Rev. Bruce Reyes-Chow, a former moderator of the Presbyterian Church-USA and a proponent of churches' use of technology. Reyes-Chow's webinar recommended the use of Zoom for worship and

---

4. For my dissertation research, I interviewed thirty-four subjects representing twenty-five congregations in the United Church of Christ between May and July 2020. Study congregations were located across the San Francisco Bay Area to limit the amount of variation in COVID restrictions between different churches. Semi-structured interviews covered the congregations' experience moving online during the pandemic, decisions they had made about worship and meetings, congregational response, challenges, and new learning. I offer this material as an anecdote and an example and make no claims that the experiences of my interview subjects are generalizable beyond this denomination or this geographical area.

5. Practices here include all aspects of public in-person worship services, especially the ritual of Communion, but also including financial giving. Many churches were very concerned about a drop-off in giving, either because people would be suffering financial harm during the pandemic or because people would not have the ordinary opportunities to give during in-person worship services or some combination of the two. However, studies have since suggested that for most churches, giving did not decline significantly during the pandemic. See Eagle et al., "Financial Impacts of COVID-19 on United Methodist Churches in North Carolina."

meetings, and all of the interview subjects who attended the webinar adopted Zoom for those purposes after the webinar. To use Zoom for these activities, congregations were required to purchase one or more paid licenses, as the free version of Zoom did not allow for enough participants at once, nor did it allow for meetings longer than forty minutes.

This is not necessarily a criticism of those churches or of any organization that used Zoom or other paid online meeting platforms to continue meeting and working remotely during the pandemic. Indeed, it is hard to imagine how any church could have avoided moving services and meetings online when all of our in-person gathering options were constrained. However, acquiring those paid Zoom accounts (or in some cases, paid accounts with other providers of online video conferencing software) had a lasting impact on churches.[6] In follow-up research, all of the congregations in my study are still paying for accounts with those platforms three years later, and all of my interview subjects reported continuing to meet online for some or most of their meetings. There are significant benefits to this practice in some types of increased accessibility, especially to members with mobility or immune system disabilities as well as increased access for parents with kids at home. But in most cases, decisions were not made explicitly to benefit those people. Instead, meetings simply continued online because they were already online, carried by institutional momentum. Additionally, most of my interview subjects reported participating in more meetings per week than they had prior to the pandemic, perhaps because online meetings seem like less of a burden and are thus easier to justify.

Anecdotally, it seems to be the case that the actual content and structure of meetings and gatherings online are shaped by the tools offered by the specific platform used to facilitate them. Features such as breakout rooms, whiteboards, and a chat feature shaped and continue to shape the services and meetings that take place over Zoom or other online video conferencing platforms.[7] Again, this is not necessarily a criticism of any of these practices. I'm certain that our practices in the physical space of our churches are also shaped by what is possible in that space. But it is important to be conscious of the ways that the platform is shaping our practice so that churches are

---

6. Increased use during the pandemic had a major impact on the corporations offering online meeting platforms as well. Zoom's profits increased by over 300 percent during 2020 and, while the growth has leveled off, they have remained high rather than declining. See Richter, "Zoom's Post-Pandemic Growth Slows to a Crawl."

7. Little research has been published about this shaping effect specific to churches, but plenty of work has referenced the way that these platforms shaped education during the pandemic, much of which can be applied to churches as well. For example, see Tamura-Ho, "Zoom Affects"; or Simmons, "Teaching and Learning in Zoom Networking Environments."

able to evaluate their practices in light of their theological and ethical commitments.

Video Infrastructure

In my study, some congregations were already live streaming worship prior to the pandemic, but most were not. In the early days of the shelter-in-place order, any congregation that had not already been live streaming worked quickly to decide how to live stream worship. Most streamed to YouTube (owned by Google) or Facebook (owned by Meta), or chose to use a video conferencing platform like Zoom to have "meeting-style" worship rather than a live stream. For those using Zoom or similar products, the financial aspect of the decision has already been discussed above; for those using Facebook Live, YouTube, or another streaming platform, some churches paid for special access while others did not, relying on the ad-supported platform to distribute the video stream to those seeking it. Some congregations chose to use streaming distribution services like Streamyard, Wirecast, Boxcast, or OBS Studio to live stream the worship service simultaneously to multiple platforms. Of those example platforms, only OBS is free; the others require a license fee which ranges from an annual fee of $300 per year to $1,000 or more per year.

All of the churches in my study, however, made significant infrastructure purchases to support online worship. From microphones and cameras to tripods, ring lights, cables, and even furniture, worship leaders worked hard to communicate what they saw as the essence of worship through a screen. As some congregants joined online worship via smartphones, my study participants reported trying to communicate via symbols and space use that would be visible and understandable on those small screens, most especially by moving the leaders closer and closer to the cameras so they would seem personal and present for viewers. Leaders also reported feeling pressure to present an online service that seemed professional and well-produced, especially in light of how many skillfully produced streaming movies and shows people were watching in the early shelter-in-place phase of the pandemic.

Many of those initial changes made to communicate worship on screens remain in place even after the churches re-introduced in-person worship. In the Bay Area, one congregation in my study moved the pulpit to stand right behind the communion table for visual appeal on camera and has left it there even as the majority of the congregation has returned to in-person worship. Several of my interview subjects (of multiple genders) described new makeup routines they adopted to look more "camera-ready," routines they are continuing to this day because the cameras continue, even while worship has shifted to a hybrid mode.

The "adjacent businesses" in this section are a little less straightforward than in the section on online meeting platforms. The companies that supply material goods (microphones, cameras, etc.) are financially incentivized for their consumers (churches) to be happy with their products, but they also want to sell newer and better products periodically and to have their clients continue to purchase from them. Churches in my study described wondering if worship would be better, clearer, more compelling if the cameras were sharper, if there were more angles or changing images, if the microphones were more dynamic and the sound more expertly mixed into the live stream. Many congregations that went for live streamed worship instead of Zoom worship ended up streaming directly to Facebook Live, where the financial connection is a little different. Facebook is primarily ad-supported, so getting more viewers to pay attention to a video (like a worship service) means those viewers also pay attention to the ads that Facebook populates around the screen. YouTube is a similar story, although viewers can subscribe to a premium service that removes ads, and some churches opted to pay for a premium account in order to have better storage and linking options. It is worth noting the class implications that divide viewers who subscribe to premium service to avoid ads and those who watch the free version, which includes advertising.

Several of my interview subjects in the Bay Area reported conversations in their individual churches about whether or not streaming to Facebook implied a support of Facebook, its parent company Meta, and the founder/owner Mark Zuckerberg. "Obviously we don't want to be supporting all of that," the pastor of a congregation near Silicon Valley commented. "But it's where people are."[8] Streaming content to Facebook does generate advertising revenue for the company, so a congregation is functionally and financially supporting Facebook by streaming services there even if they are not directly paying the company for access to the platform. It is also worth noting at this point that several congregations in my study reported members of their communities joining Facebook or learning to use YouTube in order to participate in online worship, thus generating more ad revenue for those companies.[9]

---

8. Subject 4, interview by author, Berkeley, CA, via Zoom, May 8, 2020.

9. Social media companies saw record profits during the first two years of the COVID-19 pandemic, although the subsequent two years have seen some shrinking and challenges. See Duffy, "How Big Tech's Pandemic Bubble Burst."

Social Media Companies and "Reach"

One of the major themes that participants in my study brought up was new access to multiple metrics of a church's "reach." For most churches that had not been streaming services prior to the pandemic, the question of "metrics" went as far as counting the number of people present in worship each week, if that. A number of churches did not even track numbers of worshipers, or counted only a few times a year. Interview subjects in Bay Area UCC churches reported taking a kind of intuitive pulse of the congregation on Sundays, that the sanctuary would feel "warm" when people were happy and content with their church and that those intuitive checks were more important than numerical metrics. But online worship, whether live streamed or delivered via video conferencing, created access to multiple new metrics and simultaneously made it much more difficult for leaders to get intuitive feedback from worshipers. In lieu of that informal energy check, churches began to rely more on the kind of numbers that were newly available. They were able to count the number of total views of an online worship service, which corresponded only loosely to the number of in-person worshipers pre-pandemic (since some "views" represent whole households with multiple people, while others may have been streaming the service on two devices at once, counting as two "views"). But they were also able to distinguish between live views and post-stream views, to count the number of states or countries where viewers were located, to see how long each viewer stayed with the worship service on average, and to distinguish between views from "followers" who were connected via social media and others.

The availability of these metrics led some of the participants in my study to report seeking out viewers and/or members from farther afield. Many study participants described being reunited with former members who had moved away from their local area, in some cases decades ago, through online worship. "Maybe they're looking for familiarity because everything in the pandemic is so strange," one pastor speculated about former members joining online worship in an interview in June 2020.[10] I would hesitate to judge anyone harshly for seeking connection, familiarity, and comfort during those stressful early months of the pandemic. However, it represents a major shift for congregations in the UCC to intentionally seek to recruit members and participants who do not live in their local area rather than trying to help them connect to churches local to those members. Access to online worship flattened the distinctions of distance, which may have unintentionally caused a concentrating effect, further separating resource-rich congregations from resource-poor ones since congregations

---

10. Subject 10, interview by author, Berkeley, CA, via Zoom, May 22, 2020.

with the resources to invest in upgraded camera, sound, and editing technology, excellent streaming services, and advertising to put their online worship service in front of new potential members are in a position to attract more people, many of whom may choose to give money to the online church rather than another church in their locality.[11] In fact, in addition to those churches in my study that reported growing online participation from these former members and people at a distance, several congregations in my study lamented being on the losing end of this equation, as they saw some regular members slip away from their online services and toward others with more highly polished services, or toward churches they had been a part of in the past.

For some of the churches in my study, this shift represents a new vision of having a "global audience," as one participant described. "We're seeing people from Kenya, from Indonesia. It's amazing!"[12] But even the notion of having an "audience" is a significant and identity-challenging shift for congregations in the United Church of Christ. The history, theology, and organizational structure of this denomination all emphasize shared power and collective decision-making among a community of members who know and trust each other. Congregations in this denomination have members, participants, elected leaders, and pastors, but have not traditionally thought of themselves as having an audience.

The congregation I serve as co-senior minister, First Congregational Church of Berkeley, has wrestled with this question in significant ways over the past three years as we have received interest in membership from people who participate solely online. And while we seek to serve their needs through our online offerings, we have chosen to at least try to encourage those people to seek church community nearby when possible. We find deep value in being able to meet each other's physical needs at a local level by offering rides to appointments, bringing meals to people after surgery, showing up in person to each other's major life events, and working together on local issues that matter to us. Our vision of church is fundamentally localized and physical; while we recognize (and mourn) that some people have limited access to a church like ours in their local area, and while we

---

11. The COVID-19 pandemic seemed to have the effect of concentrating wealth in several sectors. In personal finance, the already-wealthy increased their wealth, and although in the short term some impoverished individuals found improved finances, the gap between rich and poor widened in the long term. See Kartashova and Zhou, "Wealth Inequality and Return Heterogeneity During the COVID-19 Pandemic." In the restaurant sector, researchers found that successful restaurants that already had infrastructure for online sales fared well, while smaller restaurants suffered, and many closed. See Madeira et al., "Impact of Pandemic Crisis on the Restaurant Business."

12. Subject 18, interview by author, Berkeley, CA via Zoom, June 5, 2020.

would never turn someone away who is choosing to participate in our online services at a distance, we do not actively look for members who are not local, and we do try to encourage people to find local communities of faith if at all possible.

However, we also recognize that for some people, the barriers to finding an in-person church are significant. We have LGBTQ+ participants who live in conservative or rural areas of the United States, where no local church would offer them a genuinely affirming welcome.[13] These people face a choice between participating online in the life of a church like ours, avoiding church altogether, or hiding aspects of their lives in order to participate in a local church. Likewise, some local members are participating primarily online for a few important reasons. One of those is the situation of people with disability and chronic illness: For some, attending services in person is still unsafe due to risk of encountering COVID or other illnesses, while for others, the energy expenditure to travel to church and participate in person is impossible. Still others are caring for an ill family member, managing family COVID risk with an immune-compromised member of the household, or even dealing with sensory disabilities that make attending in-person worship services difficult. My congregation has several members who prefer attending online because of hearing challenges. Their ability to turn up the volume on the online service and turn on the automatic captioning available through our Facebook Live stream offers a level of access that we simply cannot match in person. For those members and for many others, attending online services is an essential accessibility option. Maintaining a robust online presence allows us to continue to include and welcome those members who cannot attend in person.

Working through social media companies is, for many churches, the easiest and most straightforward way to offer online access to worship services. Whether most of the online participants are local to the church or live at a distance, whether the online service is accessed primarily by regular participants or serves as a "front door" through which visitors enter before coming to an in-person service, social media companies offer a level of familiarity that most churches find they cannot reject. However, it is essential that we are aware of the ways that offering our services through those platforms serves to produce revenue for those companies via advertising, which we have no control over. Whether the ads are placed directly into churches' videos (as on YouTube) or set alongside the streaming video (as

---

13. This is not universally the case, but researchers find that the availability of LGBTQ-affirming churches across the country is spotty, with many areas where a person would have to travel an hour or more to access an affirming religious community. See Woodell et al., "Reconciling LGB and Christian Identities in the Rural South."

on Facebook or Instagram), participants in online worship are "paying" for their access by receiving advertising messages.

Other Businesses

Most churches in my survey described an increasing reliance on other technology companies during the pandemic as well. One important category of these companies is database management software, used by churches to keep records of some combination of the following: members' and participants' contact information, attendance patterns, giving records, pastoral care information, event registration, volunteer management, and sometimes communications. Smaller churches often keep track of some or all of this through simple spreadsheets while mid-sized and larger churches tend to use specialized church management software such as Planning Center, FaithTeams, Elvanto, Breeze, Servant Keeper, Tithe.ly, and Realm (the software my own congregation uses). The pandemic seems to have made church leaders worry more about keeping records of members and their attendance online. Several congregations in my study upgraded to a higher level of service or changed church management software systems to something with more capacity for tracking and reporting. "We're not seeing folks in person, of course," one pastor shared in my study, "and we're afraid that we won't notice if someone slips away. So we have to keep track."[14]

It might be worth noting here that none of these software options are perfectly adaptable, so congregations that choose them may shape their behavior partly on what is offered in their software. Built-in language can end up shaping the way a congregation communicates about aspects of their collective practice since it is difficult in many software packages to customize the language used. For example, in my own congregation, we prefer to use the language of "sustaining giving" to describe people's annual and ongoing financial support, and we ask people to make "commitments" for the following year. But our software uses the language of "tithe" and "pledge," so we also have to use that language to communicate to the majority of the congregation that uses the online giving option. Likewise, software that uses language like "attendance" can have a subtle disempowering effect when people "check in" as present. We may wish to emphasize people's participation and leadership, rather than their mere presence, but the software comes with its own language that we have to adapt to.

Fundamentally, in the online space, leaders found it difficult to gauge and evaluate how people were responding to the service. In an in-person

14. Subject 13, interview by author, Berkeley, CA, via Zoom, May 29, 2020.

experience, leaders often express that things feel meaningful, that people are hushed or focused or engaged, that something energetic seemed to be happening. Online, this information was much harder to access for leaders, who found themselves relying more and more on metrics. Churches that kept numbers-only tracking pre-pandemic moved to attempting to track names instead; churches that kept names looked more closely at patterns. A greater focus on metrics is not necessarily a negative thing for churches, but it may be a problem if that attention displaces a focus on identity and mission, evaluating programs and worship services by how well they communicated a church's most cherished goals. "How many people came?" is only one question we can ask of our programs, but it is one that is easy to answer from a software perspective. "How faithful was that worship service?" is much harder to quantify and capture in software.

One final piece of technological business that churches engage with is the ecosystem of Christian music copyright conglomerates with whom churches report song usage in order to pay royalties and fees. The biggest of these are Church Copyright Licensing International, Christian Copyright Solutions, and OneLicense. Each company represents different rights, so churches often need a combination of licenses from these or other licensing organizations in order to use the music they wish in their worship services. These licensing companies offer annual licenses that allow you to use anything in their catalogs as well as event-specific licenses for one-time use. Churches are thus faced with a decision with regard to music: use only music old enough to be beyond copyright, use only music covered by one license or another, or use a variety of music, requiring multiple licenses with the financial implications this brings.

Music copyright conglomerates thus shape Christian worship practice by shaping the financial implications of music choices. The pandemic shift to online worship intensified the pressure of music copyright as well because online worship is "searchable" in a new way. There are two types of music copyright: original recording copyright, which applies to nearly all recorded and published music, and lyrics and music composition, which applies to any new performance of a copyrighted song.[15] During the pandemic, many churches found their streaming worship taken down from streaming platforms due to copyright claims from holders of original recording copyright, claiming the churches were playing pre-recorded music in their services. Copyright holders were using AI tools to trawl through any online video and automatically claim copyright violation every time the tool identified the use of copyright material.

15. "Navigating Church Streaming Copyright Issues."

My own congregation experienced this many times, despite our use of recordings only of our own live performances of music, nothing pre-recorded or published. We would get a notification, nearly always through Facebook, saying that our worship had been made unavailable due to copyright restriction. We would have an opportunity to dispute, which we always did, and inevitably the video would be returned to public view, since we were not actually infringing on an original recording copyright. Most of the time, the music we were challenged about was one of our church musicians playing a piece of classical music, too old to be covered under lyrics and music copyright anyway. But the cost of the staff time to dispute those claims and ensure our worship services remained online was not insignificant.

Because of this, my church, and I suspect others as well, began to consciously or unconsciously choose music we thought would be less likely to provoke a copyright dispute. We might choose original music or lesser-known pieces rather than better-known classical music pieces, regardless of whether they would suit the mood and movement of the worship service. And while the actual cost of paying to use or stream a piece of pre-recorded music might be minimal, the cost in time and effort often seemed too much for us. So when we would have a guest speaker who would request to use a piece of pre-recorded music in the service to illustrate a point in the sermon, we would decline. Pre-pandemic, although we were streaming our services, the main worship gathering was in person, so if the sound was removed from the online service for a short period, that might not shape our choices as much as it did during fully online worship. And while we have returned to in-person worship, the online component remains, as it does for many churches, and it retains a greater importance than it had before the pandemic. So our choices are still being shaped by those copyright conglomerates in a more substantial way than they had been before.

Conclusions

As this review has demonstrated, technology is an important part of the Church Industrial Complex, a part that was both revealed and strengthened by the experience of the COVID-19 pandemic. From the infrastructure needed to stream worship online to the software that runs donations, database management, and attendance gathering, from music copyright to online meeting platforms, the technology that is a part of the Church Industrial Complex functions as any other Church Industrial Complex machinery does: it shapes practices and decisions made by those in churches. As churches moved their worship, meetings, and other practices online, technology deeply influenced the specific ways in which churches were able to practice. It is not necessarily the case that any of those influences were problematic, but churches and their leaders must be aware of the influence that technology has on their practices in order to evaluate choices based on the churches' mission and identity rather than simply on efficacy and easy-to-access metrics. Our day-to-day work may depend on our use of these technologies, but our faithful practice depends on our critical analysis of the ways those tools are shaping and influencing us.

Bibliography

Colwell, Kelly. "Co-Creating Virtual Community: A Grounded Theology of Mission for San Francisco Bay Area Congregations in the United Church of Christ During the COVID-19 Pandemic." PhD diss., Graduate Theological Union, 2022.

Duffy, Clare. "How Big Tech's Pandemic Bubble Burst." *CNN Online*, January 22, 2023. https://www.cnn.com/2023/01/22/tech/big-tech-pandemic-hiring-layoffs/index.html.

Eagle, D. E., et al. "The Financial Impacts of COVID-19 on United Methodist Churches in North Carolina: A Qualitative Study of Pastors' Perspectives and Strategies." *Review of Religious Research* 64 (2022) 399–420.

Eby, Kate. "Coronavirus Timeline: Tracking Major Moments of COVID-19 Pandemic in San Francisco Bay Area." *ABC 7 News*, March 15, 2023. https://abc7news.com/timeline-of-coronavirus-us-coronvirus-bay-area-sf/6047519/.

Kartashova, Katya, and Xiaoqing Zhou. "Wealth Inequality and Return Heterogeneity During the COVID-19 Pandemic." FRB of Dallas Working Paper No. 2114, November 1, 2021. https://ssrn.com/abstract=3967802.

Madeira, Arlindo, et al. "The Impact of Pandemic Crisis on the Restaurant Business." *Sustainability* 13 (2021) 40.

"Navigating Church Streaming Copyright Issues." *Missional Marketing*, January 3, 2021. https://missionalmarketing.com/navigating-church-streaming-copyright-issues/.

Richter, Felix. "Zoom's Post-Pandemic Growth Slows to a Crawl." *Statista*, February 27, 2024. https://www.statista.com/chart/21906/zoom-revenue/.

Simmons, Marlon. "Teaching and Learning in Zoom Networking Environments." In *Handbook of Curriculum Theory, Research, and Practice*, 833–44. Cham: Springer International, 2024.

Tamura-Ho, Akio. "Zoom Affects: Discipline, Dislocation, and Digital Surveillance During COVID-19 Remote Learning." Senior Capstone Project, spring 2023. https://educationstudies.yale.edu/sites/default/files/files/Akio_Tamura-Ho_FinalCapstone.pdf.

Woodell, Brandi, et al. "Reconciling LGB and Christian Identities in the Rural South." *Social Sciences* 4 (2015) 859–78.

Chapter 10

Mentoring for Village Leadership
Refounding Seminary in the Ways of Kinship

JOHN NELSON WITH JIN S. KIM
AND LAURA NEWBY

Preface

Underground Seminary was founded in 2014 by the Rev. Dr. Jin S. Kim, senior pastor of Church of All Nations in Minneapolis, and a 1.5 generation Korean immigrant.[1] It was co-founded by Laura Newby and me (John Nelson), both of us Euro-Americans and long-time disciples of Pastor Jin. He had a vision for a different kind of seminary where Western assumptions did not inform the purpose or pedagogy.[2] He envisioned an environment

---

1. The term "1.5 generation" refers to immigrants who moved to a new country between the ages of six and twelve, and therefore have characteristics of both first generation- and second-generation immigrants, while not feeling fully at home in either culture. They have been shaped by the language and cultural traits of their country of origin in their childhood while they have also had to learn a new language and culture in the formative years of adolescence. As a result, they exist in a liminal space between cultures, which gives them a unique perspective on both.

2. By "Western" we mean a cultural genealogy that begins with the Athenian philosopher Plato (which includes Socrates and Aristotle and is spread by Aristotle's pupil, Alexander the Great), is inherited by the Roman Empire, and then spreads north in its wake to what is today Western Europe. Characteristics include dualism, abstraction, universalism, and supremacy, and it eventually leads to individualism, interiority, and rationalism. Through settler colonialism, the West spread to North America, Australia, New Zealand, and South Africa. Today much of the world is impacted by Westernization through neoliberal globalism. We are aware of criticisms of the use of this category,

that nurtured leaders capable of cultivating genuine kinship, even in the midst of suffering and adversity. For Pastor Jin, this type of leader in the US American context of individualism and religious professionalism, what this book calls the Church Industrial Complex, would have to be non-anxious, winsome, critically discerning, courageous, loving, resilient, and adaptable. In short, he wanted to form the type of differentiated leaders common in healthy communal cultures with an unbroken lineage of village life.

I knew nothing about village-style leadership before coming to Church of All Nations (CAN), and it has taken me years to really begin to understand it. Pastor Jin has opened me to an experience of life, spirit, and kinship that I didn't know was possible. He has also given me an entirely different framework for understanding history, theology, cosmology, culture, community, leadership, and the church. Everything written in this essay I learned from him.

Pastor Jin invited Laura and me to launch Underground Seminary with him in 2014. Co-founding the seminary served our own ongoing learning as much as it was an invitation to collaborate in this new ministry for others. Through Pastor Jin's teaching, Laura was the first to understand the brokenness of Western civilization as manifest in her body and to humbly ask for another path forward. Whereas my learning for years had remained more academic, she began with her own body, and therefore had a deeper and more comprehensive grasp of what we were doing. She advocated for an alternative to the Western university model of our seminaries—not just in content, but in pedagogy. She has always had a better sense of what our seminary students actually need. Our approach to leading Underground Seminary is completely collaborative, and Laura's voice, insights, and analysis are also woven throughout this chapter. For us, it doesn't matter who writes, but a trusted disciple often serves this role because Pastor Jin, as the mentor, is occupied leading a real community.

To interrogate the Church Industrial Complex, this essay will argue, is to interrogate the foundations of the Western tradition and its cultural manifestations. That critique includes seminary education, but it also includes the academic constraints for writing. I am still in recovery from this more individualistic style of writing, and this essay is worse for it where that style seeps in. I regret the passages where I may sound more like a detached, white anthropologist than a disciple. But where there is a sense

---

but believe it remains important to particularize the cultural categories that lead to whiteness and white supremacy. The West gaslights subjects by presenting as normative and universal, even as it has specific historical roots. In reality, it represents a deviation from widespread communal ways of being and it is not a historical inevitability.

of immediacy, spirit, courage, kinship, deference, and gratitude that comes through, that is Pastor Jin and our CAN community.

Introduction

We are grateful for this important collection of essays and are honored to offer a contribution reflecting on our experience launching Underground Seminary. The central thesis of this book, that churches have fallen captive to the Church Industrial Complex, is one that we wholeheartedly affirm. This Industrial Complex, according to the editors of this book, "explores how institutions with a purpose external to themselves can become focused on their own self-perpetuation—pursuing power, growth, and profits—in ways that may well contradict and undermine that original purpose."[3] This is more obvious in evangelical megachurches that have adopted a corporate model, but it is also present in the mainline church in the United States where there are concerns about future viability.[4] Churches are desperate for any type of growth, even if it is contrived and unsustainable, and they are terrified of decline and death, even if that passing is part of an organic life cycle that could naturally compost into something new. In this way, the church is one more institution captive to the anxiety of the cutthroat world of neoliberal capitalism,[5] trying to figure out how to compete in the market economy—both with other churches and with all other forms of commitment, distraction, and coping. We take it as a given, then, that the majority of churches in the US are captive to the logic of the Church Industrial Complex.

"Growth" in the context of capitalism will never prove sustainable over the long term because it is not maturation as understood in biology, ecology,

---

3. Sheryl Johnson, email to author, September 6, 2022.

4. Anxiety about attendance, membership, and money pervades church life in the US, whether it's about continual growth or stanching atrophy, decline, and death. Notice, for example, all the hand-wringing about the demise of the mainline denominations, and all the efforts put into reversing this trend—grants, programs, dissertations, books, and conferences. For discussions on mainline decay, see Hudnut-Beumler and Silk, *Future of Mainline Protestantism in America*.

5. Political theorist David Harvey, in *A Brief History of Neoliberalism*, defines *neoliberalism* as "a theory of political economic practices that proposes that human well-being can be best advanced by liberating individual entrepreneurial freedoms and skills within an institutional framework characterized by strong private property rights, free markets, and free trade." But this process is one that requires "'creative destruction,' not only of prior institutional frameworks and powers but also of divisions of labor, social relations, welfare provisions, technological mixes, ways of life and thought, reproductive activities, attachments to the land and habits of the heart," 2–3.

or developmental psychology.[6] Capitalist growth is obsessive, grasping for survival out of anxiety, akin to cancer in that it eventually destroys its host.[7] Healthy organic growth always requires letting go; it requires death in various forms. This is what leads to a deeper, more complex, and more interconnected flourishing of life. Jesus understood this: "If any want to become my followers, let them deny themselves and take up their cross and follow me. For those who want to save their life will lose it, and those who lose their life for my sake will find it" (Matt 16:24–25). The antidote to the toxins of neoliberalism in church life is to form leaders who are not insecure about job loss, money, a bad reputation, or even death and mortality.[8] Leaders able to embrace this call—to endure suffering, slander, and insecurity for the sake of their people—will be able to transform an existing church culture away from self-preservation, or be able to found a whole new culture around service to others. This type of community, where members serve one another and the local ecosystem without anxiety about the self, we call a village.[9]

---

6. See Fritjof Capra and Pier Luigi Luisi's discussion, "From Quantitative to Qualitative Growth," in *Systems View of Life*, 368–69.

7. See Kovel, *Enemy of Nature*. He argues, "Capital is not in itself a living organism, needless to say. It is, rather, a kind of relationship like that set up by a cancer-causing virus that invades living human beings, forces them to violate ecological integrity, sets up self-replicating structures, and polarizes the giant force field. It is humanity living as capital, people who become capital's *personifications*, that destroy ecosystems," 39.

8. We interpret "take up the cross" literally, which goes against the more common metaphorical interpretations in the West. If we become attached to any form of privilege, security, reputation, or even life itself, we will betray the people for self-preservation. The acceptance of death and mortality is at the heart of discipleship, and it is motivated by a profound love of life. Christianity's alignment with temporal power and privilege throughout history has led to docetic readings of Jesus and his ministry, which has undercut this straightforward reading—it has abstracted Jesus's words either spiritually (e.g., evangelical and Pentecostal traditions) or theologically (e.g., mainline liberal traditions). But for Jesus and early Christians, death was a very real possibility and had to be accepted in order to live a spirit-filled life of village renewal amid imperial inhumanity and violence. Pastor Jin teaches and models all of this. A shortened life of integrity and dignity (e.g., speaking the truth, loving one's neighbor regardless of consequences to self) is better than a longer life of compromise and humiliation. A grasping of life leads to a slow death of spirit, while an acceptance of mortality leads to a courageous and spirit-filled life. This is the lesson of Jesus, of many of the early Christian leaders, of countless Christians around the globe who have risked their lives for their neighbor in the face of colonialism and empire, and of more recent Christian leaders in the West like Dietrich Bonhoeffer and Martin Luther King Jr. For a non-docetic reading of Jesus's life and ministry that grounds the call of discipleship in a literal reading of "take up the cross," see Myers, *Binding the Strong Man*.

9. For powerful descriptions of village life, see Prechtel's *Secrets of the Talking Jaguar*, and *Unlikely Peace at Cuchumaquic*.

Our conviction is that the church is fundamentally a village renewal movement that historically emerged to counter the traumatizing and isolating effects of the Roman Empire with humane ways of relating.[10] Traditional and Indigenous peoples have the cultural technology to pass on the ways of kinship to each generation.[11] It is this transmission of communal culture that empires attempt to destroy—first through colonial violence, displacement, laws, and policing, and later through gaslighting, propaganda, and assimilation. The result is a domesticated "community" of mostly powerless individuals that mirrors the surrounding culture. In our context of cultural loss—of a forgetting of the ways of kinship—leaders are forged by being mentored into the ancient ways of village leadership. Such leaders can re-found genuine community. We will outline this argument throughout this chapter and conclude with learnings out of our ten-year experiment at Underground Seminary.

The "Fall": From Kinship Clans to the Earliest States

Kinship cultures are not only the norm throughout the majority of human history—they are our evolutionary baseline.[12] As Indigenous peoples understand, to live the way of kinship *is* what characterizes a human being.[13] Such kinship living, though, goes against our assumptions in state societies, and especially in the West. What we take to be natural, normative, inevitable, desirable, or advanced has been shaped by the most inhumane among us who live for the extraction of human and natural resources and who will do so by any means necessary.[14] A healthy kinship culture provides the tools

---

10. Jesus's ministry in rural Galilee began with exorcizing imperial demons and healing people from colonial trauma so they could restore village life together. The apostle Paul followed Jesus by attempting to re-found "right relating" (*dikaiosune*) through village renewal (what he called *ekklesia*) in urban centers across the Roman Empire, founding communities that included people in the Jewish diaspora as well as peoples from other conquered nations (*ta ethne*). This movement was rooted in earlier attempts by the ancient Hebrew people to reclaim the ways of kinship in the wake of imperial trauma. See Horsley, *Jesus and the Politics of Roman Palestine*; and Elliott, *Liberating Paul*.

11. See Yunkaporta, *Sand Talk*.

12. This is the argument of Paul Shepard in *Coming Home to the Pleistocene*. See also his *Nature and Madness*.

13. See Van Horn et al., *Kinship*.

14. Historically, the elites have successfully distorted our vision and broken our spirits so that: (1) we struggle to see the violence that upholds our entire way of life; (2) if we do see it, we no longer believe another way of being is possible; and (3), in the

to nurture and cultivate humane beings as they grow and mature into full adulthood.[15] Our bodies hold this knowledge: we just have to recover it. But accumulated ancestral attachment and acute trauma, not to mention the ongoing pressures and violence from the state, make this recovery difficult. With trauma comes reflexes of fear, inwardness, defensiveness, reactivity, and co-dependence, which block the flow of spirit necessary for kinship.[16] The work of recovering kinship is both ancestral excavation—tapping into the vital life force buried within us—and healing from trauma.

Defining kinship cultures is bound to be reductive given the diversity of these cultures that exist, but for the sake of understanding we will offer a few general characteristics.[17] First, kinship cultures carry a deep belief that *the earth is sacred*, a communion of living beings existing in a complex web of interdependent mutuality. Second, they nurture humility and reverence for this life force through *ritual practices for the well-being of all*. Third, kinship cultures tend to be *egalitarian, but with mature elders*, who are selected based on maturity. Fourth, *cooperation and advocacy for others are primary values*, and so they are the most affirmed and rewarded in the community, while selfish behaviors are discouraged through mechanisms of social shame.[18] Fifth, this shared communal ethos enables a *gift economy*, where goods and services are exchanged without explicit calculation of personal benefit, each member trusting the community to meet one's needs. Sixth, the result of these practices is *sustainable mutuality*, where all benefit from the right balance and constructive tension held between community members. Seventh, the net result of these characteristics is that these cultures are *relatively peaceful*. Finally, these are *oral cultures* with much longer historical memories, passed down through story, myth, language, and ceremony.

---

case that a persuasive visionary rises among us, we are incapable of living into a vision of a more humane way. "Prophets" are simply those who emerge in state societies in a specific time and place to remind people who they actually *are* as human beings, and then challenge the people to live into it. See Quinn, *Ishmael*, 85–86.

15. See Shepard, *Nature and Madness*, 1–17.

16. See Walker, *Complex PTSD*, for his description of the four Fs that come from childhood trauma: fight, flight, freeze, and fawn. For a helpful overview of trauma and the body, see van der Kolk, *Body Keeps the Score*.

17. We have learned these characteristics from our own experiences over the years at Church of All Nations, a multicultural community with East Asian immigrant roots and Indigenous teachers.

18. As Yunkaporta explains, in kinship "containing the excesses of malignant narcissists is a team effort . . . engaging with them alone is futile—never wrestle a pig, as the old saying goes; you both end up covered in shit, and the pig likes it . . . . All Law-breaking comes from that first evil thought, that original sin of placing yourself above the land or above other people." *Sand Talk*, 27–28.

If we take this list seriously, then what constitutes an "advanced" culture today in the West is backward. Our metric for highly evolved, mature, or advanced cultures should be those with the ability to live sustainably in a land base, or those cultures that most enable their members to have intimate and satisfying relationships. According to James Scott, we began regressing from this way of being just five thousand years ago, when the first state apparatus emerged in the city of Uruk, complete with tax collection, social stratification, officials, and walls.[19] This new arrangement was a shift from horticultural village societies to agriculturally based city states, with a new elite class who attained their status through the commandeering of labor and extraction from the land.[20] Trauma, violence, fractured relationships, spiritual dullness, alienation, and an inability to live sustainably on a landbase were the characteristics of these supposedly advanced human communities. The city became sacred rather than the earth. The local ecology was degraded, wetlands drained, soil overused and stripped of nutrients, and forests clearcut.[21] Ziggurat temples became the central location of divinity, rather than the whole of creation.[22] The ritual power of priests and ceremonies was leveraged to solidify belief in the new order of things, with all resources flowing to the mythologized divine center.[23]

The "fall" is not a universal, personal, and one-time event, as it has often been portrayed in Judeo-Christian traditions of the West since Augustine; instead, it is a devolution into hierarchy, slavery, war, empires,

---

19. Scott, *Against the Grain*, 7, 118. James W. Perkinson also summarizes this transition (in dialogue with Scott) in *Political Spirituality for a Century of Water Wars*, 179–82.

20. Permanent settlement and domestication of plants first began seven thousand years earlier, a departure from Pleistocene nomadic hunter gatherer lifeways. Yet, an attuned ecological balance still largely remained. Kinship continued intact. These settled villages were a combination of the best of both hunting and gathering and diversified subsistence horticultural lifestyles. The break with kinship didn't begin to occur until the rise of the state apparatus. See Scott, *Against the Grain*, 58–63, 120–21. Over the next three thousand years these states spread across the Fertile Crescent, from Egypt to Assyria to Babylon to Persia before turning northwest to Greece and Rome, and eventually north into the rest of Europe. The genealogy of the West begins with the first cities in Mesopotamia.

21. Montgomery, *Dirt*, 27–81.

22. Evan Eisenberg, in *Ecology of Eden*, 69–142, summarizes this as a shift from "Mountain" as the sacred center (an *axis mundi* representing the whole of creation) to "Tower," a temple/ziggurat in the center of the city trying to steal the power of the Mountain through mimicry.

23. For a summary of these early effects and characteristics of civilization, see Diamond, "Introduction," 1–48.

desertification, and surplus agriculture that is historic, collective, and ongoing.[24] It refers to a massive cultural transformation among a people that changed how they relate to the world around them and to each other, along with their understanding of what it means to be human. Indigenous author Jack Forbes calls it *wetiko*, or "cannibal sickness."[25] It is seeing oneself as separate from creation, and then in this state of dysregulation and alienation, consuming others to stabilize oneself. This aberration within the human species is a deadly rupture in kinship-based symbiotic relationships, an imbalance and misattunement leading to objectification and commodification and resulting in destruction and alienation. "Sin" is the biblical language for this break of kinship.

Defecting from Empire: Coming under a Lineage of Spirit

The struggle to come out of empire has existed since the rise of extractive state societies five thousand years ago. There is a long history of "civilized" people—those assimilated into a state—resisting in order to carve out the space needed to reclaim traditional kinship ways of being. Because writing was largely a tool of the elites in the first three thousand years of this history, however, most of the stories of the earliest attempts at imperial defection have been lost, along with their lessons.[26] This is where the Bible is an important resource. When read within this much larger historical and geographical context, we find valuable lessons for this work of decolonization and village renewal. While much of the Hebrew Bible supports centralized state formation that began under David in Jerusalem, there are also ancient stories of resistance to coercive attempts at domestication.[27] This "little tradition," which advocates kinship over state, survived between the lines of

---

24. See Myers, "Fall," 636; and Howard-Brook, *Come Out, My People*, 22–46.

25. Forbes, *Columbus and Other Cannibals*.

26. "The original crimes of civilizations, conquest and political repression, were committed in silence and that is still their intention, if not always their result. For most of the victims, through most of human history, could not and cannot read or write. Those people who *could* write, the scribes and priests of Egypt, Babylonia, or China, were rarely disposed to record the attitudes of those they taxed, subordinated, and mystified. . . . History, then, has always been written by the conqueror; the majority of people have traditionally remained silent, and this is still largely the case." Diamond, "Introduction," 2–4.

27. These attempts were by external colonial regimes and by internal domestic monarchy. See Howard-Brook, *Come Out, My People*; and Perkinson, *Messianism Against Christology*.

the elite scribal "great tradition."[28] It is rooted in pre-state Indigenous and nomadic, symbiotic lifeways, carrying memories of kinship ways of being.[29]

The resistance to extractive agricultural states begins with the Hebrew midwives' resistance to the Egyptian pharaoh in Exod 1 (likely Ramses II, ca. 1304–1237 BCE). This is the backdrop of an early paradigmatic story of liberation—Moses's defection to lead an escaped slave movement in the Sinai desert. Moses is ethnically a Hebrew, an enslaved people under Egypt. Taken in by Pharaoh's daughter, he grows up wealthy in Pharaoh's palace (Exod 2:5–10). He makes a sharp turn from a privileged and assimilated minority to a conscientized resistor when he sees an Egyptian overseer beating a fellow Hebrew (Exod 2:11). Moses kills him and flees to the desert in Midian (Exod 2:12–15). There, he is taken in by Jethro, a local priest, and then marries Jethro's daughter, Zipporah (Exod 2:16–22; 3:1). Through his marriage, Moses becomes part of an "uncivilized" clan of nomads living outside of state control, where he lives for forty years (see Acts 7:23)—a prolonged rite of initiation under his mentor, Jethro.[30] Through this mentorship, Moses is schooled in a kinship way of being that lived in symbiotic relationship with the land.[31] Moses learns intensive relationality, adaptability, and resilience. He becomes skillful and cunning when necessary for survival, and he becomes generous and hospitable when relating with kin. He becomes a mature adult in a way only kinship societies can midwife.[32]

---

28. Richard A. Horsley uses "the great tradition" to refer to the elite scribal tradition connected to the temple in Jerusalem, and "the little tradition" to refer to prophetic movements at the popular village level. See his *Jesus and the Politics of Roman Palestine*, 95–96.

29. The disruptive current of the little tradition is so strong that James Perkinson suggests that "the bible is arguably the world's first resistance tract." Perkinson, *Messianism Against Christology*, 10.

30. See Perkinson, *Political Spirituality for a Century of Water Wars*, 182.

31. Scott, *Against the Grain*, 83–92, speculates on the differences between "civilized" (i.e., domesticated) and Indigenous people—differences physically, in behavior, and at the level of consciousness. He concludes that the transition to civilization "represented a concentration of our species' attention to and practical knowledge of the natural world, a contraction of diet, a contraction of space, and perhaps a contraction, as well, in the breadth of ritual life." Moses, then, was going through a deprogramming and transformation of consciousness that opened his attention to the regular communication and gifts that were all around him on the land and in the people of the land.

32. Shepard describes the culmination of this process of *ontogenesis* in kinship societies: "'It seems to me that the *highest* order of maturity is essential to the achievement of a reality relatedness with that which is *most unlike* oneself.' Maturity emerges in midlife as the result of the demands of an innate calendar of growth phases, to which the human nurturers—parents, friends, teachers—have responded in season. It celebrates a central analogy of self and world in ever-widening spheres of meaning and participation, not an ever-growing domination over nature, escape in abstractions, and

Jethro is an elder in a community that has chosen to "go feral" and live off the land with the help of herd animals, rather than suffer the humiliation of life in settled extractive agricultural societies.[33] By coming under Jethro's guidance, Moses finds dignity and recovers his spirit. This training prepares him to liberate his own people from the imperial captivity of their minds, bodies, and spirit.

The point here is that by coming under the nomad and priest, Jethro, and growing into the lineage of spirit that he has carried and passes on, Moses is equipped to lead his own people into a liberation of spirit. Moses is not selfmade, nor does he receive special charisms directly from Yahweh; rather, through a forty-year crucible, he is initiated into another way of being under an elder. When Moses returns to Egypt and confronts Pharaoh, eventually winning his peoples' release (Exod 4:18—12:42), he is not inviting them to return to who they were before. This is not possible. Their land and spirit have been stripped bare. He invites them into Jethro's lineage of spirit that he now carries, even though Jethro is a foreigner. The Israelites will now undergo a similar apprenticeship to the land and community for forty years in the Sinai desert, just as Moses had done for forty years in the Midian desert. Only then, after the passing of a generation, will they be sufficiently purged of the spirit of empire to relate in a good way with the land and community—through hospitality, attentiveness, and mutual aid rather than competition, extraction, and hierarchy.

The name for this way of the spirit that was passed on was Sabbath-Jubilee, with a central practice of "release" or letting go, whether of land, wealth, or possessions (see Exod 16, 23; Lev 25; Deut 15).[34] In Sabbath-Jubilee, security is not found in what is owned but in the shared wealth of the community. Early Israel emerged as a re-tribalizing social experiment designed to free people from the grip of imperial control and dehumanization through the reclamation of kinship.[35] From the lens of state society,

---

existential funk." *Nature and Madness*, 14.

33. "Going feral" was common in the early state period. See Scott, *Against the Grain*, 219–56.

34. On the Sabbath-Jubilee tradition, see Myers, *Biblical Vision of Sabbath Economics*. Perkinson, in *Political Spirituality for a Century of Water Wars*, 244–45, refers to it as a "schoolhouse of the sevens," referencing the "comprehensive ritual regime to maintain the Sinai method." These are a series of "releases" of labor, land, and animals in order to keep spirit and resources flowing in the community.

35. This argument was first put forward by Norman Gottwald in his influential book, *Tribes of Yahweh*. The Canaanite highlands, unlike the lowland plains, had yet to be conquered for intensive agricultural production by surrounding empires. There they practiced diversified subsistence agriculture alongside herding in a way that cooperated with the local ecology while meeting community needs. From the historical record, it

also known as the "civilized," these village kinship cultures appear as "uncivilized" or "barbarian." Because they exist outside the control of the state and rely more on embodied sensation and flow, they have always been interpreted as dangerous, exotic, naive, chaotic, lawless, or even savage. In fact, the entirety of Western civilization has been built on this anxiety—fear of the "wild," "primitive," or "foreign," both without and within.[36] Further, just as the way of kinship cannot be interpreted or understood from within an imperial context, neither can it be recovered from imperial resources once lost. This is why *wetiko* spreads so quickly. The devastation and forgetting is almost total. One way it can be recovered by imperialized subjects, as we see in the story of Jethro and Moses, is through defection and mentorship from somebody without who still retains kinship. The lineage of Spirit resurfaces amid the soulless wreckage of empire when a mature person not fully domesticated by the state—an elder from an intact kinship community—takes defectors into a prolonged period of mentorship and initiation.

The Church Industrial Complex: Navigating the Great Tradition and Westernization

In traditional village contexts, defection and reschooling are not necessary. There is a whole cultural process that supports what Paul Shepard calls ontogeny, or "coming into being"—maturing into secure and healthy adults grounded in a sense of connection with all of creation.[37] But when this connection is broken, as it has been in the West, the childish narcissistic impulses remain. Pastor Jin points this out regularly and warns that, in this respect, many Christian leaders are no different than the general populace. Since there is no pathway for emotional maturity in an individualistic society, most of us have not become adults. We are stuck in individualism, insecure at our core, codependent on congregants' approval, and participants in the crass transactionalism of US American society. Our infantilization is covered over by rules, feigned expertise, specialization, job or relational status, money, charisma, respectability, etc. Where leaders do not grow into

---

appears Israel managed to sustain this confederacy of highland tribes for two hundred years until, in the face of Philistine threat from the outside, they made the ill-fated choice for monarchy. From 1043 BCE onward, Israel came under increasingly centralized state control, and the people once again began to groan under the weight of an oppressive rule.

36. On the external fear of the "primitive" in the West, see Williams, *Savage Anxieties*. On the internal fear of the "primitive" in the West, see Kovel, *Radical Spirit*, 208–25; Dodds, *Greeks and the Irrational*.

37. Shepard, *Nature and Madness*, 6.

emotionally mature adults, neither do the people, and so genuine kinship or sustainable village life becomes impossible.[38]

Jesus lived and ministered in a context of imperial trauma, broken kinship, and cultural loss. The Galilean people were bruised and battered by repeated Roman conquests of their land and an economy that reduced many of them to tenant farmers or day laborers. The temple, rebuilt in grand Hellenistic fashion by Herod the Great (37–4 BCE), was a colonial tool of Rome and a source of great wealth for the priests and temple leaders. In the midst of this "great tradition," we read in Mark's Gospel that Jesus chooses to apprentice under John the Baptist in the wilderness (Mark 1:9). John, the text makes clear, is resurfacing the lineage of Spirit first opened through Jethro's mentoring of Moses.[39] Jesus is initiated into this tradition through baptism into the Jordan River (Mark 1:9–11).[40] And this passing on of spirit is forged into durable character through forty days of testing and letting go in the wilderness (Mark 1:12–13). Jesus returns emptied of personal ambition but filled with the Spirit and with an unbreakable sense of connection to his new prophetic lineage, to the people, and to the land. He then embarks on his three-year ministry of mentoring a new generation of disciples, exorcizing imperial spirits, and healing through restoring peoples' connection to kinship. His ministry is village renewal.[41]

The US Church Industrial Complex is a continuation of the "great tradition" in the Bible—from the first temple of David, to the second temple

38. Other challenges to kinship are boundaries and itinerant ministry. Given the widespread infantilization in American society, including among leaders, safe professional distance ("boundaries") is necessary to prevent misconduct, but it also blocks the chance at deeper healing, transformation, and kinship that only comes through full immersion in the lives of the people. In healthy society, the most mature have a durable character that makes them trustworthy and resilient. They are the ones elevated to leadership and are able to be close to the people in order to nurture the village. The other barrier to constructing a village is that mainline pastors are itinerant, relocating to serve a new congregation every few years. This shields a deeper knowing of oneself that comes from living with the same people for decades. The pastors don't fully mature and the people don't have stable, mature, dependable leadership to trust for the long-term.

39. Mark quotes the prophet Isaiah (Mark 1:2; Isa 4:3), then has John dressed as the prophet Elijah (Mark 1:6; 2 Kgs 1:8) and reenacting the experience of Moses's group of escaped slaves in the desert during their forty years of re-schooling (Mark 1:6b; Exod 16:31–36). As Horsley states, "The Gospel of Mark portrays Jesus [through John] as a prophet like Moses and Elijah, carrying out a renewal of Israel in opposition to the rulers of Israel." *Jesus and the Politics of Roman Palestine*, 11.

40. See Myers, "Toward Watershed Ecclesiology," 200–217. He argues that in Mark's baptism narrative, "Jesus was en-spirited from 'below' through a deep submersion *into* his beloved homeland, grounding him in the storied Jordan watershed of his ancestors through which Creator still speaks," 206.

41. Horsley, *Jesus and the Politics of Roman Palestine*, 44–47.

of the Persian, Greek, and Roman empires. These traditions were in place to grant legitimacy to the centralizing state powers of their time, whether domestic or foreign. The role of temple leadership is to use the stories of the sacred scriptures to interpret the present oppressive systems as willed by God and to offer rituals to help the people cope. If this is done well, then the religious leaders find economic security within empire and the people find meaning and occasional relief amid the anxieties caused by empire. Under this framework, the point of seminary education today is to form competent leaders for our current temples—large evangelical churches and mainline denominations. Emotional maturity is not necessary for this work. Aspiring religious leaders are given skills for ministry, from biblical and theological knowledge to preaching to liturgy to counseling to management. If they successfully domesticate the wild and unsettling sacred stories in the Bible, thereby further domesticating their people, they are rewarded with a middle-class lifestyle.[42]

Underground Seminary was founded in 2014 in response to the current captivity of seminary education to the Church Industrial Complex, but its real origins begin earlier. In 2004 Pastor Jin and a group of second-generation Christians of a Korean immigrant church in Minneapolis launched Church of All Nations (CAN). Birthed with a blessing by the first-generation mother church, CAN was founded as a multicultural community to combat the structural sin of racism in American society and to do the "ministry of reconciliation" (2 Cor 5:11–21). Recognizing that they still carried the cultural gifts of kinship, they decided to share those gifts with others. Within a few years there were over twenty-five nations represented in the membership, including a growing number of European Americans, historically more assimilated in US society. Just as the apostle Paul, a member of the Jewish diaspora, offered his cultural gifts to the gentiles—those who were more thoroughly Hellenized—so CAN was a diasporic community with a strong communal ethos offering the way of kinship to Westernized people.

As a Presbyterian Church (USA) congregation, this was done within the mainline framework of leadership and ministry. But it was soon clear that the pastoral formation offered by conventional seminaries was

---

42. The prophetic "little tradition" of the Bible, from the Exodus account to the prophets to Jesus to the early church, point to the liberation of spirit and restoration of kinship. This results in communal lifestyles of mutual aid and simplicity that consume less and in the courage and capacity to speak truth out of love for neighbor. Such lifestyles threaten capitalism, which thrives on individualism (each person needs their own personal resources), coping with the consequent feeling of alienation (more consumption), and on silence (not naming the carnage capitalism leaves in its wake). Our denominations, churches, and people are shaped by deeply ingrained capitalist assumptions and so will choose and reward leaders who don't disrupt these assumptions.

insufficient for leading a diverse, communal, and truth-telling space. Pastor Jin launched a residential internship program to mentor seminary graduates into this type of ministry, but the imperial assumptions and desires from formation in our current seminaries were too deep.[43] Further, Pastor Jin expected affirmation from the broader church for the internship program but soon recognized that the apprenticeship model, with personalized authority in himself as the mentor, was perceived as a threat by a Western denominational institution with individualistic and rationalist assumptions:[44] Ministers were to be trained through an academic approach to Western theology in a university model, healing was to be outsourced to professional therapists, and discipleship was to be replaced with "spiritual formation."[45] It was also viewed as presumptuous for a leader to invite others, like the apostle Paul had, to "be imitators of me, as I am of Christ" (1 Cor 11:1). And when Pastor Jin's mentorship was coupled with the expectation that the interns live communally, learning to trust the community for food, transportation, and housing, it was interpreted as potentially dangerous and exploitative.[46]

---

43. For example, we came with a concern for respectability, desire for specialization and expertise, habits of transactionalism, assumptions of an individualistic middle-class lifestyle, and a need for security.

44. Individualism maintains the self as the primary locus of authority while rationalism emphasizes academic learning as primary. Even in the process of pastoral formation, the student gathers knowledge as a consumer and the self is left intact. In East Asian mentoring, on the other hand, the mentee chooses—with agency and humility—to come under a chosen mentor, giving them primary authority. The mentor is someone who is emotionally mature and differentiated, so does not need (and therefore will not exploit) the mentee. The disciple seeks to receive the spirit of the mentor, which means being reshaped at the bodily level (e.g., emotions, desires, disposition). This spirit is then expressed in the particularity of the mentee, who finds their true self in losing their artificially constructed self.

45. While therapy and spiritual formation are helpful, even necessary, what they have in common in a Western context is discomfort with personalized authority. The goal is typically to help you come to your own self-awakening insights about yourself. With this individualistic orientation, therapy and spiritual formation can easily become one more move toward interiority, innocence, and performance, further entrenching the ego within the solitary self. But in many non-Western contexts the mentor knows the disciple intimately, and their role is to tell the disciple the hard truth, to confront the layers of self-deception that must be shed in the process of maturation. Mentors are also more direct in giving advice since they have more accumulated life wisdom that makes them suitable as mentors.

46. This trust is following Jesus's style of mentoring when he instructs the disciples on their ministry as a traveling village demonstration: "You received without payment; give without payment. Take no gold, or silver, or copper in your belts, no bag for your journey, or two tunics, or sandals, or a staff, for laborers deserve their food. Whatever town or village you enter, find out who in it is worthy, and stay there until you leave. As you enter the house, greet it. If the house is worthy, let your peace come upon it, but if it

So while graduates of conventional seminaries, like myself, were simply not capable of cultivating and pastoring a diverse and intimate space rooted in kinship, Pastor Jin's attempts to mentor us within the system were met with opposition. This impasse led to the search for alternatives.

One part of this impasse is a cultural clash between East and West. The West is the primary inheritor of the genealogy of civilizational *wetiko* that began in Mesopotamia, moved around the Fertile Crescent, then migrated west through Greece and Rome.[47] But Greece also made advances in tactics of control by breaking kinship bonds in their subjects *internally*. Through Plato's dualism, Greece got their subjects to split self from community and their "rational" mind from their "primitive" body and emotions.[48] The Western person is split into two—an ideal adult self and a repressed child self. This makes the development of durable character impossible, since the repression of emotions keeps people locked in an infantilized and schizoid state of self-consciousness, anxiety, and shame.[49] Greece then gaslit their conquered subjects into believing that Greek culture represented the universal norm; therefore, this was for the peoples' good. Everyone was given

---

is not worthy, let your peace return to you" (Matt 10:9–13). Faith is learning to trust the community you serve to meet your needs, but not doing so in a transactional way. Give without expectation of return. If your needs are met in return, then stay and continue to minister. If not, move on and find a place that will receive you. It is ultimately God, then, providing for one's needs through the community. This is the lesson Pastor Jin wanted our interns to internalize. Trusting a community for your basic needs can be exploitative in some contexts, so caution may be warranted until it's clear that is not what is happening.

47. While all states are inherently exploitative, not all states attempted to destroy the capacity for kinship from within their subjects. Generally speaking, Eastern cultures continued to cultivate the capacity for kinship at the local level, whereas it was eroded in the West as part of the project of state control.

48. See "Mind and State in Ancient Greece," in Kovel, *Radical Spirit*, 208–25. Just as the poor unruly masses were controlled by philosopher kings and unruly "savages" by the "civilized," so were unruly emotions and the body controlled by reason. These are all connected, as the class hierarchies are turned inward: "One of the conditions for the emergence of a sharply differentiated self-concept (i.e., reason enthroned and passion made subordinate) appears to be the existence of sharply differentiated social distinctions—between city and country, intelligentsia and peasantry, elites and masses. And behind these distinctions lies the reality of domination," 212. "Good" imperial subjects were to internalize the policing function of empire by repressing, even dissociating from, their "primitive" emotions through abstraction into an ideal world of the forms.

49. As many non-Western cultures understand, the only way to mature is through expressing emotions within a community of mature adults who have the authority to nurture, guide, and shape a person at the bodily level over a sustained period of development—ideally as children, or later through discipleship. This leads to an integrated self, where the public presentation and internal reality are one and the same. This person is safe for the community.

the chance to assimilate into Western supremacy as long as they adopted these ways of being, which entailed killing off the ancestral spirit of their people. Greece created fragile subjects who then became codependent with each other (e.g., enmeshed, jealous, reactive, competitive) and therefore easy to dominate. Rome added an emphasis on law (*nomos*), which subjects would internalize out of fear, keeping potential chaos in check.[50]

The apostle Paul navigated all of this in his ministry. He had to learn the hard way about the added challenges of mentoring Westernized people. He was trying to teach the lost arts of kinship in his letters—greetings, deference, honor, respect, hospitality, letting go—as a response to the hierarchies, selfishness, and competition emerging in his communities. And his emphasis on "spirit" over "law" (e.g., Rom 8) is an attempt to get them to desire character, where they can trust their gut and discern the spirit, rather than clinging to rules out of more immature states.[51] Village renewal across the Roman empire required converting Hellenized people back to the ways of kinship after the individualizing separation of self from community and the dissociative split of mind from body.

While the life and teachings of Jesus are the foundation, Pastor Jin has been attempting something closer to the apostle Paul's work through the ministry of Church of All Nations. The Korean cultural gifts of kinship, such as *jeong* and *noonchi*, were opened up and shared with Western people to help them understand a communal, ancient Near Eastern faith.[52] There has certainly been, like Paul experienced, opposition from within the home culture over sharing these gifts with "gentiles," but the greater opposition has been from fellow white clergy and denominational officials over Pastor Jin mentoring white ministry candidates into the way of kinship.[53] Typi-

---

50. This is critical for interpreting Paul's diatribes against "the law" in Romans and Galatians. He wasn't nullifying the Jewish approach to law (*torah*), and therefore Judaism as a whole (as Martin Luther and much of the Protestant tradition has assumed), but rather he was arguing against those who were using the Jewish law in a forensic Roman way for the purpose of control. See Elliott, *Arrogance of Nations*; Kahl, *Galatians Re-Imagined*.

51. This is the distinction Paul is making between "milk" and "solid food" in 1 Cor 3:1–3, along with the "weak" and the "strong" in Rom 14.

52. *Jeong* is the unspoken feeling of kinship. It's hard to translate in full in English, but its meaning encompasses affection, warmth, camaraderie, loyalty, and trust. *Nunchi* is related to emotional and social intelligence. It's the ability to sense the spirit of a space, which includes peoples' moods and needs. People with *noonchi* intuitively read peoples' eyes and body language and through this know how to act appropriately in social space.

53. The vast cultural gap between East and West intersects with the divide between the "little tradition" and the "great tradition." The deep subconscious fear of these gatekeepers of the Industrial Complex is that some of their white candidates for ministry

cally, where the great tradition intersects with kinship peoples, the latter are assimilated into the dominant culture or they can remain among their own "primitive" communal people so long as they do not affect the status quo. On occasion, however, someone from a kinship society manages to cross the divides and mentor long assimilated state people into the ways of kinship. The "little tradition" for us is a multicultural kinship community that resists imperial assimilation, that challenges the divide-and-conquer strategies of the elites, and that mentors people into the ways of kinship with community and the earth.[54]

Underground Seminary: Mentoring for Village Leadership

It was out of these experiences that Pastor Jin and our community moved to a more explicit program of village renewal. The only way to combat the individualism and entitlement in the average US American's body, along with the accompanying sense of alienation and depression, was to have people start living together while being mentored. We now have a village with dozens of people living in a number of church-based community houses (each privately owned by church members). Our members are eager to learn the lost skills of kinship, *but* learning to navigate space and relationships in community-living triggers all the uncomfortable feelings that our repressed child self may not have integrated. Experiencing such discomfort spurs the process of re-associating with our bodies. Somatic therapy, pastoral counseling, and mentoring are all important tools employed in our church for guiding our members through the process of confronting and navigating long-suppressed emotions that inevitably arise in intimate community. This

---

would defect, convert, and be mentored into the "little tradition" way of village renewal, thereby lending this communal tradition greater credibility in a capitalist and white supremacist society. This fear of communalism is deep in the white American psyche. Every time there has been a successful socialist revolution in a non-Western nation, for example, the US has quickly intervened to undermine it. For capitalism to work, it has to maintain the illusion of inevitability among the general populace. A successful, genuinely socialist nation would undermine this, proving that alternatives are possible. See Prashad, *Washington Bullets*.

54. This is different from the "multiculturalism" lifted up in imperial contexts, whether Roman or in US American neoliberalism. This type of multiculturalism assimilates peoples from diverse cultures into the dominant Western way of being (i.e., Hellenism or whiteness), neutralizing the creative potential for cultivating alternatives inherent to genuine diversity. In this, as Pastor Jin has warned for years in our denomination, diversity becomes an interesting garnish among an otherwise bland and sterile "community" of individuals, rather than the expanding and strengthening of an alternative collective.

process requires village leaders—pastors, elders, "older siblings"—who have been mentored in the ways of the village and are grounded enough to be consistently regulated.

Pastor Jin founded Underground Seminary as a training program for this kind of leadership. It is a two-year immersive educational program into the way of Jesus and his spiritual ancestors. Our focus is on exorcism from the demonic possession of white supremacy, healing from the effects of trauma, and mentoring in the art of kinship. Unlike Western models where the professors are interchangeable and the content is the focus, Underground Seminary is, simply put, a school of mentoring into the way of Jesus. We are centered around discipleship, not ideas. Our cohort of students lives in community houses, all within a block from the church. When possible, we have future students live in our community housing for at least a year before the program so they have some time to rest, relate, receive, process, heal, and serve before intensive study. It also gives them experiences to reflect on when they begin the program.

Once our students begin to reintegrate and settle their bodies, they are ready to undo the gaslighting they have absorbed through Western supremacist and capitalist propaganda.[55] This requires radical educational approaches that: (1) confront the historical roots of our current systems, stripping them of their sense of power and inevitability; and (2) recover Indigenous knowledge that can guide us to more humane ways of being. We gather four hours a day in the mornings for four days a week in a seminar-style discussion on readings, along with movie nights, dinners, ceremony and singing, field trips, etc. Year One focuses on world history, with an emphasis on the intersection of politics, economics, culture, and religion. We spend the first few months learning about Indigeneity and traditional kinship cultures so that we can track the loss of kinship throughout history, along with the corresponding spread of *wetiko*. We do a close reading of the Bible in the second year, locating it in the larger history of the Fertile Crescent. We read the Bible in the same way we learned to read world history, with an eye to the struggle to reclaim humanity in the face of state conquest and control. Throughout, we lift up lessons contained within the scriptures about village renewal. This is all in dialogue with Pastor Jin's accumulated wisdom through more than thirty continuous years of full-time

---

55. Both white supremacy and capitalism move people away from a "gut sense" of things that are rooted in the body and our connection to the natural world. They do this by presenting a completely arbitrary and abstract ideal (e.g., white beauty standards as normative, accumulation and professional advancement as primary goals in life) through countless channels of messaging until it is assumed to be common sense, overriding our deeper gut sense.

pastoral ministry, along with the students' experiences in our church and community housing.

There are a few different streams that especially influence our approach. The first is ancient East Asian communalism, relational notions of spirit, and mentoring. Pastor Jin was born in Korea and spent his early years there. He has a lifelong mentor who comes from a powerful spiritual lineage in Korea, rooted in village life. Underground Seminary works because of this ancient communal spirit that Pastor Jin carries, along with the ancient skills of kinship he stewards. His immersion in his native Daoism informs our seminary as much as any influence, and it is our primary interpretive lens for Spirit and "the way"/*dao* of Jesus in the Bible. We are also influenced by the witness and teaching of local Dakota and Ojibwe Indigenous elders. They have deepened our conviction that the way forward amid imperial devastation and ecocide—of which they have long been on the front lines—is a return to living in kinship with the earth and all its inhabitants.[56] Finally, we have also been shaped by Dietrich Bonhoeffer, the early twentieth-century German pastor, theologian, and resistor whom Pastor Jin calls the "first post-Western theologian." Underground Seminary, Bonhoeffer's seminary experiment in Nazi Germany during World War II, challenged the strictly academic approach to pastoral formation.[57] He opposed the spiritual inwardness, abstraction, and social apathy of the church in the context of his time with a focus on community, discipleship, and the "this-worldliness" of Jesus.[58]

All of these influences help us connect with the powerful stream of eldership and discipleship throughout the Bible. The seminary experience works because Pastor Jin and a team of leaders personally mentor each student. The care these students receive from our community for a season allows them to differentiate from toxic relationships. The point of this

56. We have learned these lessons from trips to Pine Ridge Indian Reservation in South Dakota and Standing Rock in North Dakota, but mostly through relationships and collaboration with local Indigenous elders and teachers.

57. Our first community house was founded as a house for Underground Seminary and named the "Fink House" (short for Finkenwalde, the location of the seminary) in Bonhoeffer's honor.

58. In a letter from prison to his friend Eberhard Bethge, on July 21, 1944, Bonhoeffer writes of the "profound this-worldliness" of Christianity and reflects that the goal is not to be a saint (*homo religious*), "but simply a human being, in the same way that Jesus was a human being." This means getting over oneself and "living fully in the midst of life's tasks, questions, successes and failures, experiences, and perplexities." Furthermore, in living such a life, "one takes seriously no longer one's own sufferings but rather the suffering of God in the world . . . . This is faith, this is *metanoia*. And this is how one becomes a human being, a Christian." See Bonhoeffer, *Letters and Papers from Prison*, 485–86.

ministry is not permanent dependence on the mentors, but to move the students from unhealthy codependence to healthy differentiation through attachment to God. Pastor Jin teaches that God is the universe personified, and that the universe is God incarnate. Reintegrating people's minds and bodies and placing people back in the web of intimate communal life ultimately requires that they find their ground of being in the natural world. Our people struggle to access this Spirit because our capitalist bodies are wired to extract and consume, even in spirituality. We try to heal our students' "receptors" so that they can ground in the divine and in the natural, without grasping. Only then can they relate to other people, and to their own bodies, in a differentiated way that does not exploit them or others. Indigenous cultures throughout human history have had ways of helping their people make this connection—from rituals and ceremonies to rites of passage to language, food, and clothing. One way we are doing this is through permaculture—regenerating our soil, healing our water systems, and planting more perennials and polycultures, while growing food and medicine for our own use. New seasonal rituals and rhythms are emerging through this approach in an organic way that is connected to the land.[59] Learning to relate well with one local ecosystem connects people to the Spirit of the whole universe.[60]

---

59. We started doing permaculture on our church grounds to be better stewards of the two acres of land we currently inhabit and because we knew it would build community and help our people heal. It struck a chord and we quickly had a core team of twenty-five members, with forty or more people present at community-wide work days. This community-wide investment enabled us to take on a number of large projects without relying on machines, harmful chemicals, or outsourcing to professionals. We removed our Kentucky bluegrass with deeper rooted fescue and clover. We brought in a couple semi-truck loads of compost to give a quick infusion of life back into our soil (we now produce our own compost). We cut swales on hillsides to "slow, spread, and sink" the water moving through. We planted an orchard filled with fruit tree guilds. We planted berry and nut bushes all around the property. We planted perennial polycultures to attract pollinators. We built twenty-six raised beds to plant annual fruit and vegetables for our villages. The list goes on. Our property has been transformed through the diversity of plant life (and the pollinators it attracts), and we have developed basic land-based skills and yearly rhythms. The life and diversity on our grounds now mirrors our congregation, and the work has become a central part of our life together. For an introduction to permaculture, see Hemenway, *Gaia's Garden*.

60. Since the forces of colonialism, empire, and capitalism have displaced us and severed our connection to these ways of being, part of our seminary training is teaching our students how to re-place themselves and develop new healthy cultures out of the rhythms that emerge. On culture creation, Yunkaporta points out in *Sand Talk* that: "Most lasting cultural innovations occur through the demotic—the practices and forms that evolve through the daily lives and interactions of people and place in an organic sequence of adaptation. When these processes are unimpeded by the arbitrary controls and designs of elevated individuals, they emerge in ways that mirror the patterns of creation," 62.

This is all possible, not because of a particular model we have developed for church, or because of a new theology through which to understand the Bible. Pastor Jin's focus has been passing onto our students the spirit that makes leadership in kinship possible and mentoring them toward emotional maturity so that they can be adaptable and resilient. They must find security in God so that they do not need anything in particular, least of all congregants' approval. From the founding of Church of All Nations, Pastor Jin has emphasized that we have to be willing to let the local church die if the Spirit is no longer with us, or if there is a lack of healthy, differentiated leadership. This goes for any particular ministry of the church as well. Only when we do not need any particular outcome can we be trusted with leadership. The seminary works because we as leaders do not need it, and we are okay if it is a short-lived experiment. This openness allows us to be truly *for* the students, rather than using them for institutional ends. The students feel this advocacy and so are motivated to mature toward a similar level of security, grounding, and regulation in order to genuinely advocate for others. The only way to avoid all the traps of capitalism, or the Church Industrial Complex, is through this willingness to die—both institutionally and personally. We can be filled with the Spirit when we embrace our mortality.

Conclusion

If the church is fundamentally a village renewal movement to recover kinship amid the hegemonic state, and if village leadership requires leaders who are emptied of self-concern and filled with love for the people, then seminary is fundamentally about emotional maturation and character development. The university model does not bring leaders-in-training to a grounded love that will risk one's own life for a neighbor, which should be the primary requirement for Christian ministers. True mentors model a differentiated authority characterized by humility, reverence, deference, hospitality, courage, resilience, sensitivity to flow and space, emotional and bodily intelligence, and trustworthy discernment. These traits cannot be learned through the mind but must instead be received in the body. Like Jethro to Moses, Elijah to Elisha, Naomi to Ruth, John the Baptist to Jesus, and Jesus to his disciples, mentors seek to pass on their spirit. Theological training that embraces this approach might just be able to move Christians beyond the Church Industrial Complex. Leadership does not come from acquiring technique but from emptying of the self. It is rooted in a bodily recognition of our smallness in the vast universe, and through that feeling simultaneously connected to all that exists. It is this sense that enables us to sacrifice for others because they are also a part of us. We save our life by losing it (Matt 16:25). Only when leaders lay aside personal ambition and the need for personal security can they be open to the new movement of the spirit in their midst. Underground Seminary trains its students for service and village leadership. Only in the clearest renunciation of the ways of empire can we recover the gift of village life in the way of Jesus.

Bibliography

Bonhoeffer, Dietrich. *Letters and Papers from Prison*. Edited by John W. de Gruchy. Dietrich Bonhoeffer Works 8. Minneapolis: Fortress, 2010.

Capra, Fritjof, and Pier Luigi Luisi. *The Systems View of Life: A Unifying Vision*. Cambridge: Cambridge University Press, 2014.

Diamond, Stanley. "Introduction: Civilization and Progress." In *In Search of the Primitive: A Critique of Civilization*, 1–48. New Brunswick: Transaction, 1974.

Dodds, E. R. *The Greeks and the Irrational*. Berkeley: University of California Press, 1951.

Eisenberg, Evan. *The Ecology of Eden: An Inquiry into the Dream of Paradise and a New Vision of Our Role in Nature*. New York: Vintage, 1998.

Elliott, Neil. *The Arrogance of Nations: Reading Romans in the Shadow of Empire*. Minneapolis: Fortress, 2010.

———. *Liberating Paul: The Justice of God and the Politics of the Apostle*. Maryknoll, NY: Orbis, 1994.

Forbes, Jack. *Columbus and Other Cannibals*. Rev. ed. New York: Seven Stories, 2008.

Gottwald, Norman. *The Tribes of Yahweh: A Sociology of the Religion of Liberated Israel, 1250–1050 BCE*. Maryknoll, NY: Orbis, 1979.

Harvey, David. *A Brief History of Neoliberalism*. Oxford: Oxford University Press, 2005.

Hemenway, Toby. *Gaia's Garden: A Guide to Home Scale Permaculture*. White River Junction, VT: Chelsea Green, 2009.

Horsley, Richard A. *Jesus and the Politics of Roman Palestine*. Columbia: University of South Carolina Press, 2014.

Howard-Brook, Wes. *Come Out, My People: God's Call Out of Empire and Beyond*. Maryknoll, NY: Orbis, 2010.

Hudnut-Beumler, James, and Mark Silk, eds. *The Future of Mainline Protestantism in America*. New York: Columbia University Press, 2018.

Kahl, Brigitte. *Galatians Re-Imagined: Reading with the Eyes of the Vanquished*. Minneapolis: Fortress, 2014.

Kovel, Joel. *The Enemy of Nature: The End of Capitalism or the End of the World?* 2nd ed. New York: Palgrave Macmillan, 2008.

———. *The Radical Spirit: Essays on Psychoanalysis and Society*. London: Free Association, 1988.

Montgomery, David R. *Dirt: The Erosion of Civilizations*. Berkeley: University of California Press, 2008.

Myers, Ched. *The Biblical Vision of Sabbath Economics*. Washington, DC: Church of the Savior, 2001.

———. *Binding the Strong Man: A Political Reading of Mark's Story of Jesus*. Maryknoll, NY: Orbis, 1988.

———. "The Fall." In *Encyclopedia of Religion and Nature*, edited by B. Taylor, n.p. New York: Continuum, 2005.

———. "Toward Watershed Ecclesiology: Theological, Hermeneutic, and Practical Reflections." In *Watershed Discipleship: Reinhabiting Bioregional Faith and Practice*, 200–217. Eugene, OR: Cascade, 2016.

Perkinson, James W. *Messianism Against Christology: Resistance Movements, Folk Arts, and Empire*. New York: Palgrave Macmillan, 2013.

———. *Political Spirituality for a Century of Water Wars: The Angel of the Jordan Meets the Trickster of Detroit*. New York: Palgrave Macmillan, 2019.

Prashad, Vijay. *Washington Bullets: A History of the CIA, Coups, and Assassinations*. New York: Monthly Review, 2020.

Prechtel, Martin. *Secrets of the Talking Jaguar: Memoirs from the Living Heart of a Mayan Village*. New York: Penguin Putnam, 1998.

———. *The Unlikely Peace at Cuchumaquic: The Parallel Lives of People as Plants: Keeping Seeds Alive*. Berkeley: North Atlantic, 2012.

Quinn, Daniel. *Ishmael: An Adventure of Mind and Spirit*. New York: Bantam/Turner, 1992.

Scott, James C. *Against the Grain: A Deep History of the Earliest States*. New Haven, CT: Yale University Press, 2017.

Shepard, Paul. *Coming Home to the Pleistocene*. Washington, DC: Island, 1998.

———. *Nature and Madness*. Athens: University of Georgia Press, 1982.

van der Kolk, Bessel. *The Body Keeps the Score: Brain, Mind, and Body in the Healing of Trauma*. New York: Penguin, 2014.

Van Horn, Gavin, et al., eds. *Kinship: Belonging in a World of Relations*. Libertyville, IL: Center for Humans and Nature, 2021.

Walker, Pete. *Complex PTSD: From Surviving to Thriving*. Lafayette: Azure Coyote, 2013.

Williams, Robert A., Jr. *Savage Anxieties: The Invention of Western Civilization*. New York: Palgrave Macmillan, 2012.

Yunkaporta, Tyson. *Sand Talk: How Indigenous Thinking Can Save the World*. New York: HarperCollins, 2020.

Conclusion

SHERYL JOHNSON AND DANNIS MATTESON

The Business of God is an examination of the facets of the Church Industrial Complex (CIC), revealing a number of its problems. Greening's historical angle in chapter 1 shows us the early roots of the CIC by considering how the institutional church colluded with settler state-building with a Christian theology that was used to justify land stealing and resource consolidation as well as definitions of rationality that measured the humanity of non-Christians. Greening's work shows how, centuries ago, the growth of church side-by-side with industry yielded both contestation and justification. And we find that the political and economic roots of the CIC were always entangled with other Industrial Complexes as they grew and reinforced social relationships of domination.

Through Katske and Sebastian's biblical hermeneutical angles in chapters 2 and 3, we see that scripture can be used to both prop up the CIC and offer, at the same time, direction and motivation for finding our way out from under industrial structures. Katske's angle raises crucial questions for church reflection: What are we building, and to what extent are we forming our consciousness and identity around the structures we build? Can we create structures of belonging through our interconnected relationships rather than the commodities we produce? Meanwhile, Sebastian's angle reveals how scripture can return us to the deeper meanings of our rituals. Sebastian illuminates how the widow in the Gospel of Mark practically leaps off the page to disrupt rituals of giving that have come to reflect our obsession with raising capital over deepening community.

In chapters 4 and 5, Kwon and Tomszak highlight the refraction of the Catholic Church. Kwon offers facets of Catholic Social Thought to critique a morality covered over by materialism and to return Christians to a moral agency centered around social justice, solidarity, and charity. Tomszak displays how the Catholic Church has exemplified the CIC through its deceptive hoarding of wealth while, at the same time, Catholic Social Teaching and the example of the Catholic Worker offer resources to resist political and economic violence.

Stephens's angle, in chapter 6, reveals the habit of predominantly white churches that measure community vitality through the narrow logic of the market. Evaluating the life of a community by counting only dollars and heads, Stephens shows, completely eclipses the fruitfulness of less quantifiable works, especially the repairing work of racial justice. Market logic extends to church leadership too, and in chapter 7, Dodrill considers how pastoral work is degraded when pastors become managers who need to maximize profits. Has the history of settler homesteading become a predominant blueprint for the structure of the church? In chapter 8, Newton shows that when institutional survival and then dominance become the primary goal for Christian communities, we may be "owned" by neoliberal values and habits. Colwell, in chapter 9, explores the question of whether technology is truly a tool for helping communities live out the gospel in challenging times, or whether it too easily becomes an extension of the CIC.

This volume ends by examining an angle of hope and creativity amid the Church Industrial Complex. In chapter 10, Nelson, Kim, and Newby provide a picture of forming leaders to uphold kinship rather than to consolidate capital. Their particular angle enables us to imagine how many other examples are available to us when we build communities that refuse to participate in Industrial Complexes.

While examining these angles and the problem of the CIC are an important start, many areas of the Church Industrial Complex remain unexamined. For example, we need to pay close attention to, and articulate the ways that, people experience the CIC as a structure of racial, gender, and sexual domination. We also need to gather more and more examples of communities living in resistance to the CIC and creating livable environments that allow for the flourishing of human and non-human life. We need to pay close attention to the ways that the CIC interlocks with other Industrial Complexes.

The facets we have examined may also leave our readers with many other questions: Can an institution be an institution without perpetuating some kind of Industrial Complex? Must churches be institutions? Does a church need to make or handle money to be a church? What would it mean to deinstitutionalize church? Is that work necessary? Of course, many churches do operate without money and certainly in ways that are less institutional, if at all. But is that necessarily the only way to resist the Church Industrial Complex? And if we are to deinstitutionalize or otherwise resist the Church Industrial Complex, is it simply up to individual churches, pastors, or church communities? Is it possible to be a community in a capitalist, white supremacist society without being fundamentally shaped by these influences? What are the markers or signs of the CIC shaping our churches that we must not ignore? Some markers we have identified in this book include market logic viewpoints that see unceasing growth as inherently good, stability as stagnation, and decline as demise. Each community might harbor different markers, so we ask: What markers do you observe in your community? What do you imagine might exist beyond the Church Industrial Complex?

While we are not certain about the answers to many of the questions we are left with, we do know that one clear step for Christian communities is to articulate and constantly remind ourselves of what we are for. Market values will constantly be pushing their way in, trying to convince Christians that we are for growth, success, and eternal existence. But if we can be sure of who we are, we will know better who we are not.

What is it, exactly, that the church is—and is for? That is a difficult question and not one that can be answered simply. Writers from within the fields of ecclesiology, practical theology, and other disciplines have offered many useful definitions and descriptions as they strive to call the church back to itself. In Adjoa Florência Jones de Almeida's essay addressing the Non-Profit Industrial Complex, entitled "Radical Social Change: Searching for a New Foundation," the need for time as well as spirituality are put forth as two important prerequisites to be able to imagine beyond the systems within which we are so deeply embedded.[1] These elements are inherent to faith practice and should come easily in communities seeking to challenge the Church Industrial Complex. Yet, the time that it takes to step out of the many persistent demands of the status quo to envision what could be is not as common as it may appear in church contexts. Communities need only to recall familiar practices and commitments in the Christian tradition, such as times of Sabbath or periods of Jubilee. Seasons such as these challenge a reset to the order of systems and structures that have become unjust or oppressive, and they invite us to ask how they can be reclaimed and restructured.

Critics of the Non-Profit Industrial Complex also challenge Christians to see ourselves as not primarily accountable to our funders but instead to our primary constituents.[2] In the case of churches, it may appear that we are indeed doing this already because many of our church members are our

---

1. Jones de Almeida, "Radical Social Change," 187.
2. Jones de Almeida, "Radical Social Change," 186.

financial contributors. But in fact, this insight challenges the conventional association that our funders determine our work. It further challenges the common thought pattern that the more money people give, the more voice, power, and influence they should receive. When we think critically about who the "primary constituents" of church may be, we must remember that we are fundamentally called to serve God and neighbor, with special emphasis on anyone who is marginalized or in need. Our "primary constituents" may not be totally distinct from those who offer funds to our churches, but they are also not precisely the same. Separating out the question of who funds our churches from who we are accountable to and for may offer us a major shift in whose voices are prioritized and whose needs come first.

The work to resist the Church Industrial Complex should not be pursued in a vacuum. As Henry Giroux argues in addressing the Military-Industrial-Academic Complex, resistance against one form of Industrial Complex must be connected to an overall project of transforming the entire economy to be more just.[3] For churches, this is incredibly important. With a strengthened social safety net, pastors would be less reliant on their churches for their livelihoods and perhaps more willing to take risks in their churches or even possibly move outside of formal employment models entirely. If our society had fewer people facing acute forms of need, churches would be less susceptible to the perils of the Non-Profit Industrial Complex and perhaps less embedded in systems requiring grants and funding to provide band-aid solutions to address basic needs. We must not lose sight of broader economic injustice and the need to ensure that in our work to address the Church Industrial Complex, we are not becoming so self-focused that we neglect these broader needs for social justice in all forms and in all arenas.

In addition to acknowledging the church's context within the broader political and economic structures and their intersecting systems, it is also critical to attend to dynamics at the micro level. This idea that there is similarity and resonance on micro and macro scales (and everything in between), is described by adrienne maree brown in her work on Emergent Strategy. brown observes that "small actions and connections create complex systems, patterns that become ecosystems and societies."[4] To resist the Church Industrial Complex, micro-level patterns, habits, relationships, feelings, and dispositions matter, too, and they contribute to larger-scale change. Individuals and communities may feel relatively small and powerless in the face of intersecting systems and historical structures, but even

---

3. Giroux, *University in Chains*, 208.
4. brown, *Emergent Strategy*, 3.

small-scale changes can have an impact and serve as the foundation for broader change. Our principles and values should guide all that we do: Nothing is too minute to matter.

However, minute change should not be seen as a substitute for systemic change. We cannot retreat into our corners to do what we can while ignoring the broader issues that will remain. In ecclesiology, one of the images or metaphors of the church is that of the church as a foretaste or a seed of the kingdom of God. Communion can also be understood in the same way— an appetizer for, and a catalyst of, the broader and more cosmic feast that awaits. Our work to reveal and dismantle the CIC will play a similar role, furthering the work for ecclesial and broader sociopolitical transformation toward greater justice, equity, and resistance to all systems of oppression.

This work inevitably comes with risk, however. Christians may have to risk the structure of our institutions as we have known them for decades, if not centuries. Breaking away from the Church Industrial Complex may mean breaking down familiar patterns that we think of as common sense procedures for building a "successful" church or institution. If we no longer focus our work on guaranteeing institutional longevity or financial security, for example, we may risk loss of what feels comfortable and familiar. We may risk losing what feels to us like "church." And we may even risk losing the institutions that pay our bills. But if we take our authors' warnings seriously and pay attention to the many forms of violence, exploitation, and alienation left in the wake of the CIC, then refusal to participate in the CIC becomes an ethical imperative. It is important to keep in mind that, as Nelson et al. demonstrate, there are already communities doing this work.

Articulating community identity beyond the "metrics" of the CIC will be a critical and creative project for Christian churches in North America. The authors within this volume demonstrate methods for participating in this project by asking what facets of our tradition become mechanisms of the CIC and which facets of our tradition motivate us to work for liberation. For example, we can be critical of biblical interpretations that begin to sound like blueprints for industrial expansion, and instead, ask how biblical figures disrupt our physical spaces of power and domination. Our community practices and rituals can show us what we value: whether that is a balanced budget, attempts to manufacture and meet consumer demand, or efforts at upholding rituals that create opportunities for reconnection and deep solidarity. We can hold tension with our traditional church teachings, reviving their promises for reconnecting us to our values while pushing against teachings that exclude, exploit, and limit our reach to love God and neighbor. Most importantly, we can look to examples of church-in-resistance happening in our own backyards if we stay open to learning from unconventional initiatives.

Although the work to dismantle the CIC is an ethical imperative that would be worthwhile regardless of the cost, what awaits us on the other side may be even better than we could dream. Better for the planet, for marginalized communities, for those with significant privilege, for tired and worn church leaders—for us all. We might be freed from certain patterns and pressures, from unquenchable demands for more and "better," from deep wells of dissatisfaction and consumer malaise. We might be liberated from work that we know, deep down, is not congruent with our values and our faith.

There might well be long and uncomfortable "Holy Saturday" periods of waiting and uncertainty; of hopeful experimentation, followed by fizzling or firm failure; of so much grief and loss in ourselves and all around us for many worthy things, including for things that were familiar and loved despite their shortcomings. But folks might also be granted the opportunity to return to the "first things" that may have initially brought them to church or other spiritual communities: encounters with the holy, catalyzing moments of experiencing communities, boldly and bravely living into their values, and so forth. We can't know precisely what is on the other side for the church—or for anything, including ourselves—until we step out into it. We will not always get it right, but we can pray that God will receive our efforts and let us try and try and try again.

Bibliography

brown, adrienne maree. *Emergent Strategy: Shaping Change, Changing Worlds*. Chico, CA: AK, 2017.

Giroux, Henry A. *The University in Chains: Confronting the Military-Industrial-Academic Complex*. Boulder, CO: Paradigm, 2007.

Jones de Almeida, Adjoa Florência. "Radical Social Change: Searching for a New Foundation." In *The Revolution Will Not Be Funded: Beyond the Non-Profit Industrial Complex*, edited by Incite!, 185–95. Cambridge, MA: South End, 2007.

www.ingramcontent.com/pod-product-compliance
Lightning Source LLC
Chambersburg PA
CBHW021726220426
43662CB00008B/723